PEARSON EDUCATION

AP* TEST PREP SERIES

AP* AMERICAN GOVERNMENT

FOR

EDWARDS | WATTENBERG | LINEBERRY

GOVERNMENT IN AMERICA:

THIRTEENTH ADVANCED PLACEMENT* EDITION

PREPARED BY:

JOSEPH STEWART, JR.
CLEMSON UNIVERSITY

JAMES W. RIDDLESPERGER, JR.
TEXAS CHRISTIAN UNIVERSITY

REBECCA D. SMALL
HERNDON HIGH SCHOOL

KERRY L. HAYNIE
DUKE UNIVERSITY

CATHY GRIFFIN
NORTHWESTERN HIGH SCHOOL

Longman

New York   Boston   San Francisco
London   Toronto   Sydney   Tokyo   Singapore   Madrid
Mexico City   Munich   Paris   Cape Town   Hong Kong   Montreal

* AP and Advanced Placement are registered trademarks of The College Entrance Examination Board, which was not involved in the production of, and does not endorse, this product.

Preparing for the United States Government AP* Exam with Government in America: People, Politics, and Policy, Edwards/Wattenberg/Lineberry

Copyright ©2009 Pearson Education, Inc.

ISBN: 0-132-32894-1

1 2 3 4 5 6 7 8 9 10–CW–11 10 09 08

Please visit our web site at *www.pearsoned.com*

CONTENTS

About Your Pearson Text Plus Test AP Guide

Pearson Education is the leading publisher of textbooks worldwide. With operations on every continent, we make it our business to understand the changing needs of students at every level, from kindergarten to college. We think that makes us especially qualified to offer this series of AP test prep books, tied to some of our best-selling textbooks.

Our reasoning is that as you study for your course, you're preparing along the way for the AP test. If you can tie the material in the book directly to the test you're taking, it makes the material that much more relevant, and enables you to focus your time most efficiently. And that's a good thing!

The AP exam is an important milestone in your education. A high score means you're in a better position for college acceptance, and possibly puts you a step ahead with college credits. Our goal is to provide you with the tools you need to excel on the exam . . . the rest is up to you.

Good luck!

Part I

Introduction to the AP U.S. Government & Politics Examination

This section overviews the advanced placement program, introduces the types of questions you will encounter on the exam, and provides helpful test-taking strategies. It also explains the grading procedure used by the College Board. Finally, a correlation chart is provided that shows where key information commonly tested on the exam is covered in *Government in America*. Review this section carefully before trying the sample items in the following parts.

The Advanced Placement Program

This book will help prepare you to take the Advanced Placement (AP) U.S. Government & Politics Exam at the end of the year. To succeed on the exam, you need to follow a plan of curriculum review and practice. This book offers both of these. First, you will review each content area of government and politics that appears on the AP U.S. Government & Politics Exam. Then, for each section, you will complete some practice drills that replicate actual AP exam questions. You will not only receive extra, guided study for your coursework, but you will also have the opportunity to apply what you have learned in class to a testing situation. You will become familiar with the types of questions on the AP U.S. Government & Politics Exam and how to approach them. Go through each review section thoroughly and complete all of the accompanying drills. If you have difficulty with particular sections, that is your cue to refer to your textbook for a more detailed review.

For more practice, this book includes two full-length AP U.S. Government & Politics Exams. These will help you practice taking the exam under real-life testing conditions. The more familiar you are with the AP U.S. Government & Politics Exam ahead of time, the more comfortable you will be on testing day. And the more comfortable you are, the better your chances of achieving a high score.

The AP Program is sponsored by the College Board, a nonprofit organization that oversees college admissions tests. The AP Program offers high school students the opportunity to take advanced college-level courses. According to the College Board, AP courses are intended to offer a curriculum equivalent to that of an introductory college class. If you receive a grade of 3 or higher (5 is the highest possible grade), you may be eligible for college credit. Thousands of colleges and universities grant credit to students who score well on AP exams. If you are taking several AP courses and if you score well on multiple AP exams, you may even be eligible to enter college as a sophomore. Some institutions grant sophomore status to incoming first-year students who have demonstrated mastery of many AP subjects. In addition, the College Board confers a number of AP Scholar Awards on students who score 3 or higher on three or more AP exams. Additional awards are available to students who receive very high grades on four or five AP exams.

The curriculum for each of the 37 AP courses is designed by a development committee, consisting of college professors and high school teachers. Every AP course is different, and your textbook, *Government in America: People, Politics, and Policy*, is widely and successfully used in AP classes across the nation. The committee develops guidelines for a test that represents equally and accurately the skill levels of over 100,000 AP U.S. Government and Politics students across the country. Your score on the AP U.S. Government & Politics Exam reflects your abilities in comparison to other high school students enrolled in the course. Colleges use this information not only to award credit for introductory college classes but also to choose the most suitable applicants.

Why Take an AP Course?

You may be taking one or more AP courses simply because you are thirsty for knowledge. Of course, the fact that selective colleges look favorably on applicants who have AP courses on their transcripts is another powerful incentive. Because AP classes should involve rigorous lessons, they signal to college admissions officers that AP students are willing to challenge themselves to get the most from their education. Because AP course work is more difficult than average high school work, many admissions officers evaluate AP grades on a kind of curve—if you receive a *B* in an AP class, for example, it might carry the same weight as an *A* in a regular high school class. Furthermore, the score you achieve on the AP exam places you in the context of your peers across the nation and across years.

Your AP U.S. Government & Politics course teaches you many of the skills you will need in college. For example, your teacher will make writing assignments and encourage you to use resources beyond your textbook. Some of these resources may be primary sources that permit you to analyze events, issues, and data as a political scientist does. The AP U.S. Government & Politics course will challenge you to gather and consider information in new—and sometimes unfamiliar—ways. Your ability to use these methods and skills will give you an advantage as you enter college.

Taking an AP Examination

You should challenge yourself further by taking the AP U.S. Government & Politics Exam at the end of your high school course. A wealth of information—which colleges grant credit for AP exam scores, and for what score, the exam schedule, when you need to sign up, the cost, the availability of fee reductions—is available either from your AP teacher or school guidance counselor or at www.colleageboard.com or apcentral.collegeboard.com/apc/Controller.jpf. At the College Board's web sites you will have to establish an account to get access to all of the information, but there is a wealth of information, and it is free. Even if you use the web site as a primary source of information, you should also communicate with you AP teacher or school guidance counselor. There are many state and local programs that help you defray the costs of taking the exam.

When you register for the AP exam, you can arrange to have your score sent automatically to a number of colleges for free. In fact, your score can be received at colleges and universities only if it has been sent there directly by the College Board. If you would like your score to be sent to other schools, you must pay an additional fee. You can also cancel your score (you must do so before you find out your score), but either of these requests must be made directly to the College Board. Your exam grade will be sent to you by mail in early–mid July. If you simply cannot wait to find out your score, Educational Testing Service (the organization that develops and scores tests for the College Board) will release your score to you over the phone around July 1 for an additional fee.

AP U.S. Government & Politics: Course Goals

The goal of the AP U.S. Government & Politics course is to provide students with an understanding of the operation of American national government. Specifically, you will develop

- an understanding of the principal themes in U.S. government and politics

- the ability to analyze evidence—historical, quantitative, and presented graphically

- skills to express your knowledge in writing

AP U.S. Government & Politics courses vary somewhat from teacher to teacher and from school to school. Yet the focus of your course should reflect these goals, and the instruction you receive will grow out of these basic principles. The U.S. Government & Politics Development Committee has created a list of major topics and has divided them into the six groups below. These topics are the focus of your AP course, and will be revisited in questions on the AP U.S. Government & Politics Exam.

Constitutional Underpinnings of United States Government

- Historical development and adoption of the Constitution

- Separation of Powers

- Checks and balances

- Federalism

- Theories of modern government

Political Beliefs and Behaviors

- Theories of modern government, including elitist, pluralist, and hyperpluralist

- Views that people have about government and their elected officials

- Characteristics and impact of public opinion

- Voting patterns of citizens

- Characteristics of political beliefs and the differences between liberals and conservatives

Political Parties, Interest Groups, and Mass Media

- Characteristics, organization, and history of political parties

- Impact of key elections

- Voting patterns and the effect on the political process

- Laws that affect elections

- Interest groups and political action committees

- Legislation affecting the political process

- The mass media and its effect on politics

Institutions of National Government

- Characteristics and power of each institution

- Relationships among each institution

- Linkage between these institutions and the political process, political parties, interest groups, the media, and public opinion

- How public policy is formulated and implemented

Public Policy

- The nature of public policy

- The creation of public policy

- The impact of the three branches of government on public policy

- The impact of the bureaucracy on public policy

- The relationship between public policy and linkage institutions

Civil Rights and Civil Liberties

- The Bill of Rights and how it evolved

- The incorporation of the Fourteenth Amendment

- Judicial review and key Supreme Court cases

- The fight for minority rights

Using class lectures, assignments, and activities, you can immerse yourself in all six themes of AP U.S. Government & Politics. Extensive classroom preparation and your own regular practice and study will be the foundation for your success on the AP U.S. Government & Politics Exam.

Understanding the AP U.S. Government & Politics Examination

The AP U.S. Government & Politics Exam incorporates graphical, cartographic, and quantitative materials. This cross-disciplinary approach reflects the methods used today in colleges and universities to present subject matter.

The AP U.S. Government & Politics Exam takes two hours and 25 minutes. It consists of a multiple-choice section and a free-response section. You can expect to see graphs, charts, and quotations in both sections of the test. You are expected to know the foundations of U.S. government and how and why it has evolved, but this is not an exam on history. The AP U.S. Government & Politics course is a course in political science.

Section I: Multiple-Choice Questions

You will have 45 minutes to complete the 60 questions in the multiple-choice section of the test. This section accounts for 50 percent of your overall score. Each question has five answer choices, and only one choice is correct. Most of the questions in this section will be fairly straightforward. Some may require interpretation, such as determining cause and effect or drawing a comparison. Others will ask you to analyze data in charts or graphs, or to evaluate a political cartoon or other illustration. The questions vary in degree of difficulty.

Not all multiple-choice questions are the same. The AP U.S. Government & Politics Exam will contain the following types of questions:

Definition or Identification Questions

These questions ask you to recognize something and know what it is. Here is an example.

1. Class action suits

    (A) permit a small number of people to sue on behalf of all other people similarly situated.

    (B) are filed by students seeking to force a school district to offer additional sections of perpetually overenrolled courses.

    (C) have to do with constitutional issues, thus broadening the standing to sue.

    (D) are routinely filed by teachers' groups to prepare the way or strikes.

    (E) may be filed only if all of those with standing to sue agree to participate.

The correct answer is *A*. A small group of people who believe, for example, that they have been harmed by a product can sue the manufacturer on behalf of all the people who believe they were harmed. This is the definition of class action.

Cause-and-Effect Questions

This type of question asks which event caused another, or what is the result of something. Here is an example:

2. The increasing speed of technological advance

    (A)   has significantly reduced the scope of American government.

    (B)   helps reduce and accelerate government policymaking.

    (C)   has helped reduce the cost of health care in the United States.

    (D)   has dramatically affected health policy, but has had no effect on environmental and energy policy.

    (E)   has created many new practical and moral problems of the political system.

The answer is *E*. You can use the process of elimination. The scope of government has not gotten smaller; policymaking has not become faster; health care costs have risen; if technology has affected health policy, it is unlikely that it has not also affected environmental and energy policies. Answers *A–D* are obviously wrong, leaving *E*.

"Roman Numeral" Questions

Here you are given a question, then several statements, phrases, or words relating to the question. You must decide which of the statements, phrases, or words are correct. It may be one or more than one.

3. Registered voters directly elect which of the following?

    I.   The president and vice president

    II.   Supreme Court justices

    III.   Senators

    IV.   The Electoral College

(A)   I only

(B)   IV only

(C)   I and II only

(D)   III and IV only

(E)   II, III, and IV only

The answer is *D*. Registered voters vote for electors who then vote for the president and vice president. This is not *direct* election. So any choice that includes *I* is wrong (*A, C*). Justices of the Supreme Court are appointed by the president and approved by the Senate, so you can also eliminate choice *E*. Voters vote directly for both senators and, as noted above, the Electoral College.

EXCEPT/NOT Questions

In this type of question, four of the answer choices are correct, and you must find the answer that is *wrong*. Be sure to read the question carefully. Here is an example of this type of question.

4. Which of the following is NOT specifically mentioned in the Constitution, including its amendments?

    (A)   Protection against double jeopardy

    (B)   Right to bear arms

    (C)   Freedom of speech

    (D)   Right to privacy

    (E)   Right to trial by jury

The answer is *D*. Double jeopardy is addressed in the Fifth Amendment. The right to bear arms is mentioned in the Second Amendment. Freedom of speech is protected by the First Amendment. Article III provides for trial by jury. Only the right to privacy is not specifically mentioned in the Constitution.

Supreme Court Decisions

You will be asked to identify, interpret, or compare one or more well-known Supreme Court decisions. Here is an example:

5. *New York Times* v. *Sullivan* addressed

   (A)   equal opportunity in the workplace.

   (B)   libel.

   (C)   prior restraint.

   (D)   business monopolies.

   (E)   obscenity.

The answer is *B*. The Court held that statements about public figures are libelous only if made with "reckless disregard for the truth." There is no way to guess here. All the choices are topics the Supreme Court has ruled on, and all might involve a newspaper. You need to remember significant cases and the issues they address.

Graphic Questions

You can expect to see questions based on graphs, tables, and maps.

DISTRIBUTION OF INCOME AMONG FAMILIES
(percentage share by economic level)

	1970	1980	1990	2000
Lowest fifth	5.5	5.1	4.6	3.6
Second fifth	12.0	11.6	10.8	8.9
Third fifth	17.4	17.5	16.6	14.9
Fourth fifth	23.5	24.3	23.8	23.0
Highest fifth	41.6	41.6	44.3	49.6

9

6. Which of the following conclusions about income distribution is supported by the table?

   (A)   The share of income received by the lowest fifth increased, and the share received by the fourth fifth decreased.

   (B)   The share of income received by the second fifth increased, and the share received by the fourth fifth decreased.

   (C)   The share of income received by the highest fifth increased, and the share received by the lowest fifth decreased.

   (D)   The number of people earning high incomes increased.

   (E)   The middle class disappeared.

The numbers clearly show that *C* is the answer. Choice *D* might be attractive, but note that the table gives percents. Although the *percent* of families in the highest fifth increased, you know nothing about the actual number of people. Always read the questions and answer choices carefully.

Section II: Free-Response Questions

The second portion of the AP U.S. Government & Politics Exam is an hour-and-40-minute free-response section consisting of four questions, i.e. 25 minutes per question. You must answer all four—none of them is optional. You may, however, have some choice within a question. All four questions count equally, and together they account for 50 percent of your overall score.

Because the free-response questions are open-ended, this is your opportunity to demonstrate your understanding of U.S. government and politics. You will see directives like *define, identify, describe,* and *explain.* Knowing facts or terms may earn you points if the task is to *define* or to *identify*, but to *describe* or to *explain* requires using your knowledge to construct an argument. You should use your knowledge to construct a thorough and intelligent response.

1. Scan all four questions quickly to form initial impressions of the topics about which you are being asked to write. You do not have to answer the questions in the order in which they are presented. Begin with the question you think you can respond to best. (If you are to run short on time, you would rather run short on a question about which you think you know the least, than the one about which you know the most.)

2. Read and reread the question to be sure you understand exactly what is being asked. Underline directives such as *define, identify, describe,* and *explain.* These are the tasks that must be accomplished for you to earn credit for a response. You can jot notes in the margins of the exam booklet.

3. Take a couple of minutes to brainstorm about the topic. Write down the things that come to your mind. Then look them over to see which ideas will go well together to serve as examples for your response to the question and to determine the order in which you will present them. This, in essence, is the outline for your response. Remember, you have, on average, 25 minutes for each response. Five minutes invested in brainstorming and outlining up front can produce a much better response with less expenditure of time overall. But do keep track of time.

4. You may use any organizational approach that makes sense to you as long as you respond to the question and all of its parts. When in doubt, use the question format as your guide to your outline.

5. Now you are ready to begin writing. What you write is the only evidence that the reader has about what you know regarding the question that has been posed. Flesh out the ideas you used to construct your outline, using examples to bolster you points. Correctly used, appropriate examples give the reader confidence that you have an understanding of the question that merits awarding the points allocated to that part of the question. Your answer will be judged based on whether or not you have accomplished your task—to define, identify, describe, or explain—as laid out in the question. There is no need to venture beyond the scope of the question. You earn points for accomplishing the assigned tasks. You will not earn extra points, and, because each question is scored independently, you will not be able to make up for a question you feel you did not answer well enough by overcompensating on another question. Many free-response questions on the AP U.S. Government & Politics Exam will ask you to address a single topic in a straightforward way. Here is an example of such a question:

1. The system of checks and balances ensures that no branch of government has unfettered power. Describe—using examples—how each branch has exercised this power over another branch.

In your response to this question, you need to furnish *examples* that help you *describe* how each of the three governmental branches has used the system of checks and balances to wield power.

Some free-response questions are divided into several parts, or subquestions. You might be presented with a list of items, such as specific court cases or interest groups, that you are asked to address in your response. These partitioned questions often contain directives like *identify, describe,* and *explain.* Here is an example:

2. Choose two of the following Supreme Court cases.
    * *California Board of Regents* v. *Bakke*
    * *Roe* v. *Wade*
    * *Gideon* v. *Wainwright*
    * *Rust* v. *Sullivan*
    * *Miranda* v. *Arizona*
    * *Korematsu* v. *United States*

For each case you selected, do each of the following.

     a. Describe the position of each side.

     b. Describe the Supreme Court's ruling.

     c. Explain whether the ruling increased or decreased the rights of individuals.

First, you need to recognize (at least two of) the cases and choose the two you want to use in the remainder of your response. Do not be intimidated by a list of six cases. You could know absolutely nothing about four of the cases and still earn all of the points for the question. Second, you would need to describe the positions of the opposing sides in each of the two cases chosen (four descriptions).

Third, you must describe the Court's ruling, i.e. a simple statement of the Court's holding in the cases chosen. Finally, you must take a position on whether the rights of individuals were increased or decreased in each of the chosen cases and support your position. A simple statement of your conclusion about the increase or decrease of individual rights by the Court in your chosen cases would be insufficient to earn credit for the *explain* part of the question. The reader must finish your response knowing how you think rights were expanded or contracted or why you have taken the position you have for each of the chosen cases. It is often the *explain* part of a question that separates the best prepared students from the rest. You must answer all of the subquestions. Your personal opinions may affect how you explain something, but you will not be asked about your personal political opinions, so do not include them. You do not get extra credit for going beyond the scope of a question, and that just wastes your valuable time. This is a political science exam, not a forum for political position-taking.

It cannot be overemphasized, pay close attention to exactly what the question asks you to do, and do it—nothing more; nothing less! For example, in the question posed above, asking you to describe the positions of the parties in two cases, the Supreme Court's ruling, and to explain the cases' impact on the expansion or contraction of individual rights, you might know the full story of Clarence Gideon and how his case made it to the Supreme Court, but even a brilliant explanation of this saga would earn you no points because that is not requested in the question. To earn points, answer the question that is asked—not the one you wish had been asked.

Grading Procedures for the AP U.S. Government & Politics Examination

The raw scores of the exam are converted into the following five-point scale:

> 5—Extremely Well Qualified
>
> 4—Well Qualified
>
> 3—Qualified
>
> 2—Possibly Qualified
>
> 1—No Recommendation

How these scores are used in admission, credit, or placement decisions varies from college to college, with credit and placement decisions often being made at the departmental level. Some colleges give undergraduate course credit to students who achieve scores of 3 or better on AP exams. Other colleges require students to achieve scores of 4 or 5. If you are considering using your AP exam score for college credit, check with individual colleges or at www.colleageboard.com to find out their specific requirements for credit. Below is a breakdown of how the grading of the AP U.S. Government & Politics Exam works.

Section I: Multiple-Choice Questions

The multiple-choice section of the exam is worth 50 percent of your total grade. The raw score of Section I is determined by crediting one point for each correct answer and by deducting one-fourth of one point for each incorrect answer. No points are gained or lost for unanswered questions. If you have no idea what the correct answer is, do not make a wild guess—leave the answer blank. But if you can eliminate two or more of the five choices, you should make an educated guess.

Section II: Free-Response Questions

The free-response section of the exam is worth 50 percent of your total grade. It is graded by a group of AP U.S. Government & Politics instructors and professors known as "faculty consultants." Each essay may be read by anywhere from one to 20 readers. The readers do not know whose essay they are reading nor from which school the essay originates. Each faculty consultant generally will only read responses to one of the Free-Response Questions during the reading and will not know what you scored on either the Multiple-Choice part of the exam or on the other three Free-Response Questions. You begin with a 0 score on each Free-Response

Question, and earn points as you correctly respond to the question. The scale for scoring each Free-Response Question is specifically adapted to the question, e.g. one question may be scored using a "5-point rubric" while another is scored using a "9-point" rubric. Then, your score on each Free-Response Question is weighted so that it counts the same as each of the other three Free-Response Questions. These weighted scores are then summed, and this total counts the same as your total Multiple-Choice score in your final score. The Chief Reader, the person in charge of scoring all of the exams, in consultation with statisticians from the Educational Testing Service and personnel from the College Board, then determines what total scores will be required for an AP score of 5, of 4, etc. Great care goes into assuring that your score accurately reflects where you stand in relation to the other students who took the exam you did and in relation to the students who took the exam in prior years. Colleges want to know that your score of 5 means the same as the 5 presented last year from a school across the country from where you are.

Test-Taking Strategies for the AP U.S. Government & Politics Examination

To become comfortable with both the content and the format of the AP U.S. Government & Politics Exam, begin preparing for the test in advance. You want to have plenty of time to devote to each of the six main subject areas on the test while practicing your free response skills at the same time. The more relaxed study time you allow yourself, the more prepared you will be and the better you will do on the exam.

Aim to finish the review sections about a week and a half before the exam. Then take the first practice test at the back of this book. Treat the practice test exactly like the real exam. Find a quiet place where you can work without interruption and give yourself only two hours and 25 minutes. This allows you to become familiar with the actual testing conditions so that you will be less nervous on testing day.

After you have scored your practice test, take a day just to review your answers. Look at the types of questions you got wrong. Do they fall under the same content area or areas? If so, you should focus further study on those particular areas for the next two days or so. Count the number of questions you skipped. Did they fall near the end of the section? This could mean that you were running out of time. Did you feel rushed? It might be wise, then, to plan ahead of time which kinds of questions you should skip over. For example, if you got every data question right and a lot of questions about Supreme Court cases wrong, plan to skip a few of those case questions so that you can answer all of the data questions in the section. You need to make sure that you answer the questions you are more likely to know and that you skip the ones that might slow you down.

Now that you know what adjustments to make to your test-taking strategy, give yourself a few days of extra practice with your problem areas and then take the second practice test at least three days before the real exam (do not overwhelm yourself before the real thing!). Again, analyze your performance. Did your adjustments pay off? Is there anything you should do differently? Use your last few days to do any fine-tuning and to relax before the exam.

Below is a brief list of basic tips and strategies to think about *before* you arrive at the exam site.

- Try to plan your schedule so that you get *two* very good nights of sleep before exam day. On the day of the exam, make sure that you eat good, nutritious meals. These tips may sound corny or obvious, but your body must be in peak form for your brain to perform well.

- Arrive at the exam site 30 minutes before the start time. This saves you additional worry about arriving late.

- It is a good idea to have a photo I.D. with you when you arrive at the exam site. (It is essential if you are taking the exam at a school other than your own.) Carrying a driver's license or a student I.D. card will allow you to prove your identity if anyone needs such proof.

- Bring at least two pencils for the multiple-choice section, as well as two black pens for the free-response section of the exam. Make sure that your pencils are labeled #2 and that they have good erasers. The machine that scores Section I of the exam cannot recognize marks made by other types of pencils. Also, it cannot read a correct answer if a previous answer has not been erased completely.

- It is helpful to have a watch with you at the exam. Most testing rooms will have clocks, and most test administrators will give you periodic reminders of how much time you have remaining. Still, having your own watch makes it easy to keep close track of your own pace. The watch cannot have a calculator or an alarm, however, as these are not permitted in the exam room.

- Do not bring books of any kind, laptop computers, wireless instant-messaging devices, cameras, or portable radios. If you must bring a cellular phone with you, turn it off and give it to the test proctor until you are finished with your exam.

The test administrators are very clear and very serious about what is *not* allowed during the examination. Below is a list of actions to avoid at all costs, since each is grounds for your immediate dismissal from the exam room.

- Do not consult any outside materials during the exam period. Remember, the break is technically part of the exam—you are not free to review any materials at that time either.

- Do not speak during the exam, unless you have a question for the test proctor. Raise your hand to get the proctor's attention.

- When you are told to stop working on a section of the exam, you must stop *immediately*.

- Do not open your exam booklet before the test begins.

- Never tear a page out of your test booklet or try to remove the exam from the test room.

- Do not behave disruptively—even if you are distressed about a difficult test question or because you have run out of time. Stay calm and make no unnecessary noise. Remember, too, the worst-case scenario: If you are displeased with your performance on test day, you can cancel your exam scores.

Section I: Strategies for Multiple-Choice Questions

Having a firm grasp of U.S. government and politics is, of course, the key to your doing well on the AP U.S. Government & Politics Examination. In addition, being well-informed about the exam itself increases your chances of achieving a high score. Below is a list of strategies that you can use to increase your comfort, your confidence, and your chances of excelling on the multiple-choice section of the exam.

- Pace yourself and keep track of the remaining time as you complete the multiple-choice section. Remember, you have 45 minutes to answer all 60 questions. It is important that you do not get stuck on one question for too long.

- Make a mark in your test booklet next to any questions you cannot answer. Return to them after you reach the end of Section I. Sometimes questions that appear later in the test will refresh your memory of a particular topic, and you will be able to answer one of those earlier questions.

- Always read the entire question carefully and underline and define key words or ideas. You might want to circle words such as *NOT* or *EXCEPT* in that type of multiple-choice question.

- Read *every* answer choice carefully before you make your final selection.

- Use the process of elimination to help you choose the correct answer. Even if you are sure of an answer, cross out the letters of incorrect choices in your test booklet as you eliminate them. This cuts down on distraction and allows you to narrow the remaining choices even further.

- If you are able to eliminate two or three answer choices, it is better to make an educated guess at the correct answer than to leave the answer blank.

- Make yourself completely familiar with the instructions for the multiple-choice questions *before* you take the exam. You will find the instructions in this book. By knowing the instructions cold, you will save yourself the time of reading them carefully on the day of the test.

Section II: Strategies for Free-Response Questions

Here is a list of strategies that you can use to increase your chance of excelling on the free-response section of the exam.

- You have one hour and 40 minutes to outline and write four essays. This is plenty of time to accomplish your task, but not so much that you have any to waste. You must manage your time carefully.

- Be careful not to stray from the focus of the question asked. As you read a question, underline any key words and directives that indicate how you should address the material in your response. Some frequently used directives are listed below, along with descriptions of what you need to do in writing your answer.

- *compare:* address similarities and differences between two or more things

- *describe:* give a detailed account

- *identify:* give a brief definition or listing

- *explain:* communicate how or why

- As you formulate your answer, always consider whether or not it answers the question directly.

AP Correlation to Government in America: People, Politics, and Policy

The following table is intended for your use as a study device. The left column shows one way to break down into historical eras the time period covered in AP U.S. Government & Politics courses. The two columns to the right include detailed breakdowns of chapters in your textbook where you can learn more about those topics. You may want to use this table throughout the year to review what you've learned. It is also an excellent place to begin your pre-exam review of subjects.

SAMPLE AP COURSEUNITS	CORRELATIONS TO *GOVERNMENT IN AMERICA: PEOPLE, POLITICS, AND POLICY* (10th Edition)	CORRELATIONS TO *GOVERNMENT IN AMERICA: PEOPLE, POLITICS, AND POLICY* (11th, 12th, and 13th Editions)

Constitutional Underpinnings of United States Government

The Constitution

Chapter 2: The Constitution
- The Origins of the Constitution
- The Government That Failed: 1776–1787
- Ratifying the Constitution

Chapter 2: The Constitution
- The Origins of the Constitution
- The Government That Failed: 1776–1787
- Ratifying the Constitution

Chapter 4: Civil Liberties and Public Policy
- The Bill of Rights—Then and Now
- Freedom of Religion
- Freedom of Expression
- Defendants' Rights
- Trial by Jury
- The Right to Privacy

Chapter 4: Civil Liberties and Public Policy
- The Bill of Rights—Then and Now
- Freedom of Religion
- Freedom of Expression
- Defendants' Rights
- Trial by Jury
- The Right to Privacy

Federalism

Chapter 3: Federalism
- Defining Federalism
- The Constitutional Basis of Federalism
- Understanding Federalism

Chapter 3: Federalism
- Defining Federalism
- The Constitutional Basis of Federalism
- Understanding Federalism

Separation of Powers

Chapter 2: The Constitution
- The Madisonian Model

Chapter 2: The Constitution
- The Madisonian Model

Chapter 13: The Presidency
- Presidential Leadership of Congress:

  The Politics of Shared Powers

Chapter 13: The Presidency
- Presidential Leadership of Congress:

  The Politics of Shared Powers

Theories of Democratic Government	**Chapter 1: Introducing Government in America** • Democracy	**Chapter 1: Introducing Government in America** • Democracy
	Chapter 3: Federalism • Defining Federalism	**Chapter 3: Federalism** • Defining Federalism

Civil Rights and Civil Liberties

Civil Liberties and Judicial Interpretation	**Chapter 4: Civil Liberties and Public Policy** • Freedom of Religion • Freedom of Expression • Defendants' Rights • The Right to Privacy • Understanding Civil Liberties	**Chapter 4: Civil Liberties and Public Policy** • Freedom of Religion • Freedom of Expression • Defendants' Rights • The Right to Privacy • Understanding Civil Liberties
Civil Rights and the Fourteenth Amendment	**Chapter 5: Civil Rights and Public Policy** • Two Centuries of Struggle • Race, the Constitution, and Public Policy • Women, the Constitution, and Public Policy • Newly Active Groups Under the Civil Rights Umbrella • Affirmative Action • Understanding Civil Rights and Public Policy	**Chapter 5: Civil Rights and Public Policy** • Racial Equality: Two Centuries of Struggle • Race, the Constitution, and Public Policy • Women, the Constitution, and Public Policy • Newly Active Groups Under the Civil Rights Umbrella • Affirmative Action • Understanding Civil Rights and Public Policy

Political Beliefs and Behaviors

Citizens' Political Beliefs	**Chapter 6: Public Opinion and Political Action** • Measuring Public Opinion and Political Information • What Americans Value: Political Ideologies	**Chapter 6: Public Opinion and Political Action** • Measuring Public Opinion and Political Information • What Americans Value: Political Ideologies

Political Parties, Interest Groups, and Mass Media

The Mass Media

Chapter 7: The Mass Media and the Political Agenda
- The Mass Media Today

- The Development of Media Politics

- Reporting the News

- The News and Public Opinion

- The Media's Agenda-Setting Function

- Understanding the Mass Media

Chapter 13: The Presidency
- The President and the Press

Political Parties

Chapter 8: Political Parties
- The Meaning of Party

- The Party in the Electorate

- The Party Organizations: From the Grass Roots to Washington

- The Party in Government: Promises and Policy

- Party Eras in American History

- Third Parties: Their Impact on American Politics

- Understanding Political Parties

Chapter 6: Public Opinion and Political Action
- How Americans Participate in Politics

Campaigning and Elections

Chapter 9: Nominations and Campaigns
- The Nomination Game

- The Campaign Game

Chapter 7: The Mass Media and the Political Agenda
- The Mass Media Today

- The Development of Media Politics

- Reporting the News

- The News and Public Opinion

- The Media's Agenda-Setting Function

- Understanding the Mass Media

Chapter 13: The Presidency
- The President and the Press

Chapter 8: Political Parties
- The Meaning of Party

- The Party in the Electorate

- The Party Organizations: From the Grass Roots to Washington

- The Party in Government: Promises and Policy

- Party Eras in American History

- Third Parties: Their Impact on American Politics

- Understanding Political Parties

Chapter 6: Public Opinion and Political Action
- How Americans Participate in Politics

Chapter 9: Nominations and Campaigns
- The Nomination Game

- The Campaign Game

- Money and Campaigning

- The Impact of Campaigns

- Understanding Nominations
  and Campaigns

**Chapter 10: Elections and
Voting Behavior**
- How Americans Vote:
  Explaining Citizens' Decisions

- The Last Battle: The Electoral College

Chapter 11: Interest Groups
- The Role and Reputation of
  Interest Groups

- Theories of Interest Group Politics

- What Makes an Interest Group
  Successful?

- The Interest Group Explosion

- How Groups Try To Shape Policy

- Types of Interest Groups

- Understanding Interest Groups

National Government

Chapter 12: Congress
- The Representatives and Senators

- Congressional Elections

- How Congress Is Organized
  To Make Policy

- The Congressional Process

- Understanding Congress

**Chapter 9: Nominations
and Campaigns**
- The Nomination Game

• The Campaign Game

Chapter 10: Elections and Voting Behavior
• The Last Battle: The Electoral College

Chapter 13: The Presidency
• The Presidents

• Presidential Powers

• Running the Government: The Chief Executive

• The President and National Security Policy

• Power from the People: The Public Presidency

• The President and the Press

• Understanding the American Presidency

Chapter 16: The Federal Courts
• The Nature of the Judicial System

• The Structure of the Federal Judicial System

• The Politics of Judicial Selection

• The Courts as Policymakers

• The Courts and the Policy Agenda

• Understanding the Courts

Chapter 15: The Federal Bureaucracy
• The Bureaucrats

• How Bureaucracies Are Organized

• Bureaucracies As Implementors

• Bureaucracies As Regulators

• Understanding Bureaucracies

	Chapter 20: Foreign and Defense Policymaking	**Chapter 20: Foreign and Defense Policymaking (ed. 13: Foreign Security Policymaking)**
	• American Foreign Policy: Instruments, Actors, and Policymakers	• American Foreign Policy: Instruments, Actors, and Policymakers
Balance of Power	**Chapter 13: The Presidency** • Presidential Leadership of Congress: The Policies of Shared Powers	**Chapter 13: The Presidency** • Presidential Leadership of Congress: The Policies of Shared Powers

Public Policy

Policymaking in a Federal System	**Chapter 12: Congress** • How Congress Is Organized To Make Policy • The Congressional Process	**Chapter 12: Congress** • How Congress Is Organized To Make Policy • The Congressional Process
	Chapter 13: The Presidency • Presidential Leadership of Congress: The Politics of Shared Powers	**Chapter 13: The Presidency** • Presidential Leadership of Congress: The Politics of Shared Powers
	Chapter 15: The Federal Bureaucracy • Bureaucracies As Implementors	**Chapter 15: The Federal Bureaucracy** • Bureaucracies As Implementors
Formation of Policy Agendas	**Chapter 7: The Mass Media and the Political Agenda** • The Media's Agenda-Setting Function	**Chapter 7: The Mass Media and the Political Agenda** • The Media's Agenda-Setting Function
	Chapter 8: Political Parties • The Party in Government: Promises and Policy	**Chapter 8: Political Parties** • The Party in Government: Promises and Policy
	Chapter 9: Nominations and Campaigns • Money and Campaigning	**Chapter 9: Nominations and Campaigns** • Money and Campaigning
	Chapter 11: Interest Groups • How Groups Try To Shape Policy • Types of Interest Groups	**Chapter 11: Interest Groups** • How Groups Try To Shape Policy • Types of Interest Groups

	Chapter 19: Policymaking for Health Care and the Environment	**Chapter 19: Policymaking for Health Care and the Environment**
	• Health Care Policy	• Health Care Policy
	• Policymaking for Health Care	• Environmental Policy
	• Environmental Policy	• Energy Policy
	• Understanding Health Care and Environmental Policy	• Groups, Energy, and the Environment
		• Understanding Health Care and Environmental Policy
Foreign Policy	**Chapter 20: Foreign and Defense**	**Chapter 20: Foreign and Defense Policymaking Policymaking (in 13th ed: Foreign Security Policymaking)**
	• American Foreign Policy: Instruments, Actors, and Policymakers	• American Foreign Policy: Instruments, Actors, and Policymakers
	• The Politics of Defense Policy	• The Politics of Defense Policy

Part II

Topical Review with Sample Questions and Answers and Explanations

This section is keyed to the chapters in *Government in America*. Part II overviews important information in bullet form and provides sample questions for every question type, plus additional review items on core concepts. Use these practice questions to arm yourself thoroughly for all kinds of test items you will encounter on the AP examination. Answers and explanations are provided for each question for your further review.

CHAPTER 1

Introducing Government in America

Government, Politics, and the Policymaking System

The formal institutions, processes, and procedures within which public policies are made are **government** and **politics**. In the United States the institutions are Congress, the president, the courts, and the federal bureaucracy, and the process by which these leaders are selected and policies are pursued is politics. This **policymaking system** brings together the interests and concerns of the people, the linkage institutions, and the policymaking institutions to create and monitor public policy.

A **democracy** is a form of government in which policymaking reflects the will of the people. The United States is not a **direct democracy,** however. Instead, the American system is based on **representation**—citizens elect representatives to make political decisions for them. The authors of the Constitution were hesitant to vest too much power in the majority of uneducated Americans at the end of the eighteenth century, so they designed a system that, while democratic in nature, would remove politics from direct public control. Over time, the American political system has evolved into its own form of democracy that draws upon some of the elements of a traditional democracy.

Democracy: Traditional Democratic Theory

- **Right to vote:** The public has the right to **vote** for government representatives.

- **Opportunities for political participation:** Citizens must have equal opportunities to express their **political views** by such means as voting or joining political groups such as **political parties.**

- **Political awareness:** The public should be informed about various political and social issues to formulate judgments and make **informed decisions.**

- **Influence over the political agenda:** The issues taken up by the government should reflect the needs of the people.

- **Citizenship:** All people subject to the laws of a nation must have the opportunity to become citizens and to possess all the **rights of citizenship.**

- **Majority rule:** Decisions are made by a vote of the **majority** to reflect the will of the largest percentage of citizens.

- **Minority rights:** The American political system protects some rights of the **minority** against the majority. Freedom of speech and of petition, for example, allows the minority to express its opinions despite **majority rule.**

Three Contemporary Theories of American Democracy

Two main competing theories describe contemporary American politics: pluralist theory and elite theory.

Pluralist Theory

- The political system is composed of groups representing **competing interests.**

- The existence of such groups indicates that the government allows sufficient access to policymaking.

- Interests of the public may be more widely represented in government.

- Power is **decentralized** so that no one body or group has too much influence over policymaking.

Elite and Class Theory

- Government favors only a narrow percentage of the public, primarily the **wealthy.** Wealth is directly proportional to political influence.

- Many political groups may exist, but the distribution of government resources among them is not necessarily equal. The more wealth and influence a group has, the more it benefits from the government.

- Groups do not have equal access to policymaking or equal power.

- **Big business** plays a prominent role in politics because corporations that have money also have power.

Hyperpluralism

Political theorists have developed a third concept of American politics, called **hyperpluralism.** According to hyperpluralism, the proliferation of political groups has weakened the government. With so many interests vying for political influence and so many points of access in government, power is decentralized, and, ultimately, policies become muddled and therefore less effective.

American Political Culture and Democracy

American democracy is held together by a unifying **political culture**, a common set of political values that are widely shared in the nation. These cultural values include liberty, equal opportunity and political equality, individualism, belief in a free-market, laissez faire economy, and populism.

In recent years, some scholars have worried that a polarization has taken place within the nation, threatening a division that might jeopardize the nation's health. Other scholars disagree, saying there is little evidence of irreconcilable differences among groups.

Challenges to Democracy

Modern democracies face numerous challenges from a variety of sources:

- **Increased Technical Expertise**: An increase in the knowledge base makes it difficult for average citizens to make informed decisions.

- **Limited Participation in Government**: Citizens do not take full advantage of participation opportunities, as demonstrated by poor voter turnout.

- **Escalating Campaign Costs**: An increase in the costs of running for office makes candidates increasingly dependent on PACs and further removed from democratic theory.

- **Diverse Political Interests**: Diversity of population can lead to weak coalitions, which may result in policy gridlock.

The Scope of Government in America

The scope of responsibilities of the United States' government includes economic, military, and domestic activities. However, **individualism** in America makes the scope of the United States government comparatively small in relation to other democracies.

For Additional Review

After reviewing the relevant pages of your textbook, make a chart that shows the important characteristics of the pluralist theory, the elite and class theory, and hyperpluralism.

Multiple-Choice Questions

1. Which of the following best illustrates elite theory?

   (A) The idea that large interest groups such as AARP (The American Association of Retired Persons) dominate government decision-making.

   (B) The idea that a small group of wealthy individuals dominate government policy-making.

   (C) The idea that contending interests are so strong within the United States that government is often weakened.

   (D) The fact that more than 20,000 special interest groups lobby Congress each year.

   (E) The idea that because of technologies such as the internet and television, Americans are increasingly isolated from their government, jeopardizing the strength of traditional groups in society.

2. All of the following are characteristic beliefs associated with American political culture EXCEPT

   (A) liberty.

   (B) equality of opportunity.

   (C) individualism.

   (D) government regulation of the economy.

   (E) political equality.

3. According to pluralist theorists, which of the following statements describe the American political system?

   I. The public interest is normally served in the United States through a process of bargaining and compromise.

   II. Organized interest groups fairly shape the public agenda by broadly representing the interests of Americans.

   III. Multiple small groups among the wealthiest one percent of the public are in some way responsible for most policymaking.

   IV. Policymaking reflects the desires of those who control many of the largest corporations in the United States.

   (A) I and II

   (B) II and III

   (C) I and III

   (D) II and IV

   (E) III and IV

4.All of the following are examples of public policy EXCEPT

(A) The president issues an executive order requiring corporations doing business with the government to have affirmative action hiring plans.

(B) Congress writes a law requiring lobbyists to disclose which interest groups employ them.

(C) The Supreme Court upholds the death penalty for a murder conviction.

(D) The Federal Trade Commission writes a rule that corporate claims in television ads be true.

(E) The American Association of Retired Persons passes a rule giving access to their insurance policies only to dues paying members.

5. Democratic theory includes which of the following?

(A) "one person, one vote"

(B) freedom of religion

(C) equality of economic condition

(D) a bicameral Congress

(E) a republican form of government

6. Basic functions common to all national governments include all of the following EXCEPT

(A) collecting taxes.

(B) maintaining a national defense.

(C) providing universal health care.

(D) preserving order.

(E) socializing young citizens.

7. Members of single interest groups

(A) work to limit the bias in national laws favoring married couples.

(B) lobby the government to enact laws limiting the percentages that credit card companies can charge to finance monthly balances.

(C) regulate the discount rate that the government charges to banks for the loans that they choose to make.

(D) are reluctant, usually, to compromise on the issue that defines their narrowly defined goal.

(E) have bound together in recent years to "bundle" soft money contributions to presidential candidates.

8. All of the following can create public policies EXCEPT

(A) Congress.

(B) the president.

(C) an interest group.

(D) the courts.

(E) the bureaucracy.

9. Which characteristic of American politics is concerned with the rights of the minority?

(A) the election process

(B) the Congressional policy-making process

(C) interest group bargaining and compromising on political issues

(D) the president altering his policy proposals in response to public opinion

(E) the Bill of Rights guarantee of civil liberties

10. Government has grown to be big and active because

   I. The public expects government to solve problems

   II. It is hard to cut programs such as Social Security and national defense

   III. Democrats, the party of big government, have been in power in recent years

   IV. The government is committed to reducing income inequality

(A) I and II.

(B) II and III.

(C) III and IV.

(D) I, II and III.

(E) II and IV.

Free-Response Questions

1. At the end of the Constitutional Convention, Benjamin Franklin said that the Founders had created "a republic, if you can keep it."

   a. Define a republican form of government. Explain how a republican form of government fits with the principles of a democracy.

   b. Identify one change in the institutional arrangements of American government and explain how that change has moved us away from the Founders' concept of a republican form of government.

c. Identify a second change in the institutional arrangements of American government and explain how that change has moved us away from the Founders' concept of a republican form of government.

2. Elite/class theory and pluralist theory are two competing views of American politics.

   a. Describe two ideas associated with elite theory.

   b. Describe two ideas associated with pluralist theory.

   c. Which one of the theories best characterizes American government? Support your argument by providing two reasons why the theory you have chosen best characterizes American government.

ANSWERS AND EXPLANATIONS

Multiple-Choice Questions

- **1. (B) is correct.** Elite theory holds that a small group of wealthy and well-placed individuals dominate government decision-making. As a result, group activities and lobbying by varying interests have little impact.

- **2. (D) is correct.** Americans generally believe that a largely unregulated economy, similar to a laissez faire system, would be in the national interest. To the extent that government regulates the economy, Americans often believe that economic health is jeopardized.

- **3. (A) is correct.** Elite theorists believe that the government is mainly controlled by an elite and wealthy minority, most of whom are involved in big business while pluralists think political power is more generally distributed. Statements I and II are therefore correct while II and IV are more reflective of elite theory.

- **4. (E) is correct.** The AARP is an interest group and therefore cannot make policies that would be binding on all citizens, but rather are limited to making rules that apply only to members of their organization on issues over which they have control. The other answers have to do with government organizations engaging in legitimate activities that are universally applicable in their contexts.

- **5. (C) is correct.** A democracy is founded on the needs and wants of the people. All people may not have the same needs, but the closest representation of the whole populace is the majority. Therefore, in a theoretical democracy, decisions are made by majority rule.

- **6. (C) is correct.** While universal medical care might be desirable, and while all governments provide some social services, not all governments can afford universal coverage. The other four answers all characterize basic functions of a national government.

- **7. (D) is correct.** Single interest groups tend to be associated with hyperpluralism. Because they are formed around one narrowly defined issue, they rarely engage in the compromises characteristic of pluralistic bargaining. Single interests are not related to marriage characteristics or on interest rates charged by banks.

- **8. (C) is correct.** The formal governmental actors have the power and authority to produce public policies. Interest groups can affect public policies, but do not have the power or authority to create public policies.

- **9. (E) is correct.** The Bill of Rights was added to the Constitution to protect the expression of unpopular ideas among other things. These rights are not dependent on majoritarian concerns, but are designed to protect the rights of the minority. The other examples are related to processes that reflect broadly held policy preferences.

- **10. (A) is correct.** Government is big and active because people expect government to take action, and once programs are enacted it is hard to scale them back. The other choices are simply factually incorrect.

Free-Response Questions

This rubric provides examples of many, but not all of the possible correct responses to the free-response questions. Occasionally, there will be weaknesses pointed out in the suggested answer, providing students with examples of what to avoid.

1.

a. A republican form of government is one in which the people are represented by elected representatives. In the United States Government, that means that instead of people speaking for themselves in government decision-making, the people elect Representatives who represent them. In a representative government, the Congress members should attempt to represent the will of their constituents.

b. The Founders originally set up the election of Senators so that it was done indirectly by legislatures in the states. The 17th Amendment changed all of this, and now U.S. Senators are directly elected by the people in the states. This moved us away from the original intent of the Founders, who wanted the government not to be directly controlled by the people.

c. Another change in institutional arrangements is the media. The media consists of newspapers and television networks, and the Founders did not have TV. The media provide coverage of the news and tell people what is happening in the world. They are for profit businesses and so they are sometimes not reliable and often have a very liberal bias except for Fox News that provides fair and balanced coverage. *This answer incorrectly identifies the media as an institutional change. The media have changed but this part of the answer is not responsive to the question.*

2. The United States is not a pure democracy because many people do not vote and many who do vote are not very well informed. In a pure democracy, people would participate at much higher levels than they do in the United States. As a result, political observers have come up with other ideas to describe politics in the United States. Two of those ideas are elitism and pluralism. *This is a nice concluding paragraph, but does nothing to add to the substance of the response.*

Elitist theory argues that there is an economic elite that makes all of the important decisions for the nation. It argues that elections are not important because the elite always controls the decision-making process no matter which party wins elections.

In pluralism, the average citizen can play a role in politics by joining and participating in groups. In elitism, the average citizen does not play a role in politics. In pluralism, parties and elections are important because the government responds to whichever party wins. That way, government policy can become a reflection of what the people want.

Of the two, I believe that elitism is the most accurate view. In the United States, it seems like the wealthy always get what they want. Taxes for the rich are down, the disparity between rich and poor is the largest in any nation of the world. The war in Iraq is obviously something that was fought only to protect the oil interest of the very rich. Therefore, we have an elitist form of government. *This portion of the answer fails to provide a second reason in support of the elitism argument.*

CHAPTER 2

The Constitution

The foundation of the American political system rests on the **Constitution,** a document originally consisting of just seven articles that laid out the basic structure of the government. It established the United States as a **federal republic** composed of three branches: the **legislative, executive,** and **judicial.** Over time, the Constitution has been amended to account for the growth of the nation and changes to the political system.

The Origins of the Constitution

- Declaration of Independence (1776)

    - Lists grievances against the king of England

    - Justifies revolution

    - The idea of **natural rights**

- Philosophy of John Locke

    - Rights that are derived from people's basic moral sense supersede the authority of a government.

    - **Consent of the governed:** A government is legitimate only if the people approve of it (social contract).

    - **Limited government:** Because natural rights are superior to a government, governments should have limited power.

    - Government should protect people's property.

- American Revolution ends in 1783

The Articles of Confederation

- Established the first government of the United States (enacted in 1781)

- Designed to preserve the independence of the states

- A national government without any centralized power proves to be ineffectual.

National Government under the Articles of Confederation

- **Unicameral** national legislature

- No executive or judicial institutions

- Most power rests with state legislatures.

- No power to tax

- No regulation of foreign or interstate trade

- No national currency

- No national defense

Weaknesses of the Articles

- Without the power to **collect taxes,** the national government had few financial resources with which to repay its war debts.

- The development of a national economy was inhibited also by the government's inability to establish and **regulate trade.**

- The Articles **prevented the formation of a unified nation** out of a collection of states with different political, economic, and social concerns.

Consequences of the Weaknesses of the Articles

- **Shays' Rebellion** was not easily quelled, because the government had no power to raise a militia. The incident provided the final proof that the Articles were not a sufficient plan of government.

- **Annapolis Convention** in 1786 attempted to suggest reforms of the Articles, but it was determined instead to ask Congress to schedule a convention for 1987

Making a Constitution: The Philadelphia Convention

Many issues were hotly debated during the writing of the **Constitution.** In effect, the framers faced the momentous task of defining the nature of government. They did, however, agree on some basic principles:

- The government should check the **self-interest** of the people yet protect their **individual liberties** and advance **natural rights** such as equality.

- **Factions** should not be allowed to create political conflict and thereby undermine the government.

- No one faction should have the opportunity to prevail upon the others.

Philosophical Differences among the Founders

- Although the 55 founders at the Constitutional Convention were almost all wealthy and well-educated, they had divergent views about major issues, including:

  - Human nature

  - Political conflict and the nature of **factions**

  - Purposes of government

  - Nature of government

The Agenda in Philadelphia

Two plans were proposed to ensure **equal representation** of the people in the legislature: the Virginia Plan and the New Jersey Plan.

- **Virginia Plan:** Representation in the national Congress should be determined by the **population** of each state. Thus, larger states such as Virginia and Pennsylvania would have a greater number of representatives than less populous states such as New Jersey and Georgia.

- **New Jersey Plan:** Each state should be allowed the same number of representatives in the national Congress. Under this plan, all states, regardless of size or population, would have an equal voice in policymaking.

- **The Connecticut Compromise,** or Great Compromise, established a **bicameral legislature.** The **Senate** would include two representatives from each state as per the New Jersey Plan, and representation in the **House** would be determined by the population of each state.

- The **Three-Fifths Compromise** mandated that only three-fifths of slaves be counted in determining state representation (this was repealed by the **Fourteenth Amendment** in 1868).

- **The Economic Issues**

   - The authors identified interstate tariffs, worthless paper money, and economic recession as serious problems of the American economy. These concerns led the Philadelphia delegates to strengthen the economic powers of the new national government to address these problems.

- **The Individual Rights Issues**

   - The **writ of habeas corpus** cannot be suspended.

   - **Bills of attainder,** which punish people without a trial, cannot be passed.

   - **Ex post facto laws,** which are retroactive criminal laws, are prohibited.

   - **Religious qualifications** cannot be used as a prerequisite for public office.

   - All citizens are entitled to a **trial by jury** in a criminal case.

The Madisonian Model

- James Madison warned that both the majority (poorer and less-educated Americans) and minority (the wealthy elite) factions could pose a threat to the stability of a government.

- To protect government from the will of the majority, the president would be chosen by the **Electoral College,** and, until the Seventeenth Amendment in 1913, senators would be chosen by states' legislatures, not directly by the people.

- Madison proposed that the national government be divided into three branches: the **executive, legislative,** and **judicial.** Each branch would have its own powers and responsibilities.

- A system of **checks and balances** would ensure that no branch could become more powerful than the others. The majority or the minority might be able to take control of any one branch but not necessarily the whole political system.

- Establishing a **federal** system of government allowed power to be shared between the national and state levels of government.

Checks and Balances

Legislative Branch

- House and Senate can veto a bill of the other house.

- Senate approves presidential nominations for judges and other officials

- Can impeach the president

- Controls the budget

- Can pass laws over a president's veto with a two-thirds majority

Executive Branch

- Can veto bills passed by Congress

- Nominates judges and other government officials

Judicial Branch

- Can declare laws passed by Congress to be unconstitutional

- Can declare acts of the president to be unconstitutional

- Note that the Constitution did not grant to the courts the power to check the other branches. The Supreme Court did not assert its authority to declare laws **unconstitutional** until the case of *Marbury* v. *Madison* in 1803.

Republican Form of Government

- Established that the government would be one of elected representatives

Ratifying the Constitution

The approval of at least nine states was needed to ratify the Constitution, and it did not come easily.

Anti-Federalists

- Feared that the Constitution **favored an elite minority**

- Believed that the Constitution failed to protect too many **individual freedoms**

- Believed that a strong central government would limit the power of the states

- Published scathing articles and political cartoons denouncing the Constitution as a tool of the aristocracy

Federalists

- Published a series of articles called the **Federalist Papers** to defend the Constitution

- Asserted that the Constitution would benefit the growing middle class of tradesmen as well as the wealthy plantation owners

- Promised to add a **bill of rights** to guarantee individual liberties

- The Constitution was ratified in 1787, largely because the authors promised to add a bill of rights.

- It established the United States as a **federal republic** in which power would be divided among levels of government.

- The Constitution is considered a **"living document"** because it can be amended as the United States grows and changes.

- **Formal amendment process**

  - Proposal

    - By Congress with a 2/3 vote in each House

    - By National Convention called by 2/3 of states

- Ratification
    - By ¾ of state legislatures
    - By Conventions in ¾ of the states
- **Informal amendment process**
    - **judicial interpretation (established in *Marbury* v. *Madison*)**
    - **changing political practice, technology, and increased demands on policymakers.**
    - Over the years, it has become **more democratic** than the authors intended.

For Additional Review

Make a chart comparing and contrasting the Articles of Confederation and the Constitution. How did they organize government differently? In what ways did the Constitution amend the failures of the Articles?

Multiple-Choice Questions

1. Under America's first constitution, the Articles of Confederation,
    - (A) the national government dominated state governments.
    - (B) the executive branch had more power than Congress.
    - (C) Congress was a unicameral body.
    - (D) states were represented in Congress proportionally according to population.
    - (E) reflected the Founding Father's belief that a national standing army was necessary.

2. Which of the following Founders was the "principal architect" of the Constitution?
    - (A) Edmund Randolph
    - (B) George Washington
    - (C) Thomas Jefferson
    - (D) Alexander Hamilton
    - (E) James Madison

3. The Three-Fifths Compromise at the Constitutional Convention

   (A) allowed cloture to be invoked, ending a filibuster in the Senate, with the support of 60 senators.

   (B) prescribed the proportion of states required to ratify a constitutional amendment.

   (C) provided a formula by which slaves would be counted for apportioning the House of Representatives.

   (D) established the percentage of votes necessary for electors to be chosen under the original provisions of the Electoral College system.

   (E) established the percentage of members of the House required to pass a bill raising revenue.

4. Any law passed by a legislature that punishes an individual without a trial, under the Constitution, violates the Constitutional concept of

   (A) a bill of attainder.

   (B) an ex post facto law.

   (C) double jeopardy.

   (D) eminent domain.

   (E) habeas corpus.

5. The idea of limiting the role of government to protecting "life, liberty, and property" is generally attributed to

   (A) Karl Marx.

   (B) Thomas Jefferson.

   (C) Thomas Hobbes.

   (D) John Locke.

   (E) Alexander Hamilton.

6. The outcome of a conflict between the Constitution and the states is determined by

   (A) the Connecticut Compromise.

   (B) the Supremacy clause.

   (C) *Federalist Paper #10.*

   (D) judicial review.

   (E) ex post facto laws

7.   The founding fathers designed a system of checks and balances for the national government. Which of the following best illustrates that concept?

   I.   Congress overrides a president's veto.

   II.   The Supreme Court declares a law unconstitutional.

   III. The president issues an executive order reducing the size of the bureaucracy.

   IV.   The House and Senate cannot agree on a Conference Committee report.

   (A)   I and II

   (B)   II and III

   (C)   III and IV

   (D)   II and IV

   (E)   I and IV

8. A law goes into effect declaring that a business practice that has been legal in the past will be illegal in the future, and the law is made retroactive. Why would the Supreme Court likely rule the new law unconstitutional?

   (A)   It would constitute a bill of attainder.

   (B)   It would violate double jeopardy.

   (C)   It would bypass grand jury indictment.

   (D)   It would violate the concept of eminent domain.

   (E)   It would be an ex post facto law.

9. Which plan proposed at the Constitutional Convention called for a bicameral legislature with one chamber having members from states calculated proportionally based upon population and the other having two members per state?

   (A)   Connecticut Compromise

   (B)   Virginia Plan

   (C)   Annapolis Convention Plan

   (D)   Philadelphia Plan

   (E)   New Jersey Plan

10. The case of *Marbury* v. *Madison* (1803) established which principle?

   (A)   the supremacy clause

   (B)   judicial review

   (C)   natural rights of citizens

   (D)   the writ of habeas corpus rule

   (E)   the separation of powers

1. The Constitution has had seventeen formal amendments since the adoption of the Bill of Rights, yet there are basic elements that have changed because of informal processes as well.

    A. Identify the most common means of formally amending the Constitution.

    B. Identify and explain how one informal process has changed the meaning of the Constitution even without formal amendment.

    C. Identify and explain how another informal process has changed the meaning of the Constitution even without formal amendment.

2. When James Madison proposed a new constitution, he tried to balance the need for "proper energy" in government with a clear limitation on government power as well.

    A. Identify two features Madison proposed for keeping any branch of government from becoming too powerful.

    B. Explain how each feature identified in A. balances the need for strong government with a need for limited government.

    C. Identify one feature Madison proposed for dividing powers between national and state governments.

    D. Explain how this feature balanced the need for a strong central government while assuring the states of adequate power.

ANSWERS AND EXPLANATIONS

Multiple-Choice Questions

- **1. (C) is correct.** All but one of the answer choices mis-identify a characteristic of the Articles. Only the statement that it provided for a unicameral legislature is a correct statement.

- **2. (E) is correct.** James Madison provided the intellectual impetus for the Constitution, arriving at the convention with the Virginia Plan. As a result, in terms of his impact on the Constitution, Madison was in many ways the "first among equals." The others listed had an impact on the Constitution, but their roles were far more limited than Madison's, especially Jefferson's, since he was out of the country at the time of the Constitutional convention.

- **3. (C) is correct.** Although all of the options could provide for a 3/5 ratio, only the treatment of the slaves was specified in the Constitution. As a result, the others, though they may be correct (as in the case of invoking cloture), do not stem from the Constitution.

- **4. (A) is correct.** One of the civil liberties issues addressed in the original Constitution attempted to limit the practice, common in some parts of Europe, to pass laws that singled out individuals. The idea in the United States was that such Bills of Attainder were unfair, and that laws should apply to all citizens equally.

- **5. (D) is correct.** The political theories of John Locke hold the key (OK, bad pun) to American Constitutionalism. Locke believed in a representative democracy with limited powers, concepts that underscore the Constitution. Jefferson, one incorrect answer, of course, borrowed Locke's ideas loosely in the Declaration of Independence when he wrote that governments should protect "life, liberty, and the pursuit of happiness."

- **6. (B) is correct.** One of the major features of the new Constitution, as opposed to the Articles of Confederation, was that all states would have to adopt laws that conformed to limits of the U.S. Constitution. This was a core concept of the Constitution.

- **7. (A) is correct.** Checks and balances require the interaction between two branches of government. Hence, the overriding of a president's veto by Congress or the invalidation of a Congressional law by the Supreme Court would be examples of checks and balances while presidential orders within the executive branch or conflict within the legislative branch would not.

- **8. (E) is correct.** All of the concepts listed as possible answers are core concepts in the Constitution of the bill of rights, but the definition in the frame of the question is that of an ex post facto law, something banned in the original Constitution.

- **9. (A) is correct.** The Virginia and New Jersey Plans were contradictory proposals regarding representation. Philadelphia was the city in which the convention was held while Annapolis had been the location to a failed convention in 1786. The "great compromise" that led to a senate based upon equal state representation and a House allocated proportionally based upon population was the Connecticut Compromise

- **10. (B) is correct.** The case of *Marbury* v. *Madison* was the landmark decision of the Supreme Court declaring that in was an inherent duty of the judicial branch to "determine what the law is," thus establishing judicial review.

Free-Response Questions

This rubric provides examples of many, but not all of the possible correct responses to the free-response questions. Occasionally, there will be weaknesses pointed out in the suggested answer, providing students with examples of what to avoid.

1. The Constitution is the cornerstone of American Democracy. It was written by the founding fathers to guarantee that American democracy would survive for all times. The constitution can be amended either formally or informally.

    The process for formal amendments is that it comes with (1) a bill passed by Congress and (2) the signed as an amendment by the president. It is a very difficult process and as a result, very few amendments have been added to the Constitution since the writing of the Bill of Rights. The amendment process required that Congress pass an amendment by a 2/3 vote rather than the normal majority needed for passing a law. Then the president can choose to veto the amendment or sign it into law. If the president vetoes the amendment, Congress can override it by a three-fourths vote. *The answer does not correctly identify either "proposal" or "ratification, and does state the role of states in the amendment process.*

    The constitution can be amended informally in a bunch of ways. That means that the Constitution might have changed meaning without having a formal amendment added. Like the military has an Air Force now even though the Constitution only says that there will be "an army and a navy." Mostly, this involves custom and usage. For example, a president can issue an executive order or negotiate an executive agreement with other nations. These are not part of the Constitution, but presidents have learned to use them anyway. As a result, they are, in a way, the same as formal amendments to the Constitution. *The answer does not explain how either means changes the meaning of the Constitution.*

    So, as you can see, the Constitution can be amended formally and informally.

2.

a. In order for any branch to be kept from being too powerful, Madison designed a government that included the twin concepts of separation of powers and checks and balances. In a system such as that, power is divided among three branches of government—the legislative, the executive, and the judicial. Each branch has a specific grant of power and each one is given "checks over the other. For example, Congress must approve presidential treaties and can override a president's veto. Congress can even impeach and remove a president from power. The president can veto a bill of Congress. And the Supreme Court can declare acts of the president or laws of Congress unconstitutional. In other words, this is a Madisonian design that is intended to limit the powers of each of the branches of government. *Does not explain how separation of powers keeps any branch from becoming too powerful*

b. In order to keep the federal government from gaining too much power, the Constitution created a system of federalism, that is, a system that divided power between the national government and the state governments. The powers of the national government are listed in Article 1 of the Constitution and the 10th Amendment makes it clear that powers not listed in Article 1 are reserved for the states. As a result, the concept of federalism was designed to keep the national government from becoming too strong.

In recent years, many observers have argued that the national government has become too strong. As a result, the federal design has been seen as under siege. But President Reagan designed a "new federalism, consisting of changing categorical grants to block grants that "devolved power for the national government to the states. Also, Congress passed a law that outlawed "unfunded mandates." So, the powers between the national government and the states have come more into balance.

CHAPTER 3

Federalism

In a **federal system,** government is divided between the national and sub-national levels. In the U.S., the state governments are the most important level. Local governments are units of the states. Each level of government has its own powers and responsibilities, but often their spheres overlap. This multi-level form of government, while not unique to the United States, is not the most common form of government in the world. Federalism provided the basis of compromise at the Philadelphia Convention between supporters of a strong national government and those delegates who favored retaining state traditions and local power.

Defining Federalism

- **Federal government:** Government is **divided into more than one level.** Different bodies share power over the same group of people. Every citizen of the United States must obey both federal laws and the laws of his or her state. Citizens may also vote for their representatives in both state and federal elections. Germany, Canada, and India also have federal systems.

- **Unitary government:** Only **one central government** has authority over a nation. There are no levels of government that share power. Japan, France, and Great Britain all operate under unitary governments. Most countries today have either a federal or a unitary form of government.

- **Confederation:** An association of states with some authority delegated to a national government. The states in such a system retain most of the power, but the national government is authorized to carry out some functions, such as diplomatic relations. Although rare today, many of the former Soviet republics have either stayed in union with Russia under the Russian Federation, or have formed a confederation with Russia.

Decentralized Government

A federal system of government decentralizes power.

- **Opportunities for political participation** at all levels: Citizens can run for numerous government positions or take part in campaigns at different levels.

- **Public involvement:** Citizens can elect local, state, and federal representatives.

- **Access:** A greater number of interests can be represented across levels, ensuring that the government will be more responsive to public concerns.

- **Decisions** can be made at lower levels, thereby allowing the federal government to concentrate more fully on fewer issues.

- **Parties** also function at **two levels:** The loss of any one election does not pose as serious a setback, and it is less likely that one party will dominate the whole political system.

- **Intergovernmental relations** become especially important in a federal system because of the elaborate communication necessary to share power.

Decentralized Policy

- Policymaking is **shared between levels.** Often states act as innovators by trying out new laws before they are adopted nationally.

- Policies can be made separately. For example, family and other social issues are usually addressed by state laws.

- Policies may be discussed at both levels. For example, issues of the economy, environment, and equality are addressed by both federal and state laws.

- Debate often arises over which level of government should have the authority on an issue. A major consequence of this is the development of the court system, for it is a court's ruling that determines whether a state or federal law is constitutional.

Powers Reserved for the Federal Government	Powers Reserved for State Governments	Powers Shared by the Federal and State Governments
Coin money	Create local level of government	Make and enforce laws
Regulate the economy and foreign and interstate commerce	Regulate intrastate commerce	Collect taxes
Declare war	Hold elections	Maintain courts
Manage national military	Ratify amendments	Allocate money for public needs
Direct foreign relations	Conduct social policymaking	propose amendments

The Constitutional Basis of Federalism

Supremacy Clause

- Located in Article VI

- Asserts the authority of the national government over the states: The Constitution, national laws, and treaties made by the national government should be held as the supreme law of the United States.

- In cases of discrepancy, federal laws usually supersede state laws.

Enumerated Powers

- Located in Article 1, section 8 of the Constitution

- Powers granted to the national government, and specifically to Congress

Tenth Amendment

- Located in the Bill of Rights

- Grants all powers not specifically reserved for the national government to the states

- Often cited in arguments in favor of states' rights

Implied Powers

- Established in *McCulloch* v. *Maryland*, an 1819 Supreme Court case in which the states battled the formation of a national bank

- The Supreme Court, under Chief Justice John Marshall, ruled against the states, thereby reinforcing the supremacy of the national government.

- Elastic Clause. Also called the necessary and proper clause

- Located in Article I, Section 8 of the Constitution

- Gives Congress the authority to pass any laws necessary to carry out its duties as enumerated in the Constitution

- The elastic clause, as interpreted in *McCulloch* v. *Maryland,* allows Congress to act on implied powers that are not specifically defined in the Constitution.

- Furthered by the case of *Gibbons* v. *Ogden* in 1824, expanding Congressional power to regulate commerce

Full Faith and Credit Clause

- Located in Article IV, Section 1

- Requires each state to formally recognize the documents and judgments handed down by courts in other states

- Helps coalesce the state laws under a national umbrella

Extradition

- Located in Article IV, Section 2

- Requires the return **(extradition)** of fugitive criminals arrested in one state to the state in which the crime was committed for prosecution, although it has developed as a discretionary decision

Privileges and Immunities Clause

- Located in Article IV, Section 2

- Also helps unify the states by assuring that all citizens are treated equally when they travel from state to state

Intergovernmental Relations Today

- **Dual federalism:** Each level of government has distinct responsibilities that do not overlap.

- **Cooperative federalism:** Levels of government share responsibilities.

- Shared costs: To receive federal aid, states must pay for part of a program.

- Federal guidelines: To receive funding, state programs must follow federal rules and regulations.

- Shared administration: Though programs must adhere to basic federal guidelines, they are administered according to the state's directives.

- **Fiscal federalism:** The system of distributing federal money to state governments

- About a quarter of states' fiscal spending is derived from federal aid.

- Money is distributed through relatively restrictive **categorical grants** and **block grants,** which allow states more spending discretion**.**

- **Mandates**, however, can create economic hardships for states when Congress creates financial obligations for the states without providing funding for those obligations.

FEDERALISM AND DEMOCRACY

- Federalism contributes to democracy by increasing access to the government at all levels, but it also creates disadvantages due to differences in the resources of individual states. These differences can lead to inequities among the states in areas such as education.

For Additional Review

To understand more fully the idea of fiscal federalism, brainstorm a list of some services that your state provides. Then conduct Internet research to see how those programs receive funding.

Multiple-Choice Questions

1. Which of the following forms of fiscal federalism allow the states the broadest financial discretion?

    (A) categorical grants

    (B) block grants

    (C) mandates

    (D) foreign assistance

    (E) U. S. military funding

2. The Constitution grants Congress the power to establish post offices and post roads. This is an example of

   (A) enumerated powers.

   (B) implied powers.

   (C) reserved powers.

   (D) concurrent powers.

   (E) exclusive powers.

3. In a confederation,

   (A) power is divided between a central government and regional governments.

   (B) the sovereignty within a nation is held entirely by the central government.

   (C) sovereignty is shared at the national, state, and local levels.

   (D) power is held at the regional level, with the central government exercising only such influence as the regional governments give it.

   (E) regional governments hold sovereignty regarding domestic policy while the national government holds sovereignty in national security policy.

4. The fiscal relationship between the national and state governments involves complex relationships. Which would *least* likely be favored by state governments?

   (A) unfunded mandates

   (B) categorical grants

   (C) block grants

   (D) revenue sharing

   (E) formula grants

5. "Enumerated" powers are those given to

   (A) the Supreme Court.

   (B) the federal bureaucracy.

   (C) state governments.

   (D) the military.

   (E) the national government.

6. The system of federalism that allowed states to do most of the fundamental governing from 1789 to1937 was

   (A) home rule.

   (B) regulated "marble cake" federalism.

   (C) dual federalism.

   (D) shared powers.

   (E) cooperative federalism.

7. The case of *McCulloch* v. *Maryland* (1809) ruled that

   I.   The federal government could exercise only the enumerated powers of the Constitution

   II. The implied powers in Article I of the Constitution allowed Congress to create a nationally chartered bank

   III. The state governments could levy taxes on national government institutions

   IV. Neither states nor the federal government could tax one another

   V.   The state courts had sole jurisdiction over regulatory affairs within their boundaries

   (A) I, III, and V

   (B) I and IV

   (C) II and III

   (D) II and IV

   (E) IV and V

8. "Dual federalism" refers to the fact that

   (A) the Constitution provides two layers of government in the nation—the national and the state.

   (B) there are two major forms of aid from the national government to the states—categorical and block grants.

   (C) both the national and state governments can levy taxes on citizens.

   (D) there are two distinct eras in American history—the era before cooperative federalism and the era since the development of cooperative federalism.

   (E) there is a distinct line between policies surrounding public education and private education in the states.

9. The power of the national government to regulate interstate commerce was expanded in the landmark case of

   (A) *Marbury* v. *Madison.*

   (B) *Plessy* v. *Ferguson.*

   (C) *McCulloch* v. *Maryland.*

   (D) *Miranda* v. *Arizona.*

   (E) *Gibbons* v. *Ogden.*

10. The notion that when state and federal laws conflict, the national laws will prevail is the

   (A) Necessary and Proper clause.

   (B) Supremacy clause.

   (C) Extradition clause.

   (D) Full faith and credit clause.

   (E) Privileges and Immunities clause.

Free-Response Question

1. The Constitution designed a system in which various types of powers were assigned to different levels of government. Those types of powers are variously described as:

   - enumerated powers
   - reserved powers
   - concurrent powers, and
   - implied powers

Select three of the types of powers listed above.

a. Define each of the chosen types of powers.

b. Explain how each of the chosen types of powers affects the distribution of powers between national and state governments.

2.	Cooperative federalism is a term often used to describe the complex fiscal relationship between the national and state governments. In your essay, do the following:

        a. discuss the concept of categorical grants

        b. explain an advantage and a disadvantage of categorical grants

        c. discuss the concept of block grants

        d. explain an advantage and a disadvantage of block grants

ANSWERS AND EXPLANATIONS

Multiple-Choice Questions

- **1. (B) is correct.** One of the major fiscal federalism issues in recent years is the "devolution" of powers from the national government to the states in the form of block grants. Categorical grants give very limited discretion to states while mandates leave states with no discretion. Foreign and military policies are solely the province of the national government.

- **2. (A) is correct.** The enumerated powers are listed in Article 1, section 8, and one example is the establishment of post offices and roads. Other options describe different types of power.

- **3. (D) is correct.** Under the Articles of Confederation, the state governments held the final power while the national government had only such powers as the thirteen regional (or state) governments gave it. The other definitions provided as options describe different arrangements of power.

- **4. (A) is correct.** Mandates allow the states no discretion in spending money. Of course, from the state's position, the least liked of mandates are "unfunded mandates" that require states to spend money without any financial assistance from the national government. All of the other options allow the states some modicum of control over the supervision of spending and therefore would be preferred over mandates.

- **5. (E) is correct.** This is a simple definitional question. The other options are not the correct terms to describe the definition in the root of the question.

- **6. (C) is correct.** Before the creation of cooperative federalism with the passing of "New Deal" programs in the mid-1930s, federalism generally conformed to the dual federalism model. Other answers provided describe different scenarios than the correct answer.

- **7. (D) is correct.** The *McCulloch* case is a landmark decision that had two major findings, that state and national governments could not destroy one another by taxing and that the implied powers allowed the establishment of a national bank even though that was not explicitly mentioned in Article 1, section 8. Answers I and III contradict the correct answers and answer V is not related to the decision in any way.

- **8. (A) is correct.** Dual federalism is used to describe the original view of the relationship between the levels of government as clearly separated, or layered. The other four responses also refer to contrasts between two things, but not to dual federalism.

- **9. (E) is correct.** *Gibbons v. Ogden* had to do with expanding the national government's power to regulate interstate commerce and is one of the two, with *McCulloch v. Maryland* most important early Supreme Court federalism decisions. The other court cases listed have to do with different issues.

- **10. (B) is correct.** The supremacy clause assures that states comply with guiding provisions of the national government. Where the Constitution is silent, states have a great deal of discretion in their decision-making. But where there is a Constitutional requirement, states cannot have laws that are at variance with the national requirement.

Free-Response Questions

This rubric provides examples of many, but not all of the possible correct responses to the free-response questions. Occasionally, there will be weaknesses pointed out in the suggested answer, providing students with examples of what to avoid.

1. The Constitution provides for several types of powers—including enumerated powers, reserved powers, concurrent powers and implied powers. In this essay, I will discuss enumerated powers, concurrent powers and implied powers. These are all powers that governments have. The enumerated powers are specific powers listed in the Constitution. The reserved powers are powers reserved to the government and the implied powers are powers that are implied but not expressly discussed in the Constitution. All of these powers can be powers given to the national government or the state governments. If the national government is given these powers, it becomes more powerful while if the states get these powers, they become more powerful. The implied powers were given to the national government by the Supreme Court case of McCulloch v. Maryland. In this case, the state of Maryland tried to tell the Supreme Court that the national government couldn't do anything unless the Constitution specifically said that they could do it. But the Supreme Court took a loose interpretation of the Constitution and said that if the powers were "necessary and proper," the national government could use them. This allowed the national government to establish a national bank. The reason that these powers are important in politics these days is that Republicans think that state governments should have more powers while Democrats think that the national government should have more power. With the enumerated and reserved and implied powers, the government's powers get larger or smaller. *This is the infamous one paragraph "tossed salad" essay. The essay is not organized well and terms are not defined*

2. In American politics, the priorities of government are set by the ways government spend money. A further issue concerns which level of government has the power to set those priorities by making decisions about how to spend money. These issues, where money is spent and which level of government makes decisions about where money is spent, form the basis for understanding the issues surrounding categorical and block grants.

    Categorical grants are grants from the national government to the state government for specific purposes and with strings attached. Usually, categorical grants give money to states to spend with almost no discretion—if the states agree to receive categorical grants they agree to spend the money in specific ways. In contrast, block grants are moneys given by the national government to the states for more general purposes and as a result, states will often have choices to make on how to spend block grants.

    One advantage of a categorical grant is that it allows the national government to have greater fiscal responsibility for the money that it collects. Member of Congress may feel that since they are ultimately responsible for the money that they have collected from their constituents, they should exercise specific control over how that money is spent. For example, the Interstate Highway Act is a categorical grant. As a result, if states accept money under that act, the Congress knows that it will be spent for building and maintaining the interstate highways. However, a disadvantage of categorical grants is that the states can be blackmailed by the national government. The Interstate Highway Act illustrates that as well. In order to receive that money, states must comply with all of the provisions of the grant. So, as a result, when the national government said that in order to receive this grant, states would have to raise their drinking age to 21, all 50 states complied. So, although the national government doesn't have authority to raise the drinking age, it can make the states do that with categorical grant money.

    One advantage of block grants is that it allows the states, which are closer to the people, the ability to hone the use of that money to the specific needs of the state. Northern states might have needs that are different from Southern states and Urban States might have needs that are different than Rural States. For example, if the national government wants to improve science and math education, needs might be different in a state like Texas, where a lot of student speak Spanish, than in a state like Minnesota, where language barriers are not as big an issue. The disadvantage of block grants is that the national government does not have as much control over the money and states might "waste" the free money that the federal government gave them. That would mean that the national government was not a good steward of its money.

    In all, the politics of intergovernmental relations is fascinating and reflects partisan differences as well as policy preferences. Categorical and block grants illustrate those differences very well.

CHAPTER 4

Civil Liberties and Public Policy

Civil liberties are the individual freedoms guaranteed in the Bill of Rights. They are primarily concerned with protecting citizens from too much government control. While these freedoms are specifically addressed in the first ten amendments, they are not always clearly defined, especially in light of today's social, political, and technological circumstances. Because civil liberties are rarely absolute and often conflict with each other and with other societal values, the courts must continually define and interpret the meaning and practice of these freedoms.

The Bill of Rights—Then and Now

- The Bill of Rights protects freedoms at a national level, but these freedoms were not necessarily guaranteed in some state constitutions.

- In the case of *Barron* v. *Baltimore* (1833), the Supreme Court ruled that the Bill of Rights did not protect individuals against state governments.

- In *Gitlow* v. *New York* (1925), the Court reversed its earlier decision, citing the due process clause of the **Fourteenth Amendment** as reason to protect individuals' free speech and free press rights, found in the **First Amendment,** against state government incursions.

- *Gitlow* v. *New York* began a tradition called the **incorporation doctrine,** by which the Supreme Court has gradually, on a case-by-case basis, ensured the protection of most freedoms listed in the Bill of Rights from state infringement by means of the due process clause of the 14th Amendment. The Supreme Court has not incorporated every freedom in the Bill of Rights. Instead of "total incorporation," the Supreme Court has engaged in "selective incorporation."

Freedom of Religion

Establishment Clause: In the First Amendment, prohibiting Congress from making laws establishing any religion in conjunction with the government

- Some critics interpret the clause loosely: The government should not favor one religion over another in its policies. Others, including Thomas Jefferson, argue that the establishment clause endorses the **separation of church and state.**

- The Establishment Clause is at the center of the debate over prayer in school and over federal funding to private religious schools.

- *Lemon* v. *Kurtzman* (1971): The Supreme Court allowed federal funding of parochial schools, provided that the money neither advances nor inhibits religious teaching, but instead is used for administrative purposes. In 2002, the Supreme Court also permitted state vouchers to be used for parochial schools in *Zelman* v. *Simmons-Harris.*

- *Engel v. Vitale (*1962) and *School District of Abington Township, Pennsylvania* v. *Schempp* (1963): Forbid the practice of prayer in school as a violation of the Establishment Clause and a breaching of the separation of church and state.

- Federal funds may be used to construct school buildings and to provide administrative and academic supplies, but not to endorse religious teaching.

- Student religious groups cannot be denied access to school buildings for the purpose of meeting or worship if other groups are also allowed access.

Free Exercise Clause: A First Amendment right that guarantees the freedom to practice or not practice any religion.

- The Court has upheld that the government cannot infringe on people's beliefs, but it can regulate religious behavior to some degree.

- State laws can ban religious practices that conflict with other laws, but they cannot forbid religious worship itself.

Freedom of Expression

Speech

- Courts grapple with the definition of "speech." Political protests and picketing are protected by the First Amendment, but **libel, slander,** and **obscenity** are not.

- Fraud and incitement to violence are considered action, not speech, and are not protected.

- The Constitution forbids **prior restraint,** or government censorship of the press. This policy was strengthened by the case of *Near* v. *Minnesota (*1931), in which the Court found in favor of the press.

- Prior restraint is granted in situations where **national security** might be compromised.

- As decided in *Schenck* v. *United States* (1919), freedom of speech may be curtailed when it threatens **public order.**

The Press

- Freedom of the press can conflict with the **right to a fair trial,** but the press does have a right to report on any criminal proceeding, and all trials must be open to the public. However, in *Branzburg* v. *Hayes* (1972), the Supreme Court ruled in favor of fair trial over a reporter's right to protect sources, and in *Zucher* v. *Stanford* (1978) the Court sided with the police over the press.

- ***Roth* v. *United States*** (1957): The Court asserted that obscenity is not protected under the First Amendment. However, the definition of "obscenity" continues to be a point of controversy.

- ***Miller* v. *California (1973):*** Allowed community standards, varying in different parts of the country, to be used in determining if material is obscene.

- Cases of libel are usually difficult to win because public figures must prove that the insults were intentionally malicious, as mandated in ***New York Times* v. *Sullivan*** (1964).

- Acts of symbolic speech, such as protesting and flag burning (***Texas* v. *Johnson,*** 1989), are protected under the First Amendment.

- **Commercial speech,** such as advertising, is more closely regulated by the **Federal Trade Commission.**

- Commercial speech on radio and television is regulated by the **Federal Communications Commission.** The broadcast media have significantly less freedom than do print media (*Red Lion Broadcasting Company* v. *Federal Communications Commission,* 1969), though they are not required to print replies from candidates they have criticized (*Miami Herald Publishing Company* v. *Tornillo (1974).*

Assembly

- **Freedom of assembly** includes the right to protest, picket, or hold a demonstration.

- The right to establish groups of people with similar political interests, from political parties to the Ku Klux Klan, is protected under the First Amendment (*NAACP* v. *Alabama,* 1958).

Defendants' Rights

As with free speech, the courts must continually interpret the vague language of the Constitution to apply it to today's issues and events.

- **Searches and seizures:** The **Fourth Amendment** protects citizens from **unreasonable searches and seizures.**

  - Police investigators cannot search private property without a **search warrant** issued by a court unless there is reason to believe that the evidence will disappear or be destroyed or removed in the meantime.

  - The police cannot arrest someone unless there is **probable cause** to believe that he or she is guilty.

  - The **exclusionary rule** prevents prosecutors from using evidence acquired through unreasonable search and seizure.

  - The case of *Mapp* v. *Ohio* (1961) extended the exclusionary rule to state as well as federal cases.

  - In recent years, the Supreme Court has made exceptions to the exclusionary rule. For example, when police are thought to have acted in "good faith," even if their actions technically violate the rule, the Court has allowed use of the evidence seized.

  - The **USA Patriot Act** (2001) also expanded the government's right to investigate terrorism suspects without warrants.

- **Self-incrimination:** The **Fifth Amendment** protects people from being forced to supply evidence against themselves.

  - Because a person is innocent until proven guilty, the prosecution is responsible for proving a defendant's guilt.

  - *Miranda* v. *Arizona* (1966): Established that suspects must be informed of their constitutional rights before they are questioned by the police.

- **Right to counsel:** The **Sixth Amendment** guarantees that all accused persons tried in a federal court have the right to be represented by an attorney.

  - *Gideon* v. *Wainwright* (1963): Extends this privilege to cases tried in state courts as well.

  - Most cases are settled by **plea bargaining** between lawyers instead of by a trial.

  - The Sixth Amendment requires a trial by a jury of 12 people in federal cases; in state cases this number may be fewer, and a conviction does not require a unanimous vote.

- **Cruel and unusual punishment** is prohibited by the **Eighth Amendment**, though the term is not clearly defined in the Bill of Rights.

    - In *Gregg* **v. Georgia** (1976) and *McCleskey* **v. Kemp** (1987), the Supreme Court confirmed that the death penalty does not violate the Bill of Rights —that is, it is not considered "cruel and unusual."

    - Debate over the death penalty continues as DNA tests sometimes prove the innocence of inmates on death row.

- **Right to privacy** is not specifically guaranteed by the Bill of Rights, but the Supreme Court has interpreted the first ten amendments to imply this right.

    - *Griswold* v. *Connecticut* (1965) asserted the right to privacy, which became more controversial when the principle was applied, in *Roe* **v. Wade** (1973), to forbid states from controlling abortions during the first trimester of pregnancy.

    - *Webster* **v. Reproductive Health Services** (1989): The Supreme Court upheld a Missouri law that prevented the use of state funds for abortion clinics and that prohibited state employees from performing abortions.

    - The Supreme Court, while allowing abortions, has increasingly permitted regulation of them (*Planned Parenthood* **v. Casey**, 1992).

    - Medical technology also causes debate over the right to privacy in cases of surrogate parenthood and physician-assisted suicide.

For Additional Review

Make a three-column table. In the first column, write all of the civil liberties discussed in this chapter. In the second column, list all Supreme Court cases that have addressed each liberty, including the date, the chief justice, and brief synopsis of the case. In the third column, list the corresponding amendment or any previous court cases on which the Supreme Court based its decisions about each civil liberty.

Multiple-Choice Questions

1. *Roe* v. *Wade* (1972) ruled that a woman's right to an abortion came from the

    (A) right of symbolic speech.

    (B) right of the people to "be secure in their persons, houses, papers, and effects".

    (C) "right to remain silent."

    (D) due process of law.

    (E) right to privacy.

2. In *Engel* v. *Vitale* (1962), the Supreme Court ruled that

   (A) the reciting of a state-required prayer in public school constituted an impermissible establishment of religion under the First Amendment.

   (B) the Gideon society could distribute Bibles in public schools under the free exercise clause of the First Amendment.

   (C) the eminent domain clause of the Fifth Amendment prevents government from taking religious property for public purposes.

   (D) public school children may wear crosses as necklaces as a permissible mode of symbolic speech under the First Amendment.

   (E) the Second Amendment "right to bear arms" does not apply in religious facilities.

3. The "exclusionary rule" means

   (A) the Senate has removed a member from voting membership because of a violation of ethics rules.

   (B) the House Rules Committee has refused to schedule a debate on a bill.

   (C) the bureaucracy has failed to enforce unpopular legislation.

   (D) the president has decided to "impound" some programmatic money appropriated by Congress.

   (E) evidence gathered in violation of the Fourth Amendment has not been allowed to be introduced during a trial.

4. Which of the following cases made decisions regarding the establishment of religion?

   I.   *Mapp v. Ohio (1965)*

   II.   *Texas v. Johnson (1989)*

   III. *School District of Abington Township, Pennsylvania v. Schempp (1963)*

   IV. *Lemon v. Kurtzman (1973)*

   (A) I and II
   (B) II and III
   (C) III and IV
   (D) I and III
   (E) II and IV

5. Which of the following forms of expression is protected by the First Amendment?

   (A) obscenity

   (B) libel

   (C) fighting words

   (D) symbolic speech

   (E) slander

6. Which of the following rights is protected by the Fifth Amendment?

   (A) the right of privacy

   (B) Protection against self-incrimination

   (C) the right to bear arms

   (D) the right to counsel

   (E) the right to a speedy and public trial

7. The Bill of Rights begins with the words "Congress shall make no law . . ," telling the reader that the Bill or Rights is intended to protect citizens only from the national government. Yet, most of the provisions of the Bill of Rights now limit the states as well. Which of the following provisions is most relevant in explaining that change?

   (A) the equal protection clause of the Fourteenth Amendment

   (B) the double jeopardy clause of the Fifth Amendment

   (C) the rights "retained by the people" in the Ninth Amendment

   (D) the grand jury indictment provision in the Fifth Amendment

   (E) the due process clause of the Fourteenth Amendment

8. The right of citizens to be made aware of their constitutional guarantees against self incrimination and to be represented by counsel was established in

   (A) *Gitlow* v. *New York (1925)*.

   (B) *Mapp* v. *Ohio (1965)*.

   (C) *Miranda* v. *Arizona (1966)*.

   (D) *Gideon* v. *Wainwright (1963)*.

   (E) *Lemon* v. *Kurtzman (1971)*.

9. All of the following concepts are guaranteed to a citizen accused of a crime EXCEPT

(A) a speedy and public trial by an impartial jury.

(B) security against unreasonable search and seizures.

(C) protection from capital punishment.

(D) not to be put in jeopardy of life or limb twice for the same offense.

(E) having the assistance of counsel.

10. The right of government to keep a newspaper from publishing information that would be harmful to the morale of troops deployed in a military conflict

(A) would be denied as "prior restraint."

(B) would be allowed under the "no quartering of soldiers" provision of the 3rd Amendment.

(C) would be denied as entailing a "clear and present danger."

(D) would be allowed as denying "seditious speech."

(E) would be allowed under the USA Patriot Act.

Free-Response Questions

1. The USA Patriot Act was passed after the terrorist attacks of September 11, 2001.

    a) Describe the USA Patriot Act.

    b) Identify and describe a provision in the Bill of Rights that the USA Patriot Act affects.

    c) Explain how the USA Patriot Act might limit the application of the provision in the Bill of Rights identified in (b).

2. Under the Constitution, the Supreme Court has the right of judicial review.

    a. Define judicial review.

    b. Describe the application of judicial review to the decisions in two of the following cases:

- *Brown* v. *Board of Education (1954)*
- *Engel* v. *Vitale (1962)*

- *Texas* v. *Johnson (1989)*
- *Roe* v. *Wade (1973)*

   c. Explain how each selected decision could be seen as an "activist" decision.

ANSWERS AND EXPLANATIONS

Multiple-Choice Questions

- **1. (E) is correct.** In *Roe v. Wade,* the Supreme Court extended the right to privacy to include a right to abortion. The other answers are liberties in the Bill of Rights, but are not relevant to the *Roe* decision.

- **2. (A) is correct.** The *Engel* decision was based upon the establishment clause of the Constitution. The other four possible answers have to do with religion, but do not address the issues raised in *Engel v. Vitale.*

- **3. (E) is correct.** The exclusionary rule was designed to keep law enforcement agencies from conducting searches in an irresponsible way. The other possible answers all suggest exclusions of some variety, but have nothing to do with the "exclusionary rule."

- **4. (C) is correct**. The *Schempp* and *Lemon* decisions dealt with the establishment clause, *Schempp* limiting religious activities in public schools and *Lemon* defining boundaries of excessive entanglement between church and state. The other two decisions have nothing to do with religious liberty.

- **5. (D) is correct.** Freedom of speech is subject to almost no limits regarding political speech, including symbolic acts like flag burning. Obscenity, libel, slander, and fighting words have been ruled not to be protected under the First Amendment.

- **6. (B) is correct.** The most famous provision of the Fifth Amendment is that no one is required to provide testimony against himself or herself in court. The other options are liberties protected other amendments.

- **7. (E) is correct.** The Bill of Rights has largely been incorporated to the states through the due process clause of the Fourteenth Amendment. That Amendment, adopted after the Civil War, has been ruled to make states comply with provisions of the national constitution.

- **8. (C) is correct.** *Miranda* v. *Arizona* extended the rights of the accused to those who did not know the constitution. In that case, the Supreme Court said that as fundamental as having the rights was the right to know that they existed.

- **9. (C) is correct.** Capital punishment has never been ruled to violate the cruel and unusual provision of the 8th Amendment. The other options are protected rights in the Bill of Rights.

- **10. (A) is correct.** Under the first Amendment, banning of prior restraint of publication is a very strong rule.

Free-Response Questions

This rubric provides examples of many, but not all of the possible correct responses to the free-response questions. Occasionally, there will be weaknesses pointed out in the suggested answer, providing students with examples of what to avoid.

1. In the aftermath of the terrorist attacks on the World Trade Center on September 11, 2001, Congress passed a law called the USA Patriot Act that was designed to give law enforcement agencies more power to investigate and arrest terrorists. Congress thought that under the crisis circumstances that existed, it was reasonable to give those expanded investigation powers even if it meant that some of the protections of the Fourth Amendment would be compromised. The significance of the Patriot Act was that civil libertarians thought that it provided a dangerous compromise for average citizens who might be investigated.

   The Fourth Amendment requires that if people are to be investigated, it must be with a valid search warrant signed by a judge and based upon probable cause. This Amendment was meant to keep people safe from investigations and is based on the idea that people are innocent until proven guilty.

   Some people believe that the Patriot Act compromises the Fourth Amendment too much. Critics of the Act fear that it will infringe upon some of citizens basic rights of privacy. *This paragraph fails to point out* **how** *the Patriot Act might compromise the Fourth Amendment.*

2.

   a. Judicial Review was established in the Supreme Court case of *Marbury v. Madison* early in our nation's history. In that case, the Court ruled that the Supreme Court should have the power to make sure that laws and executive actions conformed with the Constitution.

   b. In the case of *Engel v. Vitale,* the State of New York had written a law that required school children to recite a prayer at the beginning of each school day. The Supreme Court used the Engel decision to declare that law unconstitutional as a violation of the establishment clause of the First Amendment

In *Texas v. Johnson,* the court ruled that as an act of political speech, burning an American Flag is an allowable form of symbolic speech. *This paragraph correctly discusses the issue in the case, but does not explain how judicial review was involved.*

These decisions were seen as activist decisions because the Court didn't just stick to the words of the Bill of Rights. It said that there was a right that wasn't mentioned in so many words. This was seen as an activist decision.

CHAPTER 5

Civil Rights and Public Policy

The Constitution secures equal treatment under the law for all citizens. Civil rights guarantee that people are not discriminated against by the government on account of their race, religion, gender, or age. Such rights were not inherent in the Constitution, however. Many legal and political battles have been fought to extend civil rights to all groups of people in the United States.

The Constitution and Inequality

- The original Constitution did not mention equality, and only white males were allowed privileges such as voting rights.

- The **Fourteenth Amendment** first clarified the concept of equality by ensuring that all citizens must receive **"equal protection of the laws."**

- The Supreme Court's modern interpretation of equality has brought civil rights to the forefront of the political agenda.

Race, the Constitution, and Public Policy

- *Dred Scott* **v.** *Sanford* (1857) upheld the constitutionality of slavery and forbade Congress from banning it in new states.

- The **Thirteenth Amendment** (1865) outlawed slavery after the Civil War.

- The **Fourteenth Amendment** (1868) extended rights of citizenship to former slaves. With the Fifteenth Amendment guaranteeing the ability to vote, many African Americans were elected to government posts.

- In the 1876 election, a deadlock in the Electoral College led to a deal that allowed the Republican candidate, Rutherford B. Hayes, to be selected by a commission created by the House of Representatives, in exchange for the promise to withdraw federal troops from the southern states. Civil rights advances came to a halt and Jim Crow laws took effect segregating blacks from whites in the South, and preventing blacks from voting and running for public office.

- *Plessy* **v.** *Ferguson* (1896): The Supreme Court officially recognized a policy of "separate but equal" facilities, thereby allowing the practice of segregation.

The Era of Civil Rights

- *Brown* v. *Board of Education* (1954) overturned the *Plessy* decision—asserting that segregation is unconstitutional—and ordered the desegregation of public schools.

- Several more court decisions were required to enforce the *Brown* decision. Congress also passed the **Civil Rights Act** (1964), bringing the cause of civil rights to the legislative as well as the judicial agenda. The Civil Rights Act accomplished the following measures:

    - Outlawed racial discrimination in public places

    - Prohibited discrimination in employment

    - Withheld government funding from any school or institution that practiced discrimination

    - Established the Equal Employment Opportunity Commission to monitor job discrimination

    - Granted the Justice Department power to enforce civil rights laws by suing institutions still practicing segregation

- *Swann* v. *Charlotte-Mecklenberg County Schools* (1971): The Supreme Court allowed busing to be used as a means to balance racial percentages in schools.

- Other minority groups, including Native Americans, Hispanic Americans, and Asian Americans, have benefited from advances made in the civil rights movement. This legislation applies to all races and has encouraged many minority groups to speak out for their rights.

Getting and Using the Right to Vote

- The **Fifteenth Amendment** (1870) granted African Americans the right to vote,(**suffrage.**) Southern states circumvented the law by instituting **literacy tests,** which most former slaves could not pass, and **poll taxes.**

- Southern states instituted a **grandfather clause** to exempt from literacy tests illiterate whites whose grandfathers had been allowed to vote before 1860. This practice was found unconstitutional in *Guinn* v. *United States* (1915).

- *Smith* v. *Allwright* (1944): The Supreme Court outlawed the use of **white primaries** to exclude African Americans from the election process.

- The **Twenty-Fourth Amendment** (1964) outlawed the use of poll taxes to prevent poor people from voting.

- Congress passed the **Voting Rights Act** in 1965 to prevent states from using any methods to disenfranchise voters. The law provided for enforcement by allowing federal registrars to oversee elections.

Other Minority Groups

Native Americans

- Isolated on "reservations" until Dawes Act of 1887

- Given the right to vote only in 1924

- Beginning in1970, have used courts to pursue equal rights, largely through the Native Americans Rights Fund (NARF)

Hispanic Americans

- Largest minority group—have heritage from many Caribbean, Central American and South American nations

- Pursue equal rights in court through the Mexican American Legal Defense Fund (MALDEF)

Asian Americans

- Rapidly growing group

- Japanese Americans placed in isolated camps during World War II, upheld in *Korematsu* v. *U.S.*

Other groups—smaller numbers of Arab and Islamic population have faced challenges since 9/11/2001

Women, the Constitution, and Public Policy

- Women were excluded also from the rights of equality implied in the Constitution. The women's rights movement grew out of abolitionism in the 1840s, when female activists encountered discrimination among male activists.

- The **Nineteenth Amendment** (1920) granted women the right to vote.

- The **Equal Rights Amendment** (1923) was intended to enforce full equality for women, who still were discriminated against in such areas as employment. It was passed by Congress in 1972 but was never ratified by the necessary three-fourths of state legislatures.

- *Reed* v. *Reed* (1971): For the first time, the Supreme Court found a law unconstitutional based on arbitrary gender bias, and in 1976, *Craig v. Boren* established a "minimum scrutiny" standard for determining gender discrimination. Since then, it has struck down laws that discriminate against both women and men.

- Civil rights legislation barring discrimination in the workplace applies to women as well as to other minority groups, and it includes employment opportunities, equal pay, and pregnancy leave. In 1986, the Supreme Court established a woman's right to sue employers for sexual harassment under the Civil Rights Act.

- The Supreme Court has not yet ruled on the issue of **comparable worth,** which insists that women be paid the same as men for jobs that require the same skills.

- Women are allowed to serve in all branches of the military but cannot engage in ground combat.

Newly Active Groups under the Civil Rights Umbrella

- Discrimination laws prevent employers and universities from rejecting applicants because of their age. Congress also revoked the policy of mandatory retirement, unless a compelling reason can be provided based on age.

- The **Americans with Disabilities Act of 1990** protects disabled Americans against job discrimination and requires employers to provide "reasonable accommodations."

- **Gay rights** are protected by some laws but are hardly advanced by the Supreme Court. The **"don't ask, don't tell"** military policy introduced by President Clinton in 1993 bypasses restrictions on homosexuality by preventing labeling. The **right to privacy** also factors into debates over gay rights. *Lawrence* v. *Texas* (2003) overturned state anti-sodomy laws. Massachusetts, Hawaii, Vermont have each legalized some form of civil union between same sex couples.

Affirmative Action

- **Affirmative action** is a policy that attempts to go beyond preventing discrimination to provide members of groups who have suffered discrimination some compensatory treatment.

- *Regents of the University of California* v. *Bakke* (1978): A white student sued the University of California at Davis for admitting a lower scoring minority student so that the university could fulfill its enrollment quota. The Court ruled that race could be used as one factor by which to choose applicants, but that enrollment quotas were unconstitutional.

- *Adarand Constructors* **v.** *Pena* (1995): The Court ruled against set-aside contracts for minority-owned businesses, stating that even if the intent is to advance the opportunities of minorities, it still classifies people by race and is therefore unconstitutional. In recent years the court has made decisions about affirmative action on a case-by-case basis, rather than assuming a single position.

For Additional Review

Debate continues over the policy of affirmative action. Make a chart listing arguments on each side of the issue.

Multiple-Choice Questions

1. Affirmative action laws are designed to remedy which kind of discrimination?

    (A) de facto

    (B) ex post facto

    (C) de solis

    (D) habeas corpus

    (E) de jure

2. The landmark case of *Brown* v. *Board of Education* ruled that segregated schools were not acceptable because of the

    (A) Constitutional provision against Bills of Attainder.

    (B) due process of law clause of the 5th Amendment.

    (C) "involuntary servitude" clause of the 13th Amendment.

    (D) "equal protection" clause of the 14th Amendment.

    (E) command not to "deny or disparage" rights "retained by the people" under the 9th Amendment .

3. The 13th Amendment effectively invalidated which Supreme Court decision?

    (A) *Dred Scott* v. *Sandford*

    (B) *Plessy* v. *Ferguson*

    (C) *Korematsu* v. *U.S.*

    (D) *Smith* v. *Allwright*

    (E) *Guinn* v. *U.S.*

4. Which of the following are incorrectly paired?

    I.   13th Amendment—Right of Women to vote

    II.   15th Amendment—Right of African American males to vote

    III. 21st Amendment—Banning of Poll Tax

    IV. 26th Amendment—Right of 18 year-olds to vote

(A) I and II

(B) II and III

(C) III and IV

(D) I and III

(E) II and IV

5. In the case of *California* v. *Bakke,* the Supreme Court ruled that

(A) Japanese Americans could be placed in camps during World War II.

(B) migrant workers were entitled to compensation in case of injury through unemployment insurance.

(C) affirmative action admissions to a medical school could cause "reverse discrimination."

(D) women were entitled to equal pay for equal work.

(E) the "White Primary" was unconstitutional.

6. Racial discrimination in public accommodations such as restaurants and hotels was banned in

(A) the Civil Rights Act of 1964.

(B) the Open Housing Act of 1968.

(C) the 24th Amendment.

(D) the Equal Rights Amendment.

(E) *Reed v. Reed.*

7. Affirmative action refers to

   (A) the U.S. Senate approving a presidential appointment to the cabinet under its "advice and consent" function.

   (B) the president "faithfully executing" the appropriations of money under laws created by Congress.

   (C) the Supreme Court upholding a lower court decision.

   (D) interest group lobbying efforts in pursuit of the common goals of group members.

   (E) a policy giving special consideration to groups that have been disadvantaged historically.

8. The proposed "equal rights amendment" was proposed by Congress but fell three states short of the 38 needed for ratification. If adopted, the ERA would have banned discrimination based upon

   (A) race.

   (B) religious faith.

   (C) gender.

   (D) sexual orientation.

   (E) physical disabilities.

9. The biggest difference between civil rights and civil liberties is that

   (A) civil liberties protect the majority while civil rights protect minorities.

   (B) civil liberties have to do with individual protections while civil rights are protections on the basis of group attributes.

   (C) civil liberties have to do with the freedoms of expression and religion while civil rights have to do with rights of people accused of crimes.

   (D) civil liberties allow interest groups to organize into interest groups and make demands on government while civil rights allow for groups seek redress of grievances through mass protests.

   (E) civil liberties protect individual political beliefs while civil rights protect individual political actions.

10. Which Supreme Court case upheld the placing of Japanese citizens in internment camps during World War II?

   (A) *Craig* v. *Boren*

   (B) *Smith* v. *Allwright*

   (C) *Korematsu* v. *United States*

   (D) *Santa Clara Pueblo* v. *Martinez*

   (E) *Yamamoto* v. *Roosevelt*

Free-Response Questions

1. One of the key issues in civil rights had to do with gaining the right to vote for groups of citizens. African Americans and women fought for and eventually earned the right to vote through Constitutional Amendments, Supreme Court decisions, and Congressional laws. Among the issues related to voting rights are:

   - The poll tax
   - The White Primary
   - The Grandfather clause
   - Literacy tests
   - State laws prohibiting women OR Blacks OR those younger than 21 from voting
   - Discriminatory governmental practices that made it difficult to register and vote

   a. Identify and describe one Supreme Court case that declared unconstitutional one of these practices.

   b. Identify and describe one law passed by Congress that made illegal one of these practices.

   c. Identify and describe one Constitutional Amendment that addressed one of these practices.

2. Women have been participants in and beneficiaries of a civil rights movement during the past 50 years.

   a. Identify and explain the impact of the battle for the Equal Rights Amendment.

   b. Identify and explain the issue of "comparable worth".

   c. Identify and explain issues surrounding the roles of women in the military.

ANSWERS AND EXPLANATIONS

Multiple-Choice Questions

- **1. (A) is correct.** The idea of affirmative action is that preventing discrimination by law (de jure) can accomplish only so much. In order to remedy patterns of discrimination that have developed over time in fact (de facto), affirmative action is needed.

- **2. (D) is correct.** *Brown v. Board of Education* decided that the equal protection clause required desegregation of schools because "separate educational facilities are inherently unequal..

- **3. (A) is correct.** The Supreme Court, in the *Dred Scott* case, ruled that African-Americans were chattel (owned property). The Thirteenth Amendment banned slavery, thus effectively overturning the *Dred Scott* decision.

- **4. (D) is correct.** The Thirteenth Amendment was one of the three civil war amendments and banned slavery. Women received the right to vote in the 19th Amendment. The poll tax was banned in the 24th Amendment; the 21st Amendment repealed prohibition

- **5. (C) is correct.** In the case of *Regents of the University of California* v. *Bakke,* the Supreme Court found the university's quotas for enrolling minorities unconstitutional. Allan Bakke was denied enrollment in favor of a minority applicant to fulfill the university's quota, an unconstitutional "reverse discrimination.

- **6. (A) is correct.** The 1964 Civil Rights Act was a broad sweeping law that had many characteristics. Among its provisions was one banning discrimination in public accommodations.

- **7. (E) is correct.** The purpose of affirmative action is to correct for past discrimination. The other answers deal with positive, or "affirmative," things, but not with the concept of affirmative action.

- **8. (C) is correct.** All of the options have to do with different aspects of "equality," but only the rights of women were addressed in the ERA.

- **9. (B) is correct.** This question asks students to differentiate between two basic issues. While the answers all provide contrasts, only answer b is correct—civil liberties are individual rights and civil rights ban discrimination against groups.

- **10. (C) is correct.** The Japanese internment camps were upheld in the *Korematsu* decision.

Free-Response Questions

This rubric provides examples of many, but not all of the possible correct responses to the free-response questions. Occasionally, there will be weaknesses pointed out in the suggested answer, providing students with examples of what to avoid.

1. A basic right of American citizens is the right to vote. In civil rights, the first step toward making progress regarding equality is the right to participate in the elections of members of congress and other representatives. Until all groups attain the right to vote, they can never truly be equal with other groups. To attain the right to vote, a number of barriers had to be overcome, including the poll tax, the White Primary, the Grandfather Clause, and the Literacy test. Both Constitutional guarantees and laws addressing governmental practices had to be written. In short, it took concerted action of all areas of government to attain the right to vote.

a. One Supreme Court case that addressed this issue was the one that banned the White Primary. I don't remember the case name, but it said that primary elections were a basic part of the election process, so people couldn't be kept from voting in primaries because of their race.

b. The big law passed to help African American vote was the Voting Right Act of 1965. It said that states could not use literacy tests to make it hard for some people to vote and that the federal government could use voter registrars to try to get more black people to be able to vote

c. There were several Amendments to the Constitution that affected voting. The 19th Amendment gave women the right to vote, the 23rd gave the right to Washington D.C. to have electoral votes, and the 24th banned the poll tax. All of these were to expand the vote.

2. Even though women actually outnumber men in the United States, they are considered a minority group because they were denied equal rights under the law until only recently. After more than a century of political activism, women are by degrees achieving the privileges afforded them by their civil rights.

One of their big fights was a fight that women didn't win. The Equal Rights Amendment proposed by Congress and went to the states for ratification, but not enough state ratified it for it to become law. However, it did have the impact of raising the conscience of the United States and helped women make progress.

A major difference in the United States is the difference between the salaries of men and women in the work place. Although women work very hard, they often are not paid as much as men. This is because of discrimination. We need to make new laws that will let women be paid as well as men. It is unfair for women to work as hard as men and yet be paid less. *This paragraph is a polemic that does not really address the question.*

Women's rights to serve in the military are important. They should be able to be promoted to any rank just like men. It isn't fair that women can't be promoted. And we need people in our military. *This is another nonresponsive paragraph.*

CHAPTER 6

Public Opinion and Political Action

More than two centuries of immigration to the United States has created an incredibly **diverse population** of Americans. Numerous social and economic factors therefore contribute to a varied forum of **public opinion.** However, despite their differences, Americans overall share a common **political culture** based on democracy and federalism. Today, public opinion can be a powerful tool, especially during elections. Increasingly, politicians, pundits, and even voters are paying close attention to what polls tell them is the public's opinion.

The American People

- The Constitution requires that a **census** be taken every 10 years. The census collects demographic data about the population of the United States. This information is used to:

- distribute money to federal and state programs,

- **reapportion** seats in the House to each state,

- determine each state's number of electors in the Electoral College,

- redraw state and federal congressional districts,

- allocate funds for public services such as schools, roads, and public transportation.

- Census reports confirm the United States is a nation of immigrants, a **melting pot** of cultures, ideas, and people.

- According to recent census data, the percentage of minorities is increasing while the percentage of Caucasians is decreasing. This could lead to a **minority majority** in the next few decades. Also, for the first time, Hispanic Americans outnumbered African Americans.

- **Reapportionment** in the last two decades has given more seats to the increasingly populated states of **California, Florida,** and **Texas,** whereas states in the Northeast have lost seats.

- **Senior citizens** make up the largest population group by age. This gives them significant political influence. It will also put a serious strain on the Social Security system in the next few decades.

- Despite ethnic, age, and geographic diversity, the United States has a shared **political culture,** with a common set of political values that are widely shared.

How Americans Learn About Politics: Political Socialization

People learn about politics and form their political beliefs through the process of **political socialization**. There are several different means through which people informally acquire political information.

- **The family:** Families have a significant degree of influence, especially over younger members. Most people identify with the same party that their parents do.

- **The mass media:** Most Americans, especially children and teenagers, watch a significant amount of **television.** Political information is often disseminated through TV. Younger people are much less likely to watch the news than are adults, however, and as a result, the political knowledge of young people today is significantly lower than that of young people a few decades ago.

- **School:** Schools educate children in American values such as democracy and capitalism, both through academics and through practices such as reciting the Pledge of Allegiance. A good education also tends to produce more politically active and aware citizens. In addition to the influence of the educational system, young people are also influenced by members of their peer group when formulating their political attitudes and beliefs.

- **Religious** groups and associations also influence political attitudes. For example, during the last decade, fundamentalist Christians have played an ever-increasing role in the politics of the United States.

- Socialization is a dynamic process, with learning taking place over one's entire lifetime. Socialization is part of the very important nurturing process.

Measuring Public Opinion and Political Information

Polls are the most common means of assessing public opinion.

- A **random sample,** or group that statistically represents the whole population of the United States, is asked to fill out a questionnaire or answer some questions over the phone.

- A famous non-random sample, *The Literary Digest Poll* of 1936, wrongly predicted that Republican Alf Landon would defeat Franklin Roosevelt in the election that year.

- The wording of a question is critical, and ambiguously worded questions can affect the accuracy of a poll. The size of the sample can also affect the accuracy of a poll and thus the level of confidence in the poll (**sampling error**).

- Commonly, modern polls rely on **random digit dialing** to draw telephone samples.

- Some critics argue that polls allow politicians to be influenced easily by shifts in public opinion and that polls receive more media attention than do candidates' political platforms during elections. Others assert that, by advancing the public's political agenda to poll-sensitive politicians, polls advance the principles of democracy.

- Recent polls indicate that Americans have little political knowledge and little faith that the government is acting on their behalf.

- **Exit polls** are conducted by media as voters leave the voting booth to predict the outcomes of elections.

- Public opinion polls have shown a trend indicating that Americans trust government less than they used to.

What Americans Value: Political Ideologies

In recent years, more Americans have considered themselves **conservative** than **moderate** or **liberal.**

- **Conservative ideology:** Favors limited government and freedom of the private sector.

- More likely to support military spending, free markets, prayer in school, and reduced taxes.

- Opposes abortion, affirmative action, and government spending on social programs.

- **Liberal ideology:** Favors an active central government with social and economic responsibilities.

- Favors a more equal distribution of wealth, more government regulation of big business, more government spending on social programs, and abortion.

- Opposes increases in defense spending and military actions, prayer in school, and tax breaks for the wealthy.

- Women and minorities tend to be more liberal. The **gender gap** is the pattern that predicts that women are more likely to vote for a Democratic candidate; however, this was less prevalent in the 2004 elections.

- Traditionally, people of higher socioeconomic classes tend to be conservative. This trend is declining, however.

- Conservative groups tend to have more resources and therefore more political power.

- Ronald Reagan was one of the most conservative presidents of the twentieth century. Bill Clinton shifted the Democratic Party and government back to a more centrist position.

How Americans Participate in Politics

Americans express their political views and try to influence policy by voting, petitioning, participating in protests, or corresponding with their representatives.

- **Voter turnout** has been declining over the last few decades, though it is still the most common way people participate in politics. **Young people** are the group **least likely to vote.**

- **Campaign contributions** to candidates as a form of political participation are on the rise.

- **Protest** and **civil disobedience** have a long tradition in American history. Protests against globalization and war continue to be a means of political expression today.

- People of high socioeconomic status are much more likely to participate in politics, although African Americans and Hispanic Americans are becoming more active.

For Additional Review

Brainstorm a list of topics in the news. Then write down what you think the conservative and the liberal opinion about each issue would be. If you are not sure, do some library or Internet research to find out.

Multiple-Choice Questions

1. Reapportionment consists of

    (A) drawing district lines in a way to benefit one political party.

    (B) making certain that all Congressional districts are equal in population.

    (C) reallocating Congressional seats proportionally to states based upon census data every ten years.

    (D) trading votes in Congress where members agree to support each others' bills.

    (E) allocating electoral college votes across the states.

2. The nurturing process through which people learn their knowledge, feelings, and evaluations about the political world is called

    (A) political socialization.

    (B) political efficacy.

    (C) propaganda acquisition.

    (D) political ideology.

    (E) public opinion.

3. Sampling error refers to

   (A) the pollster making mistakes in selecting a sample.

   (B) the sample not being representative of the population.

   (C) coding mistakes that mean that responses are not accurately reported.

   (D) the level of confidence in the findings of a public opinion poll.

   (E) using a non-random procedure for drawing a sample of the population.

4. The failure of the *Literary Digest Poll* occurred because

   (A) the sample was too small to predict the outcome of the election.

   (B) the questions on the survey were not phrased to obtain accurate results.

   (C) mail surveys rarely can be representative of the population.

   (D) the survey over-sampled voters with high incomes.

   (E) computer technology of the day was inadequate to process the data accurately.

5. Which type of poll is most likely to be used by the media to predict the outcome of an election?

   (A) a benchmark poll

   (B) an exit poll

   (C) a matchup poll

   (D) a focus group poll

   (E) a purposive poll

6. Liberals are likely to support all of the following EXCEPT

   (A) freedom of choice in abortions.

   (B) government regulation.

   (C) increased taxes on the rich.

   (D) social welfare programs.

   (E) prayer in schools.

7. The "gender gap" refers to the idea that women

   (A) are denied equal protection of the law in economic matters in the United States.

   (B) cannot take combat roles in the military.

   (C) are more likely to vote for Democrats than are men.

   (D) are proportionally underrepresented among members of Congress.

   (E) live on average longer than men affecting their social security costs.

8. Which of the following would older Americans be more likely to support than younger Americans?

   (A) protection of Social Security

   (B) decreased military spending

   (C) gays serving in the military

   (D) increased spending on education

   (E) increased spending on environmental protection

9. Which of the following is the most common form of political participation in the United States?

   (A) expressing one's ideas in a public opinion poll.

   (B) participating in a mass demonstration.

   (C) voting in a presidential election.

   (D) contacting a public official regarding a public issue.

   (E) joining an interest group for the purpose of influencing legislation.

10. Which of the following are true?

    I. Older Americans are more likely to vote than younger Americans.

    II. Men are more likely to vote than women.

    III. Those with higher education are more likely to vote than those with less education.

    IV. Democrats are more likely to vote than Republicans.

    V. Hispanic voters are more likely to vote than non-Hispanic voters.

    (A) I and III.

    (B) II and IV.

    (C) III and V.

    (D) I, II, and IV.

    (E) II, III and V.

1. In the United States, people can participate in politics in many different ways.

   a. Describe how each of the following conventional forms of political participation might impact public policy in the United States.

   - Voting in a presidential election

   - Joining an interest group

   - Running for political office

   b. Describe how participating in a mass demonstration of protest might impact public policy in the United States.

   c. Describe the relationship between social class and participation in the United States.

   d. Explain how the relationship between social class and participation impacts American's perceptions regarding equality.

2. One of the most consistent ways that Americans learn about public opinion is through polling.

   a. Describe the advantage of a random sample for public opinion polling over a non-random sample.

   b. Describe one advantage and one disadvantage of telephone surveys compared to person-to-person interviewing.

   c. Describe what public opinion polls tell us about levels of political information that Americans have.

   d. Describe what public opinion polls tell us about political attitudes held by Americans.

ANSWERS AND EXPLANATIONS

Multiple-Choice Questions

- **1. (C) is correct.** The apportionment of seats in the House is based on the population of each state. The Constitution specifically requires that a national census be taken every 10 years. The results of the census then determine the number of seats each state receives and states are assigned a number of seats through reapportionment.

- **2. (A) is correct.** Political socialization is defined in the root of the question. Each of the other answers refers to a different concept.

- **3. (D) is correct.** In all sampling, there is a potential that the sample drawn is not perfectly reflective of the population as a whole. In random sampling, the likelihood of such error can be estimated mathematically. The other answers all can cause error as well, but they occur in ways that can not be estimated and are therefore not "sampling error."

- **4. (D) is correct.** The *Literary Digest Poll* is perhaps the most famous example of the problem of drawing a non-representative sample. By sending surveys only to those with cars and telephones during the depths of the Great Depression, the magazine unwittingly created a sample that was wildly at variance with the population as a whole. Because of that, the poll wrongly predicted that Alf Landon would win the presidency in 1936 when he actually lost in a landslide.

- **5. (B) is correct.** Exit polls are used by media on election days to predict the outcome of an election. Other possible answers are polls that can be used during campaigns, but for different purposes.

- **6. (E) is correct.** Liberals tend to favor government regulation of the economy but tend to oppose some examples of government regulation on "moral issues". As a result, liberals would favor freedom of choice in abortion, but they would not favor prayers in government –sponsored public schools.

- **7. (C) is correct.** All of the possible answers refer to differences between men and women. However, in politics, the gender gap only refers to the fact that since 1980, women have tended to be more supportive of Democrats than have men. This trend is especially strong among unmarried women.

- **8. (A) is correct.** Younger voters tend to be more supportive of expanded welfare and environmental programs while older voters tend to support more spending on defense issues and to protect their social security benefits.

- **9. (C) is correct.** There are many effective ways to participate in politics. However, only in voting do more than half of Americans participate in politics. This is not to say that voting is the most significant form of participation—others might be. However, it is the most common form.

- **10. (A) is correct.** Of the statements, the two that are correct are that older and better educated people are more likely to vote than are younger and less educated people. Women, Republicans, and Anglo voters all vote at rates higher than the contrasting groups mentioned in the answers.

This rubric provides examples of many, but not all of the possible correct responses to the free-response questions. Occasionally, there will be weaknesses pointed out in the suggested answer, providing students with examples of what to avoid.

1. Political participation is a fundamental indicator of the health of a democracy. Since in a democracy, the government should respond to the people, the people should participate at high rates. Yet, in the United States, only about half of the people vote. If voting were the only mechanism for participation, that would perhaps indicate a problem with democracy.

   Voting in a presidential election is the most common form of political participation. People can vote very easily in the United States since there is no fee for registering to vote, since the racial and gender barriers to voting have disappeared in recent years, and since we now have a motor-voter law that allows people to register even when they renew their driver's licenses. Voting is fundamental in a democracy because it allows people to elect the person who best reflects their ideas about how government should operate. By electing officials, the people have representatives in government. That is the nature of a republican government, and it is therefore a way to influence public policy. In other words, elections are the way that people can staff government with people who will do the people's business. *No description of the other two forms of conventional political participation*

   However, conventional participation, such as voting or joining interest groups, is not the only way that people can affect public policy. Through non-conventional methods such as engaging in nonviolent civil disobedience, people can also get their ideas to be noticed by government. Martin Luther King. Jr. led much of the civil rights movement by using civil disobedience. Although he and other African Americans could not win elections in the South at that time, he could use civil disobedience to gain attention for the civil rights struggle. Eventually, that attention led to national outrage and the civil rights laws were passed. So, as one can see, civil disobedience, though a non-conventional form of participation, can have influence just as a conventional method might.

   Interestingly, the two forms of participation discussed above might be seen as being tactics of people with different social status. People in higher income categories are far more likely to vote than are poor people. This fact would seem to indicate that equality cannot be realized in U.S. society. However, even poor people can engage in civil disobedience. As a result, equality might be realized.

2. A random sample is better than a non-random sample because random people can answer questions better than selected people. Random people can give "real" answers while selected people are members of the elite and don't really know what the people are thinking. As a result, a random sample gives everyone an equal chance of being selected and therefore is more likely to be representative of the population as a whole. With a non-random sample, we cannot estimate how likely the sample is to represent the people

   Telephone surveys are both great and bad. They are great because everyone with a phone can be surveyed. They are bad because people without telephones cannot be surveyed.

Surveys tell us that Americans don't know much about politics. They can't answer even simple questions well. For example, in Jay-walking, Jay Leno shows that people are really dumb in answering questions about politics. *This paragraph almost earns a point for saying that people are not well-informed. But the example is not from a survey, and there is no discussion of what polls tell us about attitudes.*

CHAPTER 7

The Mass Media and the Political Agenda

The **mass media,** including **newspapers, radio, television,** and the **Internet,** have had a profound impact on politics. In today's media-savvy world, politicians are highly visible to the public. This has both positive and negative consequences for policymakers, campaigns, and the public's trust in government.

The impact of the media on American politics is referred to as **high-tech politics**, in which the media can shape the political agenda and the behavior of policy makers.

The Mass Media Today

Political leaders have learned to use the media to set their agenda. A **media event** is an event that is staged by a political leader with the purpose of getting it covered in the media to shape an image or draw attention to a chosen issue. In addition, political leaders can more deliberately use the media to run advertisements. Such advertisements are often 30 seconds in length and such advertisements make up the majority of spending on political campaigns. Presidents also use the media to make direct appeals to the public.

The Development of Media Politics

Politics and the mass media go hand in hand. However, whereas once they worked together to communicate with the public, today they often oppose each other.

*   **Press conferences** are a common means by which presidents convey their goals and opinions to the public. However, they are a recent phenomenon begun by Franklin Roosevelt in the 1930s. FDR was also the first president to address the electorate directly through the radio.

*   The Watergate scandal and the Vietnam War changed the government's relationship with the press, as the press became more suspicious about political motives.

*   Today the media engage in **investigative journalism,** often with the intent of revealing political **scandals.**

The Print Media

*   Only a few corporations own all of the newspapers in the United States, as well as radio and television stations. These major corporations have significant control over information conveyed in the media.

- Newspaper readers tend to be politically informed, active citizens, but newspaper circulation has been declining since the advent of television.

The Broadcast Media

- Now, most Americans, especially young people, get their information from the **broadcast media.**

- Television shifts the public's focus from a politician's achievements and political views to his or her **appearance** and performance in front of the cameras.

- Cable television encourages **narrowcasting,** which allows viewers to select what information they do and do not want to see. Critics fear that this will lead to an even less informed electorate that can selectively avoid politics.

  - Media in America is free and independent because it is privately owned, but that also means it is totally dependent upon advertising. Over four-fifths of the newspapers in America are owned by large corporations (**chains**), and this applies to much of broadcast media, as well.

Government Regulation of the Broadcast Media

The Federal Communications Commission (FCC) is a regulatory agency that monitors the use of the air waves. While it is independent, the FCC is subject to many political pressures. Congress controls the funding of the agency and Presidential appointments to the agency are made with political considerations in mind. The FCC prevents monopolies, conducts periodic examinations of stations as part of its licensing authority, and issues fair treatment rules concerning access to the airwaves for political candidates and office holders. If a person is attacked on the air, they have the right to respond on the same station. However, the fairness doctrine that was once in place (required equal time to differing views) was abolished.

From Broadcasting to Narrowcasting: The rise of Cable News Channels

The first major news networks were described as "broadcasting" because messages were sent to a broad audience. With the development of cable TV, narrowcasting (media programming on cable TV or Internet that is focused on one topic and aimed at a narrow audience) is a more appropriate term. While there is now a wide variety of news programs available, the quality of content has not necessarily improved. The profit motive is still the driving force behind most news programs.

The Impact of the Internet

The Internet has made political information easily accessible. Citizens can use it to easily retrieve voting records and text of legislation for example. However, researchers have discovered that few Americans are taking advantage of the technology to be better informed citizens. The impact of the Internet on politics has been subtle.

Reporting the News

Newscasting is a business geared toward achieving high ratings. This can have detrimental consequences for both the political agenda addressed in the news and for the political knowledge of Americans.

- Profits largely determine what is considered news, and sensational, unusual, or negative events usually receive more attention than more positive or everyday policymaking does. This leads the public to believe that most of politics is scandalous and to distrust political leaders.

- Journalists usually have regular **beats** such as the White House, the Senate, or the Pentagon. Most of their information comes directly from press secretaries at these institutions. This has significant advantages for politicians, who can control how much information is reported to the public, including intentional leaks (**trial balloons**), which can gauge political reaction.

- News reporting, especially through the broadcast media, has very little depth of content. Information is reported in **sound bites,** which gloss over the complexity of issues and focus the public's attention on politicians rather than on their policies. This contributes further to Americans' lack of political knowledge.

- Sound bites allow politicians to craft political personas without having to directly address an issue. They do not have to say much when a typical sound bite is only seven seconds long.

- **Bias** is not apparent so much in the way news is presented, but it is a factor in determining what news is reported and what news is not. Dramatic stories of violence or conflict are more likely to draw an audience, so they are more likely to be featured in the news.

The News, Public Opinion, and the Media's Agenda-Setting Function

- The mass media have an enormous influence over the **public agenda.** By selecting what issues to focus on, news organizations define which are the most pressing political topics and thereby determine the political priorities of the public. By selectively assigning importance to certain issues, the media essentially tell Americans what to think.

- Politicians, interest groups, and protestors use the media to their advantage by staging dramatic **media events** to draw attention to themselves and their message.

- The media have shifted attention to individual politicians and away from government as a whole. The biggest consequence of this is the increasing amount of attention paid to the president, which as a result enhances his power.

- The media perform a watchdog function by forcing the government to be answerable to the public. However, they strongly discourage Americans from thinking critically about politics.

- At the same time, because the news is based on ratings, its content reflects what citizens want to see and read—and they seem to express little interest in politics.

Understanding the Mass Media/The Media and the Scope of Government

The media acts as a key linkage institution between the people and government. The media's watchdog function also helps to restrict politicians. The watchdog orientation of the press can be characterized as liberal or conservative.

For Additional Review

Over a period of a few days, watch the news and critique it. How much attention is given to different kinds of issues? Do you detect any bias? For each news segment, think about what is not said, or which angles might be overlooked.

Multiple-Choice Questions

1. Which of the following is most likely to be able to effectively use the national media to set the policy agenda?

   (A) Supreme Court

   (B) Congress

   (C) President

   (D) State legislators

   (E) Governors

2. Which of the following is the best example of a media event?

    (A) State of the Union Address

    (B) news report of a Presidential candidate reading to elementary students

    (C) assassination attempt

    (D) signing bipartisan legislation

    (E) private meeting with lawmakers to discuss an issue

3. The Federal Communications Commission (FCC) is which of the following?

    (A) an arm of the US Congress devoted to communications issues

    (B) a special interest group

    (C) the federal judiciary

    (D) an independent regulatory agency

    (E) a White House agency

4. Which of the following is the best example of a trial balloon?

    (A) a presidential nominee leaks the name of one of his choices for vice president to gauge public opinion

    (B) a president interviews a nominee for a federal judicial appointment

    (C) special interest groups testify in order to block a confirmation

    (D) a fake story is launched by a citizen on a Web site to criticize a politician

5. All of the following can be accurately stated about sound bites EXCEPT

    (A) presidential candidates use them to state a theme of their campaign

    (B) they are 15 seconds or shorter

    (C) they are the way many citizens learn about their candidates

    (D) they provide detailed policy information

    (E) they are used by advertisers as well as political leaders

6. What is the main focus of the media during a presidential campaign?

   (A) issues that the candidates support

   (B) background and qualification of the candidates

   (C) personality mistakes of candidates

   (D) platform of the party

   (E) accomplishments of the candidate

7. Which of the following best describes the impact of the Internet on politics?

   (A) citizens are more informed

   (B) citizens have more access to information

   (C) citizens are more likely to be liberal

   (D) citizens have more trust in government

   (E) citizens have less freedom of expression

8. Which of the following have been decreasing over the years?

   (A) news outlets

   (B) press conferences

   (C) State of the Union addresses

   (D) media events

   (E) trial balloons

Since 1986, the monthly survey of the Pew Research Center for the People and the Press has asked Americans how closely they have followed major news stories. A representative selection of their findings is presented here. The percentage in each case is the proportion who reported following the story "very closely."

The explosion of the space shuttle *Challenger* in 1986	80%
Terrorism attacks on the World Trade Center and the Pentagon (general)	78%
San Francisco earthquake	73%
Impact of Hurricane Katrina and Rita	73%
Rodney King case/verdict and Los Angeles riots	70%
Rescue of baby Jessica McClure from a well	69%
Crash of TWA flight 800	69%
School shootings at Columbine High School in Colorado	68%
Iraq's invasion of Kuwait	66%
Hurricane Andrew	66%
Sniper shootings near Washington, D.C.	65%
Debate on war with Iraq	62%
Supreme decision on flag burning	51%
Opening of Berlin Wall	50%
O.J. Simpson case	48%
Killing of Russian schoolchildren by Chechens	48%
Nuclear accident at Chernobyl	46%
2000 presidential election outcome	38%
Debate over Elian Gonzalez	33%
Iran-Contra hearings	33%
Impeachment trial of President Clinton in the Senate	32%
Iran's nuclear research program	23%
Candidates and campaigns in local districts	16%
Bush's education reform plan	14%
Congressional debate about NAFTA	13%
Passage of the Communications Deregulation Bill	12%
Election of Ariel Sharon in Israel in 2001	9%
2002 French election upset by right-wing Le Pen	6%

Source: The Pew Research Center for the People and the Press

9. Which of the following can be concluded from the table above?

(A) Supreme Court rulings get lots of attention from the public

(B) bills on deregulation are closely followed by average citizens

(C) confirmation of judicial nominees are widely watched

(D) the Presidential election coverage is important to citizens

(E) news stories on crime or natural disasters have wide audiences

10. Which of the following best describes the relationship between the media and trust in government?

(A) as the availability of news has increased, trust in government has decreased

(B) there is no relationship between the two

(C) news stories are supportive of political leaders and lead to increased trust

(D) the media has caused trust in government to rise

(E) the media has caused trust of local government to decrease more than trust of national government

Free-Response Questions

1. The independent media in American politics can both hurt candidate's chances for getting elected to office as well as help candidates' chances at getting elected to office.

a. Identify and describe two ways the media may hurt the chances of a candidate for office

b. Identify and describe two ways candidates can use the media to help their campaigns.

2. The mass media greatly impacts the course of a president's administration. Defend this statement by doing all of the following:

a. Define three of the terms below.
- press conferences
- fireside chat
- sound bites
- media event

b. For each of the term you defined, explain its impact on the course of a presidential administration.

c. Choose one of the Presidents below and explain how the media impacted the course of his administration.
- Nixon
- Kennedy
- Reagan

ANSWERS AND EXPLANATIONS

Multiple-Choice Questions

- **1. (C) is correct.** Most modern presidents have successfully used television to make direct appeals to the public. President Regan for example used prime time television to make direct appeals to citizens to take grass roots action on a political issue. Other organizations such as Congress are more decentralized and therefore have a more difficult time collectively using the media.

- **2. (B) is correct.** Media events are deliberately staged events by political figures to get attention. While the State of the Union gets broad media coverage, it is an event required by the U.S. Constitution and therefore is not the best example of a media event. Events that are not in a politicians control would not be good examples of media events, nor would events that do not get much media attention.

- **3. (D) is correct.** The Federal Communications Commission is an independent regulatory agency.

- **4. (A) is correct.** A trial balloon occurs when a political figure leaks information to the public to try to decide what the public would think if an event were to occur. Al Gore leaked his choice of Joe Lieberman as a running mate in order to see if the public approved of his choice—this type of event is referred to as a trial balloon.

- **5. (D) is correct** because it is the exception to sound bites (sound bites do not provide much information to citizens about candidates). All of the other choices about sound bites are correct.

- **6. (C) is correct.** Political races today are called candidate centered because of the focus on candidate personality, rather than issues, background or qualifications.

- **7. (B) is correct.** The Internet has not made citizens more informed or changed their opinion, but has made information more widely available.

- **8. (B) is correct.** Presidents are holding fewer regularly scheduled press conferences.

- **9. (E) is correct.** News stories that are sensational tend to have the most viewers.

- **10. (A) is correct.** Trust in government has declined as the availability of information about government has increased.

Free-Response Questions

This rubric provides examples of many, but not all of the possible correct responses to the free-response questions.

1.   The media may hurt candidates running for office through investigative journalism or allowing negative advertising to be run. Through investigative journalism, reporters will search for scandals and negative information about a candidate in order to receive higher ratings for their news programs. Such reporting can tarnish the reputation of a candidate and hurt his chances at being elected. Additionally, with the rise of the Internet, many scandals involving political figures have are have originated on Web sites only to later be picked up by the mainstream media. Negative advertisements may also be run against a candidate. Media outlets may choose to run such advertisements. Even though there is an expectation that the candidate have the right to respond, such negative advertisements often either drive down voter turnout or have a negative impact on the candidate.

On the other hand, having access to the media greatly helps candidates. Candidates can stage media events, leak trial balloons, make direct appearances on television, go on debates, or use sound bites to promote their campaigns. Media events occur when a candidate for office stages an event to draw positive attention to him or herself, such as appearing at a school or charity event. This event is covered in the media as a news story and provides attention to the candidate without the candidate having to spend any money on the campaign. Trial balloons occur when a candidate leaks information to a reporter hoping that the story will get into the mainstream media in order to gauge public opinion of a campaign event. For example, a Presidential candidate may leak information about his choice for vice president and then take polls to see if this choice helps the campaign or not.

2.   The First Amendment to the Constitution gives freedom to the press and allows media outlets to publish critical stories about the President of the United States. This freedom has an important impact on Presidents because information both flattering and unflattering about the President is widely available in the United States. Presidents have access to the media and can use this power to improve their image. At the same time the independent media is likely to publish stories that are negative in tone.

Press conferences are meetings held by the President with members of the press. They can have a negative impact on presidential approval. These meetings are not required by law or the Constitution, therefore Presidents have some control over how many press conferences are held. Presidents can also ask their press secretary to hold the meetings for them. Press conferences are frequently confrontational in nature and can lead to discussions about scandals that have been published. For example, during President Clinton's presidency he was directly asked about the Monica Lewinsky scandal in après conference in spite of the fact that he tried to turn the conversation to other topics. Because of the possibility of being questioned on scandals and unflattering events, is modern presidents have had the tendency not to hold press conferences.

The fireside chat began with FDRs presidency. These take place when presidents use the radio to communicate directly with citizens. These tend to have a positive impact on the President's term because there are no or few combative questions directed at the President. The President can set the tone of the talks and provide the information that he wants. Such " chats" are frequently used to attempt to change public opinion. FDR used fireside chats to change public opinion to favor the US entry into World War II.

Sound bites are short video clips of approximately 10 seconds and are frequently all that are shown of a president's speech on the news. These can have positive or negative impact on the president depending on how these statements are portrayed in the media. A president may choose a particular sound bite and repeat it in order to have a high likelihood that it is on the news, but also the media may choose a sound bite for the President that he is unhappy about.

CHAPTER 8

Political Parties

Political parties are the main vehicles for nominating candidates and running campaigns. They serve as **linkage institutions** that help bring the concerns of the electorate to the political arena through elections. Political parties also unite groups of politicians and the electorate by offering an ideological framework with which people can choose to identify themselves. The United States has for the most part always had a **two-party system. Party competition** is the battle between the Democrats and Republicans for the control of public offices.

The Meaning of Party

The two main political parties in the United States are the **Democratic Party** and the **Republican Party.** Democrats tend to be more liberal than Republicans, but both parties, to achieve a majority, usually remain fairly moderate. Political parties carry out the following tasks:

- **Choosing candidates:** Originally parties internally nominated their candidates to run in an election. Today, the public can choose candidates in primary elections.

- **Running campaigns:** Parties organize political campaigns and try to convince voters to elect their candidate. Today, by directly communicating with the public through television, candidates can operate more independently from their parties.

- **Providing a political identity:** Each party has an image. This offers the public a familiar ideology or platform with which they can choose to identify themselves and identify politicians. The **rational-choice theory** proposed by Anthony Downs provides a model of the relationship between parties and voters, which assumes that individuals weigh the costs and benefits of their choices and choose the party closest to them.

- **Endorsing specific policies:** Politicians of a party often support each other, because typically they agree on a general party platform.

- **Coordinating policymaking:** Through party identification, politicians in different branches of government are able to work together or support each other.

Parties, Voters, and Policy: The Downs Model

Rational choice theory explains the actions of voters and politicians. It assumes that individuals act in their best interest and weigh the costs and benefits of possible alternatives. In order to win office, candidates select policies that are widely favored. The majority of voters are in the middle ideologically, so centrist parties win elections. This has led to criticism of the two major parties for being too similar.

The Party in the Electorate

- Many voters cast their ballots on the basis of **party identification.** For instance, people who consider themselves Democrats usually vote for Democratic candidates.

- Most voters have a **party image** or perception of what the policies are that the party stands for.

- Party identification is declining, however. As of 2000, the plurality of voters considered themselves **Independent** rather than Democratic or Republican.

- **Ticket splitting,** or voting for members of different parties for different offices in an election, is also on the rise. This practice leads to a divided party government—the president may be of a different party from the majority party in Congress, for example.

The Party Organizations: From the Grass Roots to Washington

- Unlike the more formal parties of other countries, American political parties are fairly decentralized, with city, state, and national administrative bodies.

- Until the 1930s, local parties had tremendous influence over city governments. These often-corrupt **party machines** maintained their power by using the **patronage system** to reward loyal members with important positions in the government. Today local parties have declined, while county-level organizations have increased their election activities.

- Holding elections is one important task performed by the states, each of which has its own unique party organization. Each state's parties go about the election process differently, such as by choosing which type of primary to hold.

  - **Closed primary:** Only people who have already registered with the party are allowed to vote in the primary.

  - **Open primary**: Voters can choose on Election Day which party's primary they would like to participate in.

  - **Blanket primary:** Candidates from both parties are listed on the primary ballot, so voters can choose different parties' candidates for different offices.

- State parties are becoming more formally organized, but most presidential campaigning is still conducted through the candidate's personal campaign organization.

- The national party organization, or **national committee,** writes the official party platform and holds the national convention through which a presidential and vice presidential candidate are nominated. The national committee maintains the party organization during nonelection years.

The Party in Government: Promises and Policy

- Parties help members of Congress form **coalitions** that support a particular policy objective.

- However, presidents do not need to rely on party support as much as they used to because they can gain the favor of the public directly through television.

Party Eras in American History

Most democratic nations have multiparty systems that allow many interests to be represented. The United States, however, has always had a two-party system. Political scientists divide American history into **party eras** in which one party dominated politics for a significant period of time. Party eras change when a **critical election** reveals new issues and a failure of the traditional coalitions. This usually causes **party realignment,** when the party redefines itself and attracts a new coalition of voters.

- The First Party System: 1796–1824

- Alexander Hamilton's short-lived Federalist Party was the first political party.

- **Jefferson's Democratic-Republicans** maintained control of the White House.

- The Democrats and the Whigs: 1828–1856

- **Andrew Jackson** appealed to the masses rather than to the elite, and he formed a new coalition and, ultimately, the Democratic Party.

- The opposition party was the **Whig Party,** though it had little political success.

- The Two Republican Eras: 1860–1928

- The Republican Party formed out of a coalition of **antislavery** groups and nominated Lincoln as its first presidential candidate.

- The election of 1896 began another strongly Republican era during which industrialization and capitalism were advanced.

- The **New Deal** Coalition: 1932–1964

- Franklin Roosevelt brought the Democratic Party back into favor by starting scores of federal programs to combat the **Great Depression.**

- The new Democratic coalition brought together the poor, southerners, African Americans, city dwellers, Catholics, and Jews.

- Kennedy's **New Frontier** and Johnson's **Great Society** and **War on Poverty** continued the Democratic New Deal tradition.

- 1968–Present: Southern Realignment and the Era of Divided Party Government

- The states in the South have realigned and are now strongholds of the Republican party, but this has not always been true. President Nixon was able to capture the South, which had previously been solidly Democratic.

- When Nixon became President for the first time in the 20th century there was divided government. This became a frequent election pattern for most presidents that followed him.

- The trend in divided government has led many political scientists to believe that the party system has dealigned rather than realigned. **Party dealignment** means that people are gradually moving away from both parties.

Third Parties: Their Impact on American Politics

Third parties occasionally arise to challenge the two major parties, but they rarely gain enough support to put a candidate in office.

- Some parties form around a specific cause.

- Some are splinter parties, formed from smaller factions of the two major parties.

- Some form around a specific individual.

- Though they rarely win, third-party candidates do force particular issues onto the political agenda and allow Americans to express their discontent with the two major parties.

- They may also shift the votes of the electorate. Many political scientists think George W. Bush won the 2000 election because Green Party candidate Ralph Nader took votes away from Democrat Al Gore.

Understanding Political Parties/Democracy and Responsible Party Government

Political parties today are considered to be essential to a democratic system and the prevention of totalitarian rule, although the framers of the Constitution were wary of political parties.

- Critics of the two-party system allege:

- There is little choice for voters because the two parties keep to the middle of the road.

110

- There is less opportunity for political change.

- It is so decentralized that it fails to translate campaign promises into policy because politicians do not have to vote with the party line.

- The **responsible party model** is proposed by critics of the two-party system as how parties should work, including offering choices to voters and following through with campaign promises.

Multiparty systems may have these features:

Winner take all system is an electoral system in which legislative seats are awarded to candidates who come in first. In presidential elections, the candidate who comes in first gets all of the state's electoral votes.

Proportional representation an electoral system in which seats in a legislative branch are awarded in proportion to the percentage of the vote received.

Coalition government when two or more parties join together to form a majority in a national legislature.

American Political Parties and the Scope of Government/Is the Party Over?

American political parties do not require party discipline the way many European party systems do. The weak party structure of the United States makes it harder to pass legislation. Political parties have declined in strength. The political party is no longer the major source of information for citizens.

For Additional Review

Look at the list of United States presidents in the appendix at the back of your book. When did the presidency change hands between parties? What significant social and economic factors might have played a role in that transition? Note also the occurrences of third-party nominees. Select a third party that is unfamiliar to you and learn more about it in an encyclopedia or other reference book.

Multiple-Choice Questions

1. All of the following are functions of political parties EXCEPT

   (A) dictating policies

   (B) choosing candidates

   (C) running campaigns

   (D) giving cues to voters

   (E) coordinating policymaking

2. Which of the following is true of Southern states?

   (A) they have always leaned Republican

   (B) they have always leaned Democratic

   (C) they have no political leaning

   (D) they were once loyal to the Democratic party but now are loyal to the Republican party

   (E) they were once loyal to the Republican party but now are loyal to the Democratic party

3. All of the following are true of the party machine EXCEPT

   (A) they were successful in creating party loyalists

   (B) they provided jobs and favors for voters

   (C) they were corrupt

   (D) legislation has largely dismantled them

   (E) they relied on the merit principle when hiring employees

4. Which of the following is true of an open primary?

   (A) they allow cross over voting

   (B) they receive high turnout

   (C) they are the only system used to select a presidential candidate

   (D) they require that voters be registered with the party

   (E) they require voters to attend meetings in order to participate

5. Which of the following is the best definition of a realignment?

    (A) the abandonment of citizens from the two major parties to be independent

    (B) the requirement that members of a party vote together

    (C) the party that controls the White House loses control in Congress

    (D) a major ideological and demographic shift within a party

    (E) the emergence of many third parties

6. Which of the following was least likely to join the New Deal coalition?

    (A) minority voters

    (B) blue collar voters

    (C) voters without a college education

    (D) wealthy voters

    (E) liberal voters

7. Obstacles to third parties success include all of the following EXCEPT

    (A) winner-take-all rule

    (B) lack of funding from interest groups

    (C) inability to participate in the debate

    (D) lack of ballot access

    (E) inability to get media attention

8. A two-party system differs from a multiparty system in that it

    (A) encourages moderation in policymaking and discourages change.

    (B) offers voters no choice among ideologies.

    (C) usually includes a liberal and a conservative party.

    (D) relies on popular elections to change the party in power.

    (E) allows parties to choose their own leaders in the legislature.

9. Which of the following has led to ticket splitting in recent elections?

    (A) partisan dealignment

    (B) open primaries

    (C) party realignment

    (D) patronage system

    (E) closed primaries

10. The event in which the parties formally nominate their candidate for the presidency is called

    (A)   a critical election.

    (B)   a national convention.

    (C)   an open primary.

    (D)   a closed primary.

    (E)   a national committee.

Free-Response Questions

1. The power of the political party has declined over the past fifty years. Defend this thesis by defining and describing each of the terms below:

- Dealignment

- Political machine

- National party conventions

2. The Democratic and Republican parties have gone through several realignments.

    a) define realignment

    b) identify one realignment for the Democratic party and one for the Republican party

    c) explain the significance of realignments for American politics

ANSWERS AND EXPLANATIONS

Multiple-Choice Questions

- **1. (A) is correct.** American political parties may articulate policy preferences, but they are unable to dictate policy. They do however choose candidates, run campaigns, give cues to voters, and coordinate policymaking.

- **2. (D) is correct.** The South was once "solidly Democratic" but now leans Republican.

- **3. (E) is correct.** The party machines relied on the patronage system. Party machines were successful in creating party loyalists, provided jobs and favors, were corrupt and legislation has limited their efforts recently.

- **4. (A) is correct.** Open primaries allow citizens of either party to participate in the primary and this allows cross over voting, or a person of one party voting in another party's primary.

- **5. (D) is correct.** Realignments are major changes within a party. Change occurs both in the type of voters who are attracted to the party and the issues the party supports.

- **6. (D) is correct.** The New Deal coalition attracted minorities, blue collar, and lower educated and liberal voters. It did not attract wealthy voters.

- **7. (E) is correct.** Obstacles to third party success include the winner take all rule, ballot access, televised debates, and funding from interest groups.

- **8. (A) is correct.** Two-party systems encourage candidates to be more moderate.

- **9. (A) is correct.** Ticket splitting occurs because there are more citizens who are not loyal to one party over another.

- **10. (B) is correct.** Candidates for the presidency are formally selected at a national convention.

Free-Response Questions

This rubric provides examples of many, but not all of the possible correct responses to the free-response questions.

1. The power of the party has declined over the past one hundred years. This is due to a dealignment movement. Dealignment refers to the abandonment of citizen's affiliations with the two major political parties to become "independent" voters. Such independent or swing voters have hurt the power of the party because the members of the party must now battle for the ideological center in order to win an election. The party can no longer depend on large numbers of citizens to vote a straight ticket, and thus the election results become a little more unpredictable. Also Presidents are less likely to staff government with all party loyalists and more likely to turn to independents.

2. The decline of the party machine has also hurt the power of the party. The party machine can be described as a party organization with lots of power in large cities. Such a machine once guaranteed social services and jobs to new immigrants, ran conventions, and staffed city government. This created a group of party loyalists that lasted for generations. Some of these activities became illegal, causing the party to lose strength as the generations of party loyalists diminished.

    Finally, the national party convention was once a source of party strength, but this strength has diminished greatly. The national party used to determine whom the nominee would be for the presidency, with no voter involvement at all. The progressive reforms stripped this power from the party at the state level and eventually all states began holding primaries and caucuses to determine the nominee, taking the power away from the party.

A realignment occurs usually after a critical election. A realignment marks a major change in the nature of the political party. The change occurs in both the demographic groups that once supported the party as well as the agenda of the party. In a realignment usually the party that was once the majority becomes the minority. The change is national as well as local and the change is not simply marked by one election but has some permanence.

Most political scientists argue that there have been four major realigning periods. Perhaps the most remembered realignment for the Republican party took place after the election of 1860—sometimes referred to as the "birth" of the Republican party. President Lincoln had captured a new group of voters and his party dominated politics (the party realigned several times after that). Perhaps the most remembered realignment for the Democratic party was after the election of 1932. President Roosevelt began a "New Deal" coalition, which would unify the Democratic party for years to come.

3.   Realignments are significant to American politics because they mark major changes in the nature of the party and the party emerges as a completely different organization. Understanding realignments helps to explain how parties have changed. For example, it is surprising to some that Thomas Jefferson was a Democrat because he was a states' rights advocate, and the Democratic party today has advocated federal power in most domestic policy areas. The explanation for this is that the Democratic party has realigned since Thomas Jefferson was a member of the party.

CHAPTER 9

Nominations and Campaigns

To run for a political office, a person must first receive a party's official **nomination.** Then, with the party's endorsement and assistance, the candidate must **campaign** to win the support of voters. These two processes require a great deal of money and media exposure. Presidential campaigning has become a major part of the political process in the United States. **Campaign strategy** is the plan of candidates to win the election. The nomination and campaign process is so taxing that many qualified individuals make a decision not to run.

The Nomination Game

* Politicians begin their bid for a presidential nomination more than a year in advance of the election. In most other countries, campaigns are limited to only a few months.

* Most candidates have previously held a government post, such as representative, senator, governor, or military general.

Competing for Delegates

Each state selects delegates to send to the Democratic and the Republican **national conventions,** which have the supreme power to select the Presidential nominee for the party.

* A few states still use traditional **caucuses** to choose delegates. These are closed meetings of party regulars who participate in party building activities and select nominees.

* Most states now use **primaries.** Voters can nominate a presidential candidate directly, or else they can choose delegates who have pledged to vote for that candidate. State parties may have open primaries, where any registered voter can fill out a party nomination ballot, or closed primaries, where advanced party registration is required.

* The political parties in each state decide how to divide its delegates' votes. Delegates are apportioned to each candidate based on their proportion of the vote in each state congressional district. The Republican Party gives all votes to the candidate with the majority vote in each district. The Democratic Party divides delegates proportionally by district and statewide. The Democratic Party also has "superdelegates," which are not committed by primary or caucus votes, and make their own choices at the national party convention.

* The rise of primaries has allowed the electorate to take control of the election process away from political parties.

Evaluating the Primary and Caucus System

- The primary system has raised numerous criticisms:

1.   The early caucuses and primaries receive far too much media attention, which can distort campaigns.

    - This places too much attention on the outcome of early caucuses and primaries—notably in **Iowa** and **New Hampshire,** two states that are not very representative of the country as a whole

    - Candidates who do not score early victories are likely to be dismissed by the media and the public and to be unable to raise funds to continue campaigning.

    - States, to cast influential votes, try to hold their primaries early, before other states. This practice, called **frontloading,** has made the campaign process longer.

2.   The lengthy campaign and rigors of the primary season discourage some capable politicians from running.

3.   It requires and encourages an exorbitant amount of spending in campaigns.

4.   Primaries are unrepresentative of the electorate because few people vote in them, and those who do are more likely to be older and wealthier than the majority of Americans.

5.   It allows the media, which focuses on winners and dismisses losers early in the running, tremendous influence in shaping campaigns.

A **national primary** is a proposal by critics of the current system who would like to replace the extended primary calendar with a nationwide primary held on one day.

Regional primaries are another proposal that allows regions to have primaries, with rotation of the order of regional primaries every four years.

The Convention Send-Off

The delegates selected in each state's primary attend the **national convention,** where they cast their votes for their presidential candidate.

- The parties, especially the Democrats, have made efforts to **reform** delegate selection to ensure representation of youth, minorities, women, and organized labor at the convention, particularly after the **1968 Democratic National Convention** in Chicago, when violence erupted both out on the streets and inside the convention center.

- Some convention seats are reserved for **superdelegates,** party leaders and politicians who automatically earn a vote at the convention. The Democratic Party makes greater use of superdelegates than the Republican Party.

- The outcome of conventions today is usually predetermined by previous primary results, so conventions today are **media events.**

- At a national convention:

  - delegates support their candidate,

  - the party presents its official **party platform** for the next four years;

  - the winning candidate formally accepts the party's nomination;

  - The vice president is chosen, usually based on the presidential nominee's preference for a running mate.

The Campaign Game

The two presidential candidates then embark on a **national campaign** to win the votes of different groups in different regions of the country. Campaigns today are run fairly independently by each candidate.

- Modern campaign techniques include:

  - **television advertising,**

  - televised **public appearances,**

  - **direct mail** campaigns,

  - an official **web site** to advance the candidate's platform and collect campaign contributions.

- The media closely follow campaigns. Coverage focuses on the candidates' daily activities, **campaign strategies,** and poll results.

  - Studies show that voters learn more about the candidates' positions on important issues from their advertisements than from the news.

  - Critics fear that campaigns have become centered on candidates' images rather than their political beliefs.

- To coordinate a campaign, a candidate must hire a campaign team that serves both to organize his or her daily activities and to conduct **public relations.** This adds significantly to the enormous cost of a campaign.

Money and Campaigning

Candidates rely on television to communicate directly with the electorate, and air time often translates into votes. Therefore, the necessity of television has made American campaigns extremely expensive.

- Politicians spend as much time fund-raising as doing their jobs.

- In 1974, Congress passed the **Federal Election Campaign Act** to attempt to control campaign costs and donations.

    - Established the **Federal Election Commission** to enforce campaign laws.

    - Initiated public financing of elections—taxpayers can choose to donate $3 to a federal campaign fund that is divided among all candidates by checking a box on their income tax form (**Presidential Election Campaign Fund**).

- Set a limit for spending in each election by those who accept public funds.

    - Required candidates to **report all campaign contributions and how the money was spent.**

    - Individual campaign contributions were limited to $2,000.

- **Soft money** is one loophole through which businesses and wealthy individuals can make unlimited contributions.

    - Soft money is intended for a party's general use and is therefore not a donation to a specific candidate, but it can be channeled into presidential campaigns. The **Bipartisan Campaign Reform Act** (**McCain-Feingold**) attempted to ban soft money, as the candidate often rewards contributors once he or she is in office. The Supreme Court upheld the Act against a constitutional challenge in 2003.

    - A loophole in the BCRA allowed 527 organizations to form and raise unlimited amounts of money to spend on advertising and voter mobilization efforts.

- **Political action committees (PACs)** are another method, established by the 1974 F.E.C. Act, through which interest groups try to influence policy through campaign contributions.

    - To contribute to a campaign, an interest group must channel money through a PAC, which must be registered with the FEC so that it can be monitored.

    - There is **no limit** to the amount PACs can spend.

    - PACs can act independently of the candidate and his or her campaign team, by running an advertisement without the candidate's approval.

    - Candidates rely on PACs to help finance costly campaigns, and PACs allow business interests to assert themselves in the political arena.

- PACs play a greater role in congressional elections than in presidential elections, which are partially funded by the public.

- Created to provide unions and other groups the opportunity to contribute, PACs have been organized and used by businesses to affect elections.

- Despite the massive amount of money spent on campaigns and the media's constant focus on them, campaigns rarely convert voters away from their predisposed party identification.

For Additional Review

Some critics say that in the United States, the campaign never stops. Look on the web for presidential hopefuls. Also read about the financial statistics of the 2000 and 2004 elections at www.fec.gov. This information could be very helpful on a free-response question on the AP U.S. Government & Politics Exam.

Multiple-Choice Questions

1. A caucus is

   (A) held at the national level to select a nominee.

   (B) a closed door meeting of party regulars.

   (C) open to all who want to participate.

   (D) a meeting of members of Congress.

   (E) a court hearing.

2. A primary is

   (A) held at the national level to select a nominee.

   (B) a closed door meeting of party regulars.

   (C) can be open or closed.

   (D) a meeting of members of Congress.

   (E) a court hearing.

3. When the Democrats select delegates to their national convention they
   (A) require all delegates to vote based on a vote held at the state level.
   (B) use a winner take all system to allocate delegates.
   (C) mix use of proportional representation to select delegates with delegates who are not pledged.
   (D) hold a series of closed primaries.
   (E) open the convention to all who can afford a ticket.

4. Superdelegates are
   (A) used more often by Republicans than by Democrats.
   (B) used by Democrats to ensure a voice for party officials and for particular constituencies.
   (C) not able to vote at the conventions.
   (D) staff of the national parties.
   (E) used to maintain party discipline.

5. The main loophole to the McCain-Feingold legislation is
   (A) 527s.
   (B) soft money.
   (C) hard money.
   (D) bundling.
   (E) *Buckley* v. *Valeo*

6. The goal of the Federal Election Campaign Act was to
   (A) make delegate selection easier.
   (B) make campaigns more fair and transparent.
   (C) enforce party discipline.
   (D) cause a realignment.
   (E) limit the impact of the media.

7. PAC money gives the greatest advantage to
   (A) the president's party.
   (B) incumbents.
   (C) Supreme Court justices.
   (D) Cabinet nominees.
   (E) challengers.

8. Federal matching funds are available to

   (A) governors.

   (B) members of the House.

   (C) senators.

   (D) Presidential candidates.

   (E) judges.

9. Where is the first caucus held?

   (A) Iowa

   (B) New Hampshire

   (C) Washington, D.C.

   (D) Florida

   (E) South Carolina

10. All of the following are criticisms raised against the primary system EXCEPT

   (A) This process of selecting delegates is unfair because it prevents representation of minority groups at the national conventions.

   (B) Too much weight is placed on the early primaries, especially because states like Iowa are not representative of the American electorate.

   (C) It has extended the length of the campaign process to an impractical and unmanageable degree.

   (D) It prevents many qualified politicians from running, because fund-raising for and participating in primaries distracts them from their current office.

   (E) It allows the media too much power in shaping presidential campaigns.

Free-Response Questions

1. Nominating a presidential candidate occurs through an indirect process.

    a) describe the role of delegates in the nomination process

    b) define winner-take-all and proportional representation and identify where each system is used in the nomination process

    c) explain a campaign strategy that results from the indirect election process

2. In 1968 the Democratic convention erupted into chaos.

    a) explain a source of conflict at the 1968 convention

    b) describe the goal of the McGovern-Fraser commission and identify two rules that resulted from this commission

    c) Has the process of selecting presidential candidates become more democratic? Support your answer.

ANSWERS AND EXPLANATIONS

Multiple-Choice Questions

- **1. (B) is correct.** In a caucus only members who are registered with the party can participate.

- **2. (C) is correct.** Primaries can be open to any citizen or they can be restricted to members who are registered with the party.

- **3. (C) is correct.** In most states, Democrats use proportional representation to select delegates. However, a large percentage of delegates to the national convention for the Democratic party are unpledged delegates.

- **4. (B) is correct.** Superdelegates were instituted as part of a compromise between party regulars and those who wanted primaries to be the determinant of the nomination.

- **5. (A) is correct.** 527 groups are able to advertise for an issue and thus enable some to thwart the goal of the McCain-Feingold legislation.

- **6. (B) is correct.** The goal of the Federal Election Campaign Act was to make campaigns more fair and transparent.

- **7. (B) is correct.** PAC money benefits incumbents.

- **8. (D) is correct.** Federal matching funds are available for Presidential candidates who meet certain rules.

- **9. (A) is correct.** The first caucus is held in Iowa.

- **10. (A) is correct.** The Democrats mandate minority participation at the national convention and Republicans have made efforts to include minorities.

Free-Response Questions

This rubric provides examples of many, but not all of the possible correct responses to the free-response questions.

1. The selection of candidates for the presidency occurs through an indirect election. Voters are allowed to participate in primaries or caucuses at the state level. Their votes however translate into delegates that attend a national convention and cast an official vote for the nominee.

   For the Democratic party, most states allocate their delegates in proportion to voter's choices, which is proportional representation. The Republican party mostly allocates their delegates on a winner-take-all basis, meaning that the candidate who wins the most votes in a state gets all of that states delegates to the national convention.

   There are several campaign strategies that result from the rules of this contest. One is known as frontloading, in which the candidates will put all their time money and resources into states will earlier primaries and caucuses in an effort to gain momentum. Another strategy is to concentrate in states that award more delegates for the effort, such as Texas, which holds a lot of delegates in both conventions. Candidates may not campaign at all in stats with non-binding primaries.

2. The Democratic National Convention of 1968 had riots outside the convention doors, police brutality, and disorder inside the convention. There were several sources of tension which caused these riots. First, the antiwar protests of Vietnam spilled over to the convention, as the convention was viewed as resembling the establishment, pro-war position. LBJ, a Democratic president, had waged a very unpopular war. Ironically, most of the antiwar and the antiestablishment movement was associated with the Democratic party as well. Other sources of conflict included how the nominee, Hubert Humphrey was selected. Humphrey had won the nomination without competing in many primaries (Bobby Kennedy had won many primaries, but when he was assassinated Humphrey inherited his delegates). Many protesters outside the convention were demonstrating against the war, others against Humphrey's nomination. Primaries were a relatively new device at this time used to select the nominees.

The McGovern-Fraser Commission was formed after this disastrous convention. The goal of the commission was to make the party more democratic and to avoid the chaos of 1968. New rules were established to select the nominee and to decide who would serve as delegates. Because delegates to the national convention in the past were perceived to have been members of the elite, white establishment, the commission established a new rule setting quotas for female and minority delegates, so that delegates would more closely resemble the general population. The delegate count method also changed to primarily proportional representation to more accurately reflect the popular will. Some within the party were uncomfortable with these new rules, feeling that party regulars would be better equipped to decide on the nominee. Therefore, in an effort to appease these party members and get the new rules instated, a compromise was made. The compromise was a rule to allow for a percentage of the delegates to be "superdelegates." These superdelegates would be party regulars who were free to vote as they saw fit at the convention.

The process of selecting nominees is more democratic today than it used to be. This can be supported by the fact that states hold primary elections allowing average voters to have some say in the nominating process. Prior to the holding of primaries, the party had selected the nominee without voter involvement, making today's presidential selection process more democratic now than the previous system.

CHAPTER 10

Elections and Voting Behavior

Elections are the process through which power in government changes hands. Such a change is possible because elections bestow **legitimacy** both on the process and on the incoming officials, who have been chosen to lead by a majority of the people. According to the theory of democracy, elections give voters a voice in policymaking because they allow people to choose the candidate who is most likely to act in their interests or according to their political beliefs. For this to work in practice, however, candidates must represent distinct stands on the issues.

HOW AMERICAN ELECTIONS WORK

There are three kinds of elections in the United States: primary elections, general elections, and elections on specific policy issues which take place at the local level through **referendum** (state-level method of direct legislation) and **initiative petition** (voter-proposed changes in the state constitution).

Whether to Vote: A Citizen's First Choice

Suffrage has been expanded several times throughout American history. Although the Constitution left the issue up to the states, generally only white, male, property-owners had the right to vote. Today, almost **all Americans over the age of 18** can vote in elections.

- The **Fifteenth Amendment** granted suffrage to African Americans.

- The **Nineteenth Amendment** extended voting privileges to women.

- The **Twenty-Sixth Amendment** set the minimum voting age at 18.

Although more people are able to vote, fewer people are exercising this right. Some of their reasons for not voting:

- They believe that one vote in more than 100 million makes little difference.

- They are unable to take off work to vote on a Tuesday. Reformers have suggested moving Election Day to a Saturday.

- **Voter registration** is difficult or inconvenient in most states. Procedures have been made easier, especially with the **Motor Voter Act,** but turnout has still decreased.

- There is little ideological difference between the two parties' candidates.

Some reasons people are more likely to vote:

- They perceive a significant ideological difference between the two parties' candidates.

- They have a sense of **political efficacy**— they believe their vote will make a difference.

- They want to perform their **civic duty** in a democracy.

Who Votes?

- People with a college education

- Older people, especially senior citizens

- Hispanic Americans and African Americans are less likely to vote, but those with higher levels of education vote in greater percentages than educated Caucasians.

- More women than men have voted in recent elections.

- Union members

- People who are married

Politicians who rely on these voters to be elected are more likely to address their concerns in the policy arena.

- Studies show that if turnout increased among groups with low rates, Democrats would probably receive more votes.

- Reforms are unlikely because Republicans do not want to lose this advantage.

How Americans Vote: Explaining Citizens' Decisions

1. People vote according to their **party identification.**

   - A candidate of their chosen party probably shares their political beliefs.

   - They do not have to decide on or become informed about every issue.

   - This trend is declining as parties have lost some significance in the political process.

2. Voters evaluate what they know and see of the **candidates' personalities** to make a decision.

   - A candidate's appearance may play an unconscious role in voter decision making.

   - People tend to value integrity, competence, and reliability in a candidate.

128

- Voters with a college education are more likely to base their decision on a candidate's personality. They make inferences about the candidate's performance.

3. People vote for candidates who share their **policy preferences.**

   - Voters have firm policy convictions.

   - They are familiar with each candidate's policy preferences.

   - They are able to discern differences among candidates' stands on issues.

   - A person may also **vote retrospectively** by choosing a candidate who vows to continue policies helpful to him or her, or by choosing the opposition candidate who promises to change the policy.

   - Candidates may avoid taking a clear stand on a controversial issue, **making policy** voting difficult.

   - This method requires a lot of effort on the part of voters.

The Last Battle: The Electoral College

In the United States, the president is not chosen directly by the people in a popular election. The Electoral College casts the final vote. This institution was created by the writers of the Constitution to keep the presidency at a distance from the masses. It was intended to allow only the elite to choose the president.

- Each state's number of electors is equal to its total number of representatives and senators. Electors are chosen by the state party organizations.

- Almost all states are **winner-take-all:** The candidate who receives the highest popular vote in the state gets all of that state's electoral votes.

- Electors convene in December and deliver their votes to the president of the Senate (the vice president), who officially announces the majority winner at the opening of the congressional session in January.

- If no candidate receives a majority of the electoral votes (at least 270), the members of the House of Representatives vote, with each state delegation having one vote.

This system has received an enormous amount of criticism.

- It gives an unfair advantage to states with larger populations. Because they have a greater number of electoral votes at stake, large states and their policy concerns receive more attention from presidential candidates.

- A candidate may need to win in only a few large states to win the election. This neglects the less populous states (although George W. Bush used a small state strategy to win the presidency in 2000 and 2004).

- Because most large states also have large cities, the system is biased in favor of urban voters.

- It is possible to win the popular vote but lose the election because of the electoral votes. This happened to Al Gore, who won the popular vote in 2000.

For Additional Review

The 2000 presidential election was an extraordinary political event for many reasons. Not only was it one of the few elections in American history in which a candidate won the popular vote but lost the electoral vote, it was also the first presidency to be determined ultimately by the Supreme Court. Read more about the controversies of this election at www.supremecourtus.gov/florida.html and

http://www.c-span.org/campaign2000/Florida/ussupcourt.asp.

Multiple-Choice Questions

1. When does a referendum occur in the United States?

    (A)   every four years when we Presidential elections occur

    (B)   when states give voters an opportunity to vote on legislation

    (C)   when citizens sign a petition to get a third party on the ballot

    (D)   when citizens request that changes be made to the state Constitution

    (E)   when citizens change their party affiliation

2. All of the following are true of the Electoral College System EXCEPT

    (A)   It is possible to win the electoral vote but lose the popular vote.

    (B)   A majority of electors is required to win.

    (C)   Electors are awarded proportionally in most states.

    (D)   Candidates have historically focused campaigns on large states.

    (E)   Many candidates today focus their campaigns on swing states.

3. Which of the following has decreased voter turnout over the years?

   (A) expansion of those who are eligible to vote

   (B) competitive races

   (C) get-out-the-vote drives

   (D) party machines

   (E) candidate centered campaigns

4. Which of the following requires citizens to have the opportunity to register to vote?

   (A) political efficacy

   (B) civic duty

   (C) the Motor Voter Act

   (D) referenda

   (E) initiative

The demographic correlates of presidential voting behavior have changed in a number of important ways since 1960. When Kennedy was elected in 1960 Protestants and Catholics voted very differently, as Kennedy's Catholicism was a major issue during the campaign. Although John Kerry was the first major party nominee since Kennedy to be of the Catholic faith, Catholics were only slightly more likely to support him than Protestants. Today, the major difference along religious lines involves how often one attends religious services, with those who attend regularly being substantially more likely to support Republican presidential candidates. The least likely group to support Republicans these days is African-Americans. As you can see in data below, Kerry clearly drew more support from African Americans than did Kennedy. Another advantage that Democrats now enjoy is with female voters, who preferred Kerry by 7 percent more than men. Interestingly, women were actually slightly less likely than men to have supported the handsome JFK in 1960. Finally, the rapidly expanding Hispanic population in the U.S. has reshaped the electoral scene with their tendency to support Democratic candidates. Hispanics numbered only about 1 percent of voters.

	KENNEDY	NIXON	KERRY	BUSH
Protestant	36	63	40	59
Catholic	83	17	47	52
Jewish	89	11	74	25
Regularly attend religious services	49	50	39	60
Often attend regligious services	36	64	49	50
Seldom attend religious services	55	44	54	45
Never attend religious services	51	49	62	36
White	48	52	41	58
African American	71	29	88	11
Hispanic	NA	NA	57	40
Male	52	48	44	55
Female	47	53	51	48
18–29	53	47	54	45
30–44	51	49	46	53
45–64	50	50	47	52
65+	39	61	47	52
No HS diploma	55	45	50	49
High school diploma	52	48	47	52
Some college	33	67	46	54
College degree	38	62	49	50

Source: 1960 National Election Study and 2004 National Voter Exit Poll.

131

5. According to the preceding table, which group voted at the *lowest* rate?

    (A) people age 65 and over

    (B) some college

    (C) married

    (D) government workers

    (E) 18 to 20 year olds

6. According to the preceding table, which group voted at the *highest* rate?

    (A) people age 65 and over

    (B) those with some college

    (C) married

    (D) government workers

    (E) 18 to 20 year olds

7. Which of the following can be concluded from the preceding table?

    (A) Catholic voters were more likely to vote Democrat in 1960 than they were in 2004.

    (B) Jewish voters tended to choose Republican candidates in 1960 and 2004

    (C) Those who attend religious services voted Democrat in 1960 and 2004

    (D) Those with a college degree were overwhelmingly likely to vote Republican in 1960 and 2004.

    (E) Female voters voted Republican in 1960 and 2004.

8. Which of the following has increased in importance for voters?

    (A) issues

    (B) background and qualifications

    (C) personality

    (D) party affiliation

    (E) frequency of political advertising on television

9. Turnout is highest in which of the following types of elections?

    (A) open primaries

    (B) closed primaries

    (C) congressional elections

    (D) general election for the president

    (E) gubernatorial elections

10. Voters in presidential primaries are likely to be which of the following?

   (A) moderates

   (B) well educated

   (C) loyal to an interest group

   (D) young

   (E) a member of a minority group

11. Which of the following is true of some states' winner-take-all rule for Electoral College votes?

   (A) It hurts the chances of third party candidates.

   (B) It often makes it more difficult for the winner to emerge with a mandate.

   (C) It encourages campaigning in many small states.

   (D) It is simple for the public to understand.

   (E) It is used in all states.

Free-Response Questions

The demographic correlates of presidential voting behavior have changed in a number of important ways since 1960. When Kennedy was elected in 1960 Protestants and Catholics voted very differently, as Kennedy's Catholicism was a major issue during the campaign. Although John Kerry was the first major party nominee since Kennedy to be of the Catholic faith, Catholics were only slightly more likely to support him than Protestants. Today, the major difference along religious lines involves how often one attends religious services, with those who attend regularly being substantially more likely to support Republican presidential candidates. The least likely group to support Republicans these days is African-Americans. As you can see in data below, Kerry clearly drew more support from African Americans than did Kennedy. Another advantage that Democrats now enjoy is with female voters, who preferred Kerry by 7 percent more than men. Interestingly, women were actually slightly less likely than men to have supported the handsome JFK in 1960. Finally, the rapidly expanding Hispanic population in the U.S. has reshaped the electoral scene with their tendency to support Democratic candidates. Hispanics numbered only about 1 percent of voters.

	KENNEDY	NIXON	KERRY	BUSH
Protestant	36	63	40	59
Catholic	83	17	47	52
Jewish	89	11	74	25
Regularly attend religious services	49	50	39	60
Often attend regligious services	36	64	49	50
Seldom attend religious services	55	44	54	45
Never attend religious services	51	49	62	36
White	48	52	41	58
African American	71	29	88	11
Hispanic	NA	NA	57	40
Male	52	48	44	55
Female	47	53	51	48
18–29	53	47	54	45
30–44	51	49	46	53
45–64	50	50	47	52
65+	39	61	47	52
No HS diploma	55	45	50	49
High school diploma	52	48	47	52
Some college	33	67	46	54
College degree	38	62	49	50

Source: 1960 National Election Study and 2004 National Voter Exit Poll.

1. (a) Identify two groups that voted Democratic according to the preceding table in both elections. Explain why the Democratic party attracts these voters.

(b) Identify two groups that voted Republican according to the table above in both elections. Explain why the Republican party attracts these voters.

THE DECLINE OF TURNOUT: 1892 to 2004

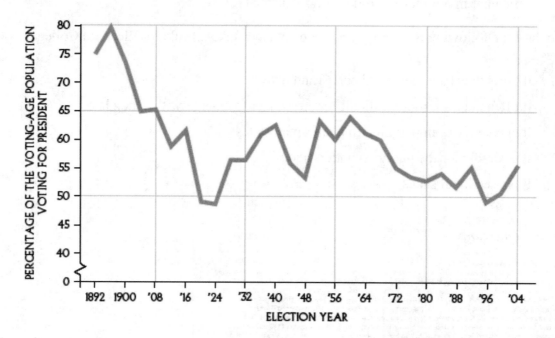

2. The chart above shows a recent trend in voting in American elections.

    a. Define voter turnout.

    b. Identify the trend in voter turnout displayed in the chart above.

    c. Identify two rules of the electoral process and explain how each impacted this trend.

    d. Describe one additional reason (not identified in c) to explain this trend.

ANSWERS AND EXPLANATIONS

Multiple-Choice Questions

- **1. (B) is correct.** Many states allow voters to vote on legislation, this is called a referendum.

- **2. (C) is correct.** The winner-take-all system is used in the Electoral College for all states except Maine and Nebraska.

- **3. (A) is correct.** As suffrage has increased, overall voter turnout has decreased.

- **4. (C) is correct.** The Motor Voter Act is a federal mandate that requires that citizens have the opportunity to register to vote at the time they get their drivers licenses.

- **5. (E) is correct.** Young people (18 to 20) voted at the lowest rate.

- **6. (A) is correct.** The elderly voted at the highest rate.

- **7. (C) is correct.** Campaigns have become more focused on candidate personality.

- **8. (D) is correct.** Voter turnout is highest in Presidential elections.

- **9. (B) is correct.** Voter turnout in primaries tends to be limited to voters in the upper socioeconomic brackets.

- **10. (A) is correct.** The winner–take-all rule hurts third-party candidates. Because third party support is frequently evenly distributed throughout the United States and not concentrated in a state, third-party candidates have difficulty winning electoral votes. Their support is not proportionally represented by the winner-take-all system.

Free-Response Questions

This rubric provides examples of many, but not all of the possible correct responses to the free-response questions.

1. The groups that voted Democratic in both elections were Jewish, African American, and the young. Jewish voters have typically favored religious freedoms and have sympathized with minority voters. These factors have attracted them to the Democratic party because the Democratic party is less likely to advocate prayer in school and supports minority rights. African American voters are attracted to the Democratic party because the Democrats advocated legislation to improve civil rights in the 1960s and currently are

more likely to support programs that help them such as affirmative action. The younger voters are more attracted to the Democratic party because the Democrats are less socially conservative.

The groups that voted Republican in both elections include Protestant, white and college educated. Protestants are more likely to support the Republican party because Republicans tend to support policies that religious individuals support—such as not allowing abortion or gay marriage and advocating prayer in school. College educated voters are more likely to have higher paying jobs which may lead them to support the low tax platform of the Republican party.

2. Voter turnout can be defined as the percentage of citizens who are eligible to vote (and have completed voter registration) who vote in a given election.

The chart above shows that voter turnout has steadily declined over the years.

There are several rules of the electoral process that impacted this trend. One is the expansion in suffrage to women, African Americans, and young (18 to 21). Each time that suffrage was expanded, the overall turnout of voters decreased. Also there are more elections today then there once were, including primary elections that are closed to members of a particular party.

There are several reasons that also contribute to this trend, including growing mistrust of the political system, growing apathy and dealignment. As citizens view elected officials in a negative light they are less likely to go to the polls to support them. Citizens are also getting more apathetic as their lives become increasingly filled with opportunities to surf the Internet or watch TV. They are less likely to make the effort to learn about the election and participate in it. Finally, fewer voters are loyal to one political party, making them less likely to care who the winner of an election is.

CHAPTER 11

Interest Groups

One of the most pronounced political trends in the last few decades is the rise of **interest groups.** Today there are more than 20,000 of these private organizations in Washington and in state capitals. Interest groups represent bodies of people with shared interests who lobby legislators on their behalf. In this sense, they are a natural part of a democracy. However, Americans tend to view them with skepticism because, most often, the language of influence is money.

The Role and Reputation of Interest Groups

- Interest groups may pursue any kind of policy, in all levels and branches of government. They differ from political parties in several ways.

- They pursue their agenda through the **political process,** whereas parties advance their agendas through elections.

- Interest groups specialize in one or two policy areas, whereas parties focus on general policies to win a majority.

- Many people criticize interest groups for fostering a policymaking system heavily influenced by the ability to raise and donate money to candidates for legislative and executive office based on money.

- Interest groups donate heavily to campaigns through political action committees (PACs) to influence legislators' voting decisions.

- The more money an interest group has, the more it is able to influence policy.

- Proponents of interest groups argue that they are effective **linkage institutions** (this term requires a brief definition)**.**

- They represent the interests of the public in the policy arena.

- Because they are carefully monitored and regulated, the methods of interest groups are much more honest than those employed by people and groups in the past.

Theories of Interest Group Politics

1. **Pluralist theory:** Interest groups are important to democracy because they allow people to organize themselves to change policies.

    - Because hundreds of interest groups must compete for influence, no one group will dominate the others.

    - Groups put up a fair fight; they do not engage in illegal activities to surpass other groups.

    - Groups are equal in power because they have different resources at their disposal.

2. **Elite theory:** There may be hundreds of interest groups, but only a select few have any real power.

    - The interests of only a handful of elites, usually business people, are almost always favored over other interests.

    - The policy battles that smaller interests do win are usually minor.

    - Power rests mostly with large multinational corporations.

    - The system of elite control is maintained by a well-established structure of interlocking policy players.

3. **Hyperpluralist theory** or **interest group liberalism**

    - **Sub governments,** or **iron triangles,** form around specific policy areas.

    - These are composed of an **interest group,** a **federal agency,** and any **legislative committees or subcommittees** that handle the policy area.

    - By avoiding having to choose between policy initiatives, the government creates conflicting policies that waste time and money.

    - Groups have too much political influence because they usually get what they want.

    - Competing subgovernments only add to the confusion.

What Makes an Interest Group Successful?

1. The **size** of the group. It is important to distinguish between a **potential group**, which is all of the people who might be members of the group, and an **actual group**, which is all the people who actually join. Interest groups organize and work for the **collective good** of the members of the group.

- **Smaller groups** are more effective than large groups.

- Smaller groups can organize more easily.

- A member of a small group is more likely to experience the group's success and, therefore, is more likely to work harder than a member of a large group. However, groups do experience the **free rider problem,** where individuals can benefit from the work of the group without actually joining the group, and according to **Olson's law of large groups**, this problem is greater with larger groups.

2. The **intensity** of the group members' feelings about the issue

- **Single-issue groups** form around a specific policy and tend to pursue it uncompromisingly.

- Single-issue groups often deal with moral issues that people feel strongly about.

- Members of single-issue groups often vote according to a candidate's stand on the group's issue.

3. The **financial resources** at the group's disposal

- Politicians are most likely to serve the needs of people or groups with money.

- Money allows groups to mobilize, conduct research, and maintain an administration.

How Groups Try to Shape Policy

Lobbying: Professional lobbyists attempt to persuade lawmakers to act on behalf of their group. The more helpful a lobbyist is the more power he or she has with a politician. Lobbyists:

- serve as policy experts in their interest area

- act as consultants who advise legislators on how to approach policy issues and debates

- mobilize support for politicians during reelection

- suggest innovative policy ideas

Electioneering: Interest groups endorse a candidate who supports their interests and work to get that candidate elected. The groups:

- encourage people to vote for the candidate

- help finance the candidate's campaign through **PACs**

- Congressional candidates have become largely dependent on PAC money.

- Most PAC money goes to **incumbents** rather than challengers.

Litigation: Interest groups use lawsuits to change policies that have already gone through the legislative process.

- Even the threat of a lawsuit may be enough to influence policymaking.

- Groups can file *amicus curiae* **briefs** to state their side in a court case and to assess the consequences of the decisions the court might make.

- Groups can also file **class action lawsuits**—suits on behalf of a larger group in the electorate.

Mobilizing public opinion: Interest groups try to influence the public because they know that politicians' careers depend on public opinion.

- Groups cultivate a positive image of themselves in the eyes of the public.

- Groups encourage public participation to advance interests from the point of view of the constituency.

Types of Interest Groups

Economic interests: business, labor, farmers

- against regulations and tax increases

- want tax advantages, subsidies, and contracts for work

- Organized labor is the second largest group (e.g., the AFL-CIO, the National Education Association). The interest group with the largest membership is the **AARP**, which represents the interests of older Americans.

- Businesses are the most widely represented interests in Washington.

Environmental interests: the fastest-growing type of interest group

- favor wilderness protection, pollution control, energy alternatives

- oppose policies that damage the environment

- examples include the Sierra Club, the Nature Conservancy

Equality interests: civil rights, women, social welfare

- Concerns center on fair treatment in jobs, housing, and education.

- Examples include the American Civil Liberties Union (ACLU), the Southern Poverty Law Center

Consumers' interests and **public interests:** the whole public benefits from certain policy actions

- product safety, which was introduced by Ralph Nader

- groups that cannot assert their interests themselves: children, the mentally ill, animals

- fair and open government; government reform

- examples include Consumer Alert, the Children's Defense Fund

For Additional Review

Make a table of several interest groups that have made the headlines recently. First define the interests of each one. Then evaluate them in terms of size, intensity, and financial resources. Was each group successful in influencing policy?

Multiple-Choice Questions

1. Which of the following is the best definition of pluralism?

   (A) a multitude of groups compete for and share power at any given time

   (B) a multitude of interest groups have the ability to form and survive

   (C) several small, single-issue groups tend to hold power

   (D) the number of groups continues to increase as society becomes more complicated

   (E) groups are multiplying and getting more intense

2. Elite theorists believe that the power of interest groups

   (A) is derived from their equal access to the government.

   (B) comes mostly from public support.

   (C) is evenly distributed among them.

   (D) reinforces a more democratic government.

   (E) is held by only a few wealthy groups.

3. The hyperpluralist theory holds that

   (A) interest group intensity places pressure on members of Congress.

   (B) the large number of groups slows down the policymaking process.

   (C) it is common for one group to rapidly split up into other groups.

   (D) many groups compete for and share power.

   (E) salient issues cause a plurality of groups to form.

4. Lawmakers often rely on lobbyists for all of the following reasons EXCEPT

   (A) to come up with new policy ideas that they can introduce in Congress.

   (B) for advice on strategies to advance or prevent a piece of legislation.

   (C) for money that would allow them to travel to their constituencies.

   (D) to encourage group members to vote for them during reelection.

   (E) for expertise on a certain issue.

5. Iron triangles are composed of

   (A) a cabinet department, a legislative committee, and a federal judge.

   (B) a corporate board, an interest group, and the speaker of the House.

   (C) a PAC, an interest group, and a congressional candidate.

   (D) an interest group, a legislative committee, and a federal agency.

   (E) a local civic group, a state legislator, and a federal department.

6. Proponents of the pluralist theory argue that for the most part, power is evenly distributed among interest groups because

   (A) the public participates equally in different types of interest groups.

   (B) all interest groups receive the same amount of federal funds.

   (C) each policy area is assigned a limited number of related interest groups.

   (D) interest groups each get the same attention from politicians.

   (E) competition prevents any one group from becoming more influential.

7. Which of the following statements accurately describe methods interest groups employ to influence policymaking?

    I.   Class action lawsuits allow interest groups to sue in the name of a larger section of the public.

    II.   Interest groups meet with judges about cases that affect their policy area.

    III.   Interest groups make almost all of their PAC contributions to incumbents rather than challengers.

    IV.   Lobbyists use their policy expertise to make themselves indispensable to politicians.

    V.   Interest groups pay committee members to review proposed legislation from a legislative point of view.

    (A) III only

    (B) I and IV only

    (C) II and V only

    (D) I, III, and IV only

    (E) II, IV, and V only

8. Interest groups do all of the following EXCEPT

    (A) link the public to the political process.

    (B) nominate candidates for elective office

    (C) try to shape specific policy goals.

    (D) play a part in political campaigns.

    (E) unite politicians with the same political ideology.

9. Which of the following interest group is known to be the largest in membership size?

    (A) National Rifle Association (NRA)

    (B) League of Conservation Voters

    (C) Christian Coalition

    (D) American Association of Retired Persons (AARP)

    (E) National Association for the Advancement of Colored People (NAACP)

10. Which of the following groups has primarily used litigation to advance its issues?

   (A) National Rifle Association (NRA)

   (B) League of Conservation Voters

   (C) Christian Coalition

   (D) American Association of Retired Persons (AARP)

   (E) National Association for the Advancement of Colored People (NAACP)

Free-Response Questions

1. Interest groups use a variety of techniques to pursue their goals. For each of the interest groups below, identify a technique that has been unique to the group's success in the policy process and explain why.

   - NAACP

   - AARP

   - NRA

Interest groups are often criticized for hurting the political process by making PAC contributions.

   - Identify one argument against allowing PACs to make contributions.

   - Identify one argument in favor of allowing PACs to make contributions.

   - Identify one law that regulates PACs and analyze its effectiveness.

ANSWERS AND EXPLANATIONS

Multiple-Choice Questions

   - **1. (A) is the answer.** Pluralists argue that political power is shared among many groups.

   - **2. (E) is the answer.** Elitists argue that political power is primarily held by the wealthy.

   - **3. (B) is the answer.** Hyperpluralists argue that the number of interest groups can slow down our system as members of congress are bombarded with competing information.

- **4. (D) is the answer.** Lawmakers do not depend on interest groups for votes since votes must come from their district.

- **5. (D) is the answer.** Iron triangles are the relationship between congressional committees, government agencies, and interest groups who work together on policies.

- **6. (E) is the answer.** Pluralists believe that power is shared and that interest groups will check one another in the policy arena.

- **7. (D) is the answer.** Interest groups frequently file class action lawsuits in an attempt to reverse policy decisions. They also solidify their relationships with members of Congress by channeling most of their campaign contributions to incumbents. Interest groups also know that policymakers are more easily influenced if they must rely on a lobbyist for information and advice about a policy.

- **8. (B) is the answer.** Interest groups do not run candidates but attempt to influence policy makers.

- **9. (D) is the answer.** The AARP is the largest interest group in the United States.

- **10. (E) is the answer.** The NAACP has used litigation in cases such as *Brown* v. *Board of Education* when other techniques were not useful.

Free-Response Questions

This rubric provides examples of many, but not all of the possible correct responses to the free-response questions.

1. The NAACP is best known for using litigation to pursue its goals. In particular, the NAACP became famous in history when its attorneys took on a class action lawsuit that reached the Supreme Court, Brown v. Board of Education 1954. Litigation is advantageous to groups like the NAACP that had attempted to use more traditional lobbying techniques unsuccessfully. Federal judges hold their positions for life and are therefore not swayed by public opinion. Supreme Court case rulings are the final legal authority in the U.S., unless overturned by a Constitutional amendment.

    The AARP is most known for its extraordinary large membership base. The members are also very active in grass roots lobbying: calling members of Congress, e-mailing, and making other similar types of contacts with law makers. The AARP is powerful because elected officials depend on their votes to get elected.

    The NRA is known for making large campaign contributions and for providing its members with information on who to vote for on election day. Campaign contributions are useful because elected officials rely on such contributions to run effective campaigns. Information is useful because it mobilizes citizens to go to the polls and support a pro NRA candidate.

2. Interest groups are often criticized for hurting the political process by making PAC contributions.

- Identify one argument against allowing PACs to make contributions.

- Identify one argument in favor of allowing PACs to make contributions.

- Identify one law that regulates PACs and analyze its effectiveness.

One argument against allowing PACs to make contributions is that it leads to corruption. Those who subscribe to this view would argue that PACs essentially buy legislation by making contributions.

One argument in favor of allowing PACs to make contributions is that making a contribution is a type of expression which is protected by the first amendment to the Constitution.

There are several laws that regulate PACs. The most recent law is called the Bipartisan Campaign Reform Act, also referred to as the McCain Feingold law. This law was designed to stop PACs from making unlimited contributions to the political party and thus banned so-called "soft money." This law has been somewhat effective; however one of the loopholes to this law is the ability of citizens to make unlimited contributions to 527 groups. These groups support issues, not specific parties, and are identified by their status in the federal tax code. By making unlimited contributions to these groups, PACs have gotten around the McCain Feingold law because the groups run similar ads to support candidates that the parties once did.

CHAPTER 12

Congress

The federal government is divided into a number of institutions of government, each with its own political role and responsibilities. The legislative branch is composed of two houses (House of Representatives and Senate). The executive branch is comprised of the president and the bureaucracy. The judicial branch is comprised of a three tiered court system, with the Supreme Court acting as the highest court of appeals. At least one third of the questions on the multiple-choice part of the AP U.S. Government and Politics Exam will address the duties of these institutions and how they function to carry out those duties.

The Representatives and Senators

Congress is composed of 435 representatives and 100 senators, for a total of 535 members.

- **Occupation:** Most are lawyers or businesspeople.

- **Party: Most election years leave** both houses about evenly split between Democrats and Republicans, with one or two independents in each.

- **Race:** The members of both houses have always been largely Caucasian. The House is more diverse than the Senate, which is almost exclusively white.

- **Gender:** The ratio of men to women in the House is about six to one; in the Senate it is about seven to one.

- **Committee work:** Most members serve on at least five committees and subcommittees; senators usually serve on more committees than representatives do. Members of Congress depend upon staff members to help them meet their obligations. Members of a personal staff help with providing services to constituents, meeting with lobbyists, and a variety of other activities, while committee staff members help with research and drafting legislation. Staff agencies, such as the *Congressional Research Service,* provide valuable information to members of Congress.

Congressional Elections

Congressional elections are held every two years in November. The most important factor that determines which candidate wins an election is incumbency. **Incumbents** are elected officials who already hold office and are running for reelection. Incumbents win reelection more than 90 percent of the time. Incumbency allows senators and representatives to gain valuable experience and bring some stability to Congress. However, this may also work to insulate members of Congress from change, making it more difficult for constituents to effect change. Senatorial races are usually intense because incumbents, who tend to have **higher profiles,** are more likely to be held accountable for public policy successes or failures. Their challengers are also more likely to be known already in the political arena, because senatorial races often draw former representatives or governors. Still, incumbents usually win, though by a narrower margin. In fact, turnover in Congress usually occurs only when members retire.

The Advantages of Incumbents

Incumbents engage in three activities that increase the probability of being elected:

- **Advertising:** Advertising makes a candidate visible to many constituents. Name recognition is an important advantage for incumbents. The number of votes a candidate receives is fairly proportional to his or her air time on television and the frequency of his or her public appearances. Advertising requires a great deal of campaign funds, particularly for senators, which explains in part why Congress is composed mostly of wealthy men.

- **Credit claiming:** Incumbents have the benefit of being able to present their **congressional record** to their constituents to demonstrate their hard work in service of the district or state. They may have helped specific people or groups sidestep bureaucratic red tape (**casework**), or they have helped with federal programs and institutions (**pork barrel**). From this record of service to the constituency, incumbents can build a more clearly defined **public image,** whereas challengers new to politics are less likely to be able to convey their position on issues to the public.

- **Position taking:** Incumbents' public image is strengthened because they have already taken a stand on issues relevant to their constituency. At election time, this can work in their favor to identify them in the minds of the public.

- **Party identification:** Voters for the most part cast their ballots along **party lines.** Thus, a predominantly Democratic district, for example, is most likely to elect and then reelect a Democratic candidate.

Defeating Incumbents

While defeating an incumbent is very difficult, occasionally incumbents are defeated. Sometimes redistricting can occur, causing an incumbent to attempt to win over an unfamiliar constituency or sometimes even compete against another incumbent. Sometimes incumbents are involved in scandals that are visible in the media, which tarnishes their name. Occasionally, the unpopularity of a president of the same party as the incumbent can have a negative impact on the incumbent's chances of success.

Open Seats/Stability and Change

When an incumbent leaves a seat open, there is more likely to be competition. However, usually the competition occurs within the primary, as most seats are safe for one party or the other. Because this is unusual, Congress does not change very much or change very often.

How Congress Is Organized to Make Policy: American Bicameralism

A bicameral legislature is divided into two houses. Legislation must pass both houses of Congress to become law. The Senate is designed to represent states and the House is designed to represent the population.

The House

A state's **population** determines how many representatives it has. A state is divided into **congressional districts,** each with an equal population. Every ten years, district lines must be redrawn according to the population data supplied by the national **census.** The political party in power in each state will try and draw district lines to their advantage, a process called gerrymandering. States therefore can lose or gain a seat in the House, but total membership remains at 435. Other characteristics of the House:

- Members tend to vote along party lines.

- Power is usually hierarchical.

- Special responsibilities include introducing revenue bills and articles of impeachment.

Key to agenda setting in the House is the **House Rules Committee**. The House Rules Committee gives each bill a rule for debate, schedules the bill on a calendar, and allows time for debate and may specify what types of amendments can be offered. The Speaker of the House chairs the Rules Committee.

The Senate

- Power is more evenly distributed among senators.

- Senators act more independently of their parties.

- Special responsibilities include approving presidential nominations, ratifying treaties, and the trial of impeached federal officials.

- Senators can **filibuster.** This power of unlimited debate means that they can talk so long that they delay or even prevent voting on a piece of legislation.

- Senators can stop a filibuster by voting for **cloture,** which halts debate. This rarely happens because it requires 60 votes; the majority party usually holds fewer than 60 seats, making cloture nearly impossible.

Congressional Leadership

The House

There are several elected positions in the House of Representatives. At the beginning of each Congressional term, the parties will meet in caucus to elect these leaders.

- The leader of the House is the Speaker of the House, who is chosen by the majority party. The Speaker presides over each session and is largely responsible for assigning representatives to committees or party positions.

- The majority leader assists the Speaker of the House in assigning majority party members to committees and scheduling legislation.

- The minority leader leads the minority party in opposing the agenda of the majority, and in choosing minority party members for committees.

- The majority and minority **whips** are responsible for "counting votes" for proposed legislation, working with members of their party to get enough votes to pass or defeat a piece of legislation.

The Senate

- The vice president of the United States is **president** of the Senate. This role is more formal than active, however. Most authority rests with party leaders in the Senate.

- The **majority leader** in both the Senate is usually the most active or seasoned member of the majority party. The majority leader manages the schedule of debate and rallies party votes for party legislation or against proposals of the minority party.

- The **minority leader** rallies the support of the minority party around legislation and acts as its spokesperson.

- **Party whip**s assist party leaders in generating support for party legislation.

The Committees and Subcommittees

Committees are the nuts and bolts of Congress. They are responsible for researching, assessing, and revising the thousands of bills that are introduced by members of Congress each year. They also conduct **legislative oversight,** which is the monitoring of federal agencies and their execution of the law. Oversight usually takes the form of investigation—often committees **hold hearings** to question agency officials about the activities of their departments. As the federal bureaucracy has grown over the last few decades, so has the process of legislative oversight.

There are four basic types of committees.

1. **Standing committees** handle a **specific policy area,** such as agriculture, finance, energy, and commerce. Both the House and Senate have standing committees. Each committee is often divided into **subcommittees.**

2. **Joint committees** are responsible for legislation that **overlaps policy areas.** They are composed of both senators and representatives.

3. **Select committees** are appointed to handle a **specific issue,** such as an investigation or impeachment trial.

4. **Conference committees** iron out the differences between the House and Senate version of a bill. They also consist of members of both houses.

Getting on a Committee

One key to a new member of Congress's success is getting on a high profile committee. Members seek committees that will help them provide opportunity to assist their constituency or publicity and help them get reelected. Committee placement is decided by the chamber leadership.

Committee Chairs and the Seniority System

Committee chairs influence the agenda of the committee. The chair is always a member of the majority party, and usually is the most senior member of the majority party on the committee. The minority party member of the committee with the longest tenure is called the ranking member. The **seniority system** was a formal rule used to select chairs, but is no longer a requirement.

Caucuses: The Informal Organization of Congress

A caucus is a group of members of Congress who share a similar interest. Each party has a caucus, and there are hundreds of caucuses, some are more active than others. The Congressional Black caucus and the Congressional Women's caucus are two examples. Caucuses may hold hearings and put pressure on committees to try to influence legislation.

Congressional Staff (Personal Staff, Committee Staff, Staff Agencies)

Members of the House of Representatives and Senators have a number of staff who assist them in serving their constituencies, researching legislation, and communicating with those who contact the office. The Committees also employ staff to organize hearings, draft reports, and perform other duties. Finally, Congress has staff agencies such as the *Congressional Research Service (CRS)* to track the progress of bills and perform research for members of Congress.

The Congressional Process

Policymaking is a slow and laborious process, and often a final bill has changed significantly from the original. The authors of the Constitution intentionally devised a complicated legislative system as a means to prevent hasty decisions and to encourage compromise in policymaking. The following diagram shows how proposed legislation usually follows a path through Congress.

1. A single member of Congress or a small group in either the House or Senate formally introduces a bill.

↓

2. The bill goes to a subcommittee of the appropriate standing committee.

↓

3. The subcommittee conducts research and holds hearings on the proposal and rewrites it as necessary.

↓

4. The approved bill then moves to the standing committee, which assesses the legislation in a formal report, rewrites the bill as necessary, and ultimately decides whether to pass it on for debate or to kill it.

↓

5. The bill is introduced for debate on the floor of the chamber. Committee members usually serve as authorities on the proposal to whom their colleagues turn, and they often rally support for it. Amendments may be added to the bill.

↓

6. If passed by both houses, the bill goes to the president for final approval as law. If different versions are passed in each house, the two bills go to a conference committee that resolves the differences between them. Then both houses vote on the final version of the bill and it is sent to the president.

Some important committees to know:

- The **House Rules Committee** reviews all bills submitted by committees before they go to the House floor, assigns them a slot on the calendar, allocates time for debate, and even decides whether the bill may be amended or not. This committee is unique to the House and has a significant degree of power.

- The **House Ways and Means Committee** writes bills concerning tax and other public revenue, which are subject to the approval of both houses.

- The **Senate Finance Committee** works in conjunction with the House Ways and Means Committee to write **tax and revenue bills.**

- The **Appropriations Committee in each house** decides how government money will be **apportioned** to federal agencies. This is the largest committee on each side, and divides into many subcommittees that attach to each of the standing committees.

Party, Constituency, and Ideology

- Members of Congress do not always vote with their party. Partisanship tends to be strongest on economic and welfare issues. On other issues, members of Congress may act more independently, especially to fulfill the needs of their constituents. Thus, although whips actively attempt to garner support for certain legislation, they are not always successful.

- When representatives or senators do act independently, what influences their vote? If the issue is of significance to their constituency, or is likely to be highly publicized, members of Congress tend to vote as the constituency would want them to. On the many other issues about which the public is less informed, congressmen and -women are more likely to vote according to their own personal views and convictions.

Lobbyists and Interest Groups

With lobbyists dominating Washington, how effective is Congress in representing the people? You should be familiar with both sides of this debate.

Congress Represents the Interests of the Electorate

- Interest groups are organized by groups of "the people" to make their views known so that policymakers will act on their behalf.

- As pluralists contend, the competition among groups for the support of members of Congress ensures that compromise will play a part in policymaking.

- The issues on which Congress focuses are as diverse as the interests pushing them to the forefront, thereby decentralizing the political agenda and power in each house.

Congress Serves the Interest Groups, Not the Public

- Critics argue that those interest groups with enough money to buy influence dominate the policy agenda and distract policymakers from the needs of the public.

- So many competing interests prevent the formation of cohesive policy. In fact, different committees may handle the same policy issue in drastically different ways.

- Ultimately the government wastes a significant amount of money by attempting to appease so many interests.

For Additional Review

As you read your textbook, keep a list of all the committees you come across. Jot down what kind of committee each is and what its role or policy specialty is. Not only will this information help prepare you for Section I of the AP U.S. Government & Politics Exam, but also it may contain good examples for use in your free-response answers.

Multiple-Choice Questions

1. Which demographic group is the most underrepresented in Congress?

    (A) African Americans

    (B) Latinos

    (C) Asians

    (D) women

    (E) upper income

2. Which of the following is most likely to determine a candidate's chance of getting elected to Congress?

    (A) their personal wealth

    (B) their connections to the media

    (C) their incumbency status

    (D) their campaign style

    (E) promises they make to the people

3. Riders are frequently unpopular with the general public because

    (A) the public does not understand them

    (B) they funnel federal money into targeted areas

    (C) they are secret

    (D) lobbyists oppose them

    (E) they are unconstitutional

4. Which of the following would be an attractive committee for a member of Congress from Montana looking to serve his or her constituency?

(A) Ways and Means

(B) Rules

(C) Education

(D) Government Reform

(E) Agriculture

POLITICAL PARTY AFFILIATIONS IN CONGRESS AND THE RESIDENCY, 1953–2001

Year	Congress	House Majority party	House Principal minority party	Senate Majority party	Senate Principal minority party	President
1953–1955	83rd	R-221	D-211	R-48	D-47	R (Eisenhower)
1955–1957	84th	D-232	R-203	D-48	R-47	R (Eisenhower)
1957–1959	85th	D-233	R-200	D-49	R-47	R (Eisenhower)
1959–1961	86th	D-283	R-153	D-64	R-34	R (Eisenhower)
1961–1963	87th	D-263	R-174	D-65	R-35	D (Kennedy)
1963–1965	88th	D-258	R-177	D-67	R-33	D (Kennedy) D (L. Johnson)
1965–1967	89th	D-295	R-140	D-68	R-32	D (L. Johnson)
1967–1969	90th	D-247	R-187	D-64	R-36	D (L. Johnson)
1969–1971	91st	D-243	R-192	D-57	R-43	R (Nixon)
1971–1973	92nd	D-254	R-180	D-54	R-44	R (Nixon)
1973–1975	93rd	D-239	R-192	D-56	R-42	R (Nixon) R (Ford)

1975–1977	94th	D-291	R-144	D-60	R-37	R (Ford)
1977–1979	95th	D-292	R-143	D-61	R-38	D (Carter)
1979–1981	96th	D-276	R-157	D-58	R-41	D (Carter)
1981–1983	97th	D-243	R-192	R-53	D-46	R (Reagan)
1983–1985	98th	D-269	R-165	R-54	D-46	R (Reagan)
1985–1987	99th	D-252	R-182	R-53	D-47	R (Reagan)
1987–1989	100th	D-258	R-177	D-55	R-45	R (Reagan)
1989–1991	101st	D-259	R-174	D-55	R-45	R (Bush)
1991–1993	102nd	D-267	R-167	D-56	R-44	R (Bush)
1993–1995	103rd	D-258	R-176	D-57	R-43	D (Clinton)
1995–1997	104th	R-230	D-204	R-53	D-47	D (Clinton)
1997–1999	105th	R-227	D-207	R-55	D-45	D (Clinton)
1999–2001	106th	R-222	D-211	R-55	D-45	D (Clinton)

SOURCES: U.S. Bureau of the Census, *Historical Statistics of the United States, Colonial Times to 1970* (Washington, D.C.: Government Printing Office, 1975); U.S. Congress, Joint Committee on Printing, *Official Congressional Directory* (Washington, D.C.: Government Printing Office, 1967–); CQ Weekly, selected issues.

Note: Figures are for the beginning of the first session of each Congress.

5. Which of the following conclusions may be drawn based on the data in the table above?

(A) The party of the president does not necessarily determine the majority party in either house of Congress.

(B) Since the 1950s, the Republican Party has usually been the majority party in the House of Representatives.

(C) In the Senate, the majority party almost always outnumbers the minority party by two to one.

(D) Voters typically do not reelect presidents who do not work well with the majority party in Congress.

(E) Most representatives in the House would probably support presidential proposals.

6. A senator can effectively prevent the Senate from voting by

   (A) conducting oversight.

   (B) filibustering.

   (C) introducing another bill.

   (D) holding hearings.

   (E) no known process, because the rules are very structured.

7. Which of the following ends debate in the Senate?

   (A) cloture

   (B) vote by the Rules Committee

   (C) conference committee

   (D) mark up

   (E) rider

8. Most of the time, members of Congress vote with

   (A) the President

   (B) their state

   (C) celebrities

   (D) their party

   (E) the lobbyists

9. After a House committee reviews a bill and writes its report, the bill goes to the

   (A) Senate.

   (B) appropriate subcommittee.

   (C) president.

   (D) floor for debate.

   (E) House Rules Committee.

10. Which of the following is the best example of legislative oversight?

   (A) The vice president presides over the senate.

   (B) The Rules Committee amends a bill.

   (C) Debate is limited.

   (D) A hearing is held to investigate misuse of funds within a federal agency.

   (E) Riders are not allowed.

Free-Response Questions

1. Occasionally, one party will have control of Congress and the Presidency. This will give the majority party advantages in Congress, yet passing legislation is still difficult.

   a) Describe the legislative advantages of the majority party in Congress with respect to both committee structure and leadership.
   b) Explain why, even with single party control, passing legislation is difficult. Use two examples to support your explanation.

2. Congress has several non-legislative functions. Describe the relevance of each of the following and provide an example:

   - oversight of the bureaucracy

   - confirmation of political appointees

   - impeachment

ANSWERS AND EXPLANATIONS

Multiple-Choice Questions

- **1. (D) is correct.** Women make up a small percentage of both the House and the Senate and do not come close to the percentage in the general population.

- **2. (C) is correct.** Incumbency is the most important determinant in a candidate's chance of getting elected.

- **3. (B) is correct.** Riders are unpopular with the general public when the targeted money does not benefit them.

- **4. (E) is correct.** Being on the agriculture committee would enable a member of Congress to assist his or her constituents in farming/ranching.

- **5. (A) is correct.** In both houses, the majority party has usually been the Democrats. However, presidents have been Republican more often than Democrat during the period shown on the table. Therefore the majority party does not necessarily have any bearing on which candidate will be elected.

- **6. (B) is correct.** The filibuster stalls the debate process and therefore prevents the Senate from voting.

- **7. (A) is correct.** A cloture (60 votes) ends a filibuster.

- **8. (D) is correct.** While party discipline is not required, on most legislative issues members of Congress will vote with their party.

- **9. (E) is correct.** After being discussed and marked up in committee, a bill goes to the Rules Committee which will schedule it for debate on the floor of the House.

- **10. (D) is correct.** Oversight committees routinely investigate claims of misuse of funds by holding hearings and asking questions of members of an agency.

Free-Response Questions

This rubric provides examples of many, but not all of the possible correct responses to the free-response questions.

1. The majority party in Congress has numerous advantages in the legislative process. All chairs of the committees come from the majority party. Committees all have more members of the majority party on them. The chair of the committee can decide to hold a vote on moving a piece of legislation to the next stage and is usually successful since he has more members from his party in the committee. The majority party also selects the Speaker of the House, who chairs the Rules Committee, schedules legislation, oversees the rules for the legislation and oversees the debate on the legislation.

   Even when one party controls both the White House and the Congress, passing legislation is still difficult. There are many things that can stop legislation from passing. First, there is no guarantee of party discipline. One defecting member of a political party has the potential to slow the legislation. Oftentimes members within a party will disagree significantly during the mark up process. One committee chair can also essentially hold a piece of legislation hostage in committee. Finally, in the Senate there are maneuvers that give the minority party power, such as filibustering. All a minority party Senator has to do is declare their intent to filibuster, and then there is a requirement that 60 votes cut off the filibuster. If the majority party does not have 60 in the Senate, passing any legislation will be difficult.

   - Congress has several nonlegislative functions. Describe the relevance of each of the following:

        1. confirmation of political appointees

        2. impeachment

2. One nonlegislative function of Congress is oversight of the federal bureaucracy. This occurs when a committee will investigate into how a federal department or agency is doing its job. Normally Congress does this by holding hearings and asking questions of federal employees.

Reports, recommendations and often new legislation is the result of this information gathering process. This is done in public and clips of these hearings are often shown on TV. One example was known as the 9–11 Commission. This commission was designed to try to figure out how our intelligence system could perform better and avoid another 9–11 catastrophe. Hearings were held and a major report was published which resulted in the reorganization of our intelligence services.

Another non legislative function of Congress is confirming Presidential appointees. This is done most often by the Senate Judiciary Committee. The committee holds a hearing and interviews the potential nominee. Former employers and those who know the nominee may also testify. The committee makes a recommendation about whether or not to approve the nominee and then the full Senate must vote by a simple majority in order for the nominee to be confirmed. One recent nomination was of Michael Mukasey to be U.S. Attorney General.

Finally, impeachment is a nonlegislative function. If the President has committed a "high crime or misdemeanor" then the House may conduct an investigation of wrongdoing. The House then votes by simple majority and the Senate can conduct a trial to see if the allegations warrant removal of the President from office. The Senate is required to vote by a two-thirds majority in order to remove the President.

CHAPTER 13

The Presidency

The president of the United States is the most powerful individual in all of American politics. The presidency as a government institution has changed dramatically since the writing of the Constitution. At that time, the president had few powers and, because he was chosen directly by the **Electoral College** without a popular vote, was far removed from the populace. Today the president is elected by the people—via electors—after a long and expensive campaign. Presidential powers have increased in the last few decades as, thanks to television, the president has become a more public figure. Questions on the AP U.S. Government & Politics Exam will test your knowledge of the powers of the president and the relationship between the president and other governmental institutions.

The Presidents: How They Got There

- **Presidents** can reach the Oval Office in different ways:

- Most are former governors or members of Congress who after being nominated by their party, campaign and win the election. Some presidents were vice presidents and took over after the death of the president.

- **Vice presidents** can also become president in the event the president resigns or is convicted in an impeachment trial.

    - **The Twenty-fifth Amendment** establishes the procedures for filling vacancies in both the offices of president and vice president. This amendment also makes provisions for presidential disability.

- The Constitution sets forth the process of **impeachment** of a president who has abused his powers or committed a "high crime or misdemeanor" worthy of removal from office.

    - The House may vote for the impeachment of the president by a simple majority.

    - The Senate conducts the impeachment trial and the chief justice of the Supreme Court presides over the trial.

    - It takes a two-thirds vote in the Senate to remove the president from office.

    - Only two presidents have been impeached, though neither was removed from office.

- Andrew Johnson was tried but not convicted in 1868.

- William Clinton was acquitted by the Senate in 1999.

Presidential Powers

The Constitution grants the president fairly limited powers that were designed to prevent him or her from gaining too much authority and thus to maintain the balance of power among government institutions. A partial list of the president's powers appears below.

- Veto proposed bills

- Report to Congress in the State of the Union address

- Nominate cabinet level government officials, Supreme Court justices, and all other federal judges

- Grant pardons for certain offenses

- Act as commander in chief of the armed forces

- Make treaties

- Serve as diplomatic representative for the United States

- Oversee the departments and agencies that make up the executive branch

This last power is one of the more overlooked responsibilities of the president. As the bureaucracy has grown, it has become nearly impossible for the president alone to execute and enforce all laws. Instead, the president now appoints numerous administrative officials, including cabinet members and department heads.

Running the Government

- **Vice presidents** traditionally have few responsibilities and little political prominence.

- They are second in line to assume the presidency if the president is unable to fulfill the duties of office.

- They are the president (chief presiding officer) of the Senate and cast a vote whenever there is a tie.

- Today, vice presidents assume more responsibilities, depending on how the president they are serving entrusts functions to them. They may serve as diplomats representing the president, take part in important policy meetings, or help raise funds for their party.

- The **cabinet** is a group of officials who act as advisors to the president. The cabinet is not mentioned in the Constitution, but it quickly became an institution that has accompanied every presidency. The modern cabinet is composed of the attorney general and the heads, or secretaries, of the 13 executive departments. The president has the power to appoint all of these officials, but each appointment must be confirmed by the Senate.

- Each cabinet member heads a **department** that deals with a different policy area. The departments, created by Congress, carry out all the administrative work necessary to enforce laws or assist the president in his executive duties.

The Executive Office of the President (E.O.P)

This is another collection of administrative and advisory bodies which assists the president in overseeing policy.

- The **National Security Council** coordinates matters of national security across agencies, including the State Department, the Department of Defense, the Treasury Department, and the intelligence agencies.

- The **Council of Economic Advisors** advises the president on economic issues.

- The **Office of Management and Budget** reviews the budgetary implications of federal programs and legislation.

- The **White House Office** includes important personal and political advisors to the president such as the legal counsel to the president, the president's personal secretary, and the chief of staff. This office takes care of the president's political needs and manages the press.

Presidential Leadership of Congress: The Politics of Shared Powers

Though not a member of the legislative branch, presidents do have a role to play in the legislative process.

1. **Acting as chief legislator**

- The power to veto legislation can be an effective tool of intimidation. Because a veto rejects a bill in its entirety, the president can have a good deal of influence over the shaping of each specific provision. If the president does veto a bill, it goes back to Congress, which, by a two-thirds vote, can override the veto. However, this rarely happens.

- The president also has the power to reject any legislation submitted at the end of the congressional session without the possibility of his veto being overruled. If he does not sign a bill submitted by Congress within 10 days of its adjourning, the bill is automatically rejected. This is a **pocket veto.**

2. **Relying on party support:** To influence policy, presidents must work closely with Congress. Specifically, they rely on close ties with members of Congress who are members of their political party. Political parties help bridge the gap between the legislative and executive branches.

   - A president and a representative of the same party were most likely elected by the same body of people, or by voters who have similar political views, so they probably share political priorities.

   - Members of Congress who support the president's legislative agenda are likely to receive support for some of their projects and initiatives in return. A close relationship with a popular president can also be beneficial to members of Congress during reelection (**presidential coattails**).

   - The president must rely on members of Congress to introduce legislation for him or her and to win support for it during the legislative process. Therefore, the president must work closely with party leaders to convince representatives to vote the party line. Even if a president's party is the majority party in either or both houses, he may not necessarily have the full support of representatives, who may not vote with the party line.

3. **Public support:** Public support for the president factors heavily in his congressional support. Representatives are much more likely to vote in favor of the initiatives of a president who is popular with the electorate, and presidents are well aware that public opinion is an incredibly powerful tool of persuasion.

   - Public approval gives a president more leeway in pursuing policy goals, because representatives are more likely to support his objectives in the hope of being reelected by an electorate that has confidence in him. Public support lends a president a greater degree of legitimacy.

   - The policies of a president who is perceived as weak are more likely to be cast into doubt by Congress, making it harder for the president to garner legislative support.

Congress is more likely to respond to the will of a president who was elected by a large margin, especially on legislation proposed early in his term.

4. **Legislative skills:** Presidents may also exert their influence over the political agenda by employing specific strategies at key times in the legislative process.

   - To strengthen a presidential coalition, presidents often bargain with representatives by offering support on one piece of legislation in exchange for receiving it on another. Members of Congress may also receive certain presidential favors, such as joint public appearances during campaigns.

   - Presidents present many proposals to Congress soon after their election during what is called the "honeymoon period," when there is a fresh sense of community in Washington.

- Presidents work hard to focus the attention of Congress on their own specific agendas. By setting priorities, they are able to concentrate their resources to push through a few key policy objectives.

The President and National Security Policy

The president is both the commander-in-chief of the armed forces and the chief U.S. diplomat. The diplomatic powers of the president include the following:

- Establishing formal recognition of other governments

- Negotiating treaties

- Formulating **executive agreements** with other foreign leaders, which, unlike treaties, do not require congressional approval; most executive agreements are administrative in nature

- Using U.S. influence to arbitrate conflicts between other nations

Military powers include the following:

- The decision to use weapons of mass destruction

- Authorizing military actions during war

- Sending troops into specific areas of conflict

The **War Powers Resolution,** passed in 1973, intended to limit this power by requiring that these troops be withdrawn within 60 days unless Congress declares war or issues an extension.

Power from the People: The Public Presidency

Because presidents know that public approval works enormously in their favor, they work hard to sell their agenda to the public. A voter's approval of the president is determined by several factors:

- Whether the voter identifies with the political party of the president

- How the president responds to economic shifts or handles other current issues

- How effective a public speaker the president is, and his appearance in front of the cameras

- Whether the president appeals to the public directly, in which case the public usually responds positively

- How the media interprets the actions of the president

The efforts of the White House to influence public opinion are not always successful, however. The public tends to be fickle in its approval, and the media often mislead the public by oversimplifying political and economic issues.

For Additional Review

As you read the chapters in your textbook about the president and presidential campaigns, keep lists of notable events or issues surrounding particular presidents to look over before the exam. The more details you have on hand during the free-response section, the higher your score will be.

Multiple-Choice Questions

1. Congress can override a presidential veto of legislation

   (A) by appealing to the U.S. Supreme Court.

   (B) by negotiating a deal with the vice president.

   (C) by getting approval of the bill in three-fourths of the state legislatures.

   (D) with a majority vote of the House Rules Committee.

   (E) with a two-thirds vote in both houses of Congress.

2. According to the Constitution, the vice president

   (A) chairs all cabinet meetings

   (B) is ineligible to run for president after two terms as vice president

   (C) is the president of the Senate

   (D) must be of the same party as the president

   (E) is an ex-officio member of the Council of Economic Advisors

3. Which of the following presidential appointments requires Senate confirmation?

   (A) press secretary

   (B) chief of staff

   (C) White House counsel

   (D) Council of Economic Advisors.

   (E) secretary of state

4. All of the following are true statements about the impeachment process EXCEPT

   (A) the chief justice of the United States presides over the trial.

   (B) the Supreme Court decides guilt or innocence.

   (C) the trial must be held in public.

   (D) the Senate serves as the jury.

   (E) the House of Representatives brings the formal charges against the president.

5. A president is most likely to gain public support for a public policy proposal by

   (A) sending the vice president out to conduct high profile town hall meetings.

   (B) placing ads in respected newspapers with large circulations.

   (C) vetoing a bill passed by Congress.

   (D) appealing to the public directly via the broadcast media.

   (E) including the proposal in his or her party's campaign platform.

6. The Twenty-fifth Amendment is significant because it

   (A) clarifies the terms under which the vice president may become president as a result of the president being disabled.

   (B) defines the line of succession to the president.

   (C) clarifies the formal roles, duties, and responsibilities of all parties involved in a presidential impeachment trial.

   (D) defines the process to be used for creating new cabinet positions.

   (E) clarifies Congress' role in the realm of U.S. foreign policy.

7. One of the primary tools presidents use to control the bureaucracy is

(A) the line-item veto.

(B) congressional oversight committees.

(C) campaign finance reform

(D) the presidential power to appoint and remove top-level administrators

(E) the presidential power to pardon.

8. Which of the following statements about the president as commander-in-chief is true?

(A) The president has the authority to declare war for up to 60 days without consulting Congress.

(B) The president can decide if and when to use weapons of mass destruction in times of war.

(C) Presidents with no prior military experience are not allowed to make major military decisions alone.

(D) The president is required by law to consult with the Joint Chiefs of Staff before deploying the military.

(E) The president is a nonvoting member of the Senate Armed Services Committee.

9. Which of the following are powers of the president?

    I.   conducting diplomatic relations

    II.   negotiating treaties

    III.   dismissing Supreme Court justices

    IV.   appointing cabinet officers

(A) IV only

(B) I, II, and III only

(C) I, II, and IV only

(D) I, III, and IV only

(E) II, III, and IV only

10. Which of the following is NOT in line of presidential succession?

    (A) chief justice of the supreme Court

    (B) secretary of state

    (C) secretary of the interior

    (D) attorney general

    (E) Speaker of the House

Free-Response Questions

1. The president is the single most powerful individual in government. Some of the president's most important responsibilities and powers fall in the area of national security.

    a. Identify and explain two national security powers or responsibilities granted to the president in the Constitution.

    b. Identify and describe two Constitutional limitations on presidential national security power.

2. The Executive Office of the President is a collection of agencies that help develop and implement the policy and programs of the president. For each of the three Executive Office of the President policymaking agencies listed below, identify and explain **two** functions it performs for the president.

    National Security Council (NSC)

    Council of Economic Advisors

    Office of Management and Budget (OMB)

ANSWERS AND EXPLANATIONS

Multiple-Choice Questions

1. (E) is correct. While a presidential veto usually effectively kills proposed legislation, Congress can override the veto with a two-thirds majority vote in both houses, and has done so in about four percent of the vetoes. The Constitution gives the president the power to veto as a means to check Congress, and it gives Congress the power to override a veto as a means of checking the president.

2. (C) is correct. The Constitution assigns vice presidents the relatively minor tasks of presiding over the Senate and voting in case of a tie among the senators.

3. (E) is correct. Because they are a member of the president's cabinet, nominees for Secretary of State, must be confirmed by the Senate. The National Security Council, the chief of staff, the White House Counsel, and the Council of Economic Advisors are considered to be part of the president's personal staff of advisors and are not required to be approved by the Senate.

4. (B) is correct. The presidential impeachment process is as follows: 1) the House votes to impeach the president; 2) the Senate carries out the impeachment trial, with the chief justice of the United States presiding; and 3) the Senate must have a two-thirds vote to convict and remove the president. The Supreme Court plays no role in this process.

5. (D) is correct. Public support is one of president's most important resources for getting their policy agenda enacted. Presidents who have the backing of the public have an easier time influencing Congress. Using the mass media to directly appeal to the public is an effective tool for gaining public support.

6. (A) is correct. The Twenty-fifth Amendment, passed in 1967, is significant because it clarifies the terms under which the vice president may become president as a result of the president being disabled. It also outlines how a recuperated president can reclaim the job.

7. (D) is correct. The power to appoint and remove top-level administrators gives the president significant influence over what the federal bureaucracy does or doesn't do.

8. (B) is correct. As commander in chief of military forces, the president decides if and when American armed forces use weapons of mass destruction in times of war.

9. (C) is correct. According to the Constitution, presidents have the power to conduct diplomacy, negotiate treaties with foreign countries, and appoint members of their cabinet. Presidents nominate federal court judges, but they cannot remove them from their seats once they have been confirmed by the Senate. In fact, once they have been nominated by the president and approved by the Senate, federal judges hold their positions for life. The Constitution specifies that Supreme Court and other federal judges have no term limit. Justices and judges can be impeached, but this has happened only thirteen times in the history of the federal courts.

10. (A) is correct. The Chief Justice is not in the line of presidential succession. The Constitution authorizes the vice president to take over the office of the presidency if the president dies, resigns, is impeached, or is otherwise unable to perform his duties. After the vice president, the succession is the Speaker of the House of Representatives, the President pro tempore of the Senate, and then cabinet members, ordered according to the date their offices were established.

Free-Response Questions

This rubric provides examples of many, but not all of the possible correct responses to the free-response questions.

1.

a. National security powers or responsibilities granted to the president in the Constitution.

- **Commander in chief**. Because the framers wanted civilian control of the military, they made the president commander in chief of the armed forces. As commander in chief, the president controls where and how the military is deployed. The president also commands the vast arsenal of weapons of mass destruction. While only Congress can declare war, the president can interject U.S. troops into armed conflict on a limited basis.

- **Diplomatic powers**. The president alone extends diplomatic recognition to foreign governments. The president can also terminate relations with other countries.

- **Power to make treaties with other nations**. The president has the sole power to negotiate treaties with other countries, although the Constitution requires the Senate to approve them by a two-third vote.

b. Constitutional limitations on presidential national security power.

- Although the president has power to deploy U.S. troops, only Congress has the constitutional power to declare war.

- Treaties that presidents negotiate with foreign countries must be approve by a two-thirds vote in the Senate.

- Congress has the power of the purse. A president's national security agenda requires a willingness on the part of Congress to appropriate the necessary funds to support it.

2. Identify and explain **two** functions each of the three Executive Office of the President policymaking agencies listed below performs for the president.

- **National Security Council (NSC).** The committee that links the president's key foreign and military policy advisors. Its formal members are the president, vice president, secretary of defense, and secretary of state. The NSC coordinates U.S. national security policy for the president.

- **Council of Economic Advisors (CEA).** Advises the president on economic policy. The CEA prepares an annual report on the state of the economy for the president. It also contributes to the president's policy on inflation and unemployment.

- **Office of Management and Budget (OMB).** Responsible for preparing the budget proposal that the president submits to Congress. The OMB also plays an important role in reviewing regulations proposed by federal departments and agencies.

CHAPTER 14

The Congress, the President, and the Budget: The Politics of Taxing and Spending

The president and Congress are responsible each year for creating the federal budget. In a balanced budget, **revenues** are equal to **expenditures.** Balancing the budget is extremely difficult, however, especially when Americans favor more federal programs but disapprove of increasing **taxes.** Spending more money than the government takes in results in a budget **deficit,** which is difficult to avoid given the demands on a large government.

Sources of Federal Revenue

Income taxes: A percentage of what a person earns goes directly to the government.

- The **Sixteenth Amendment** (1913) officially authorized Congress to collect income taxes.

- The **Internal Revenue Service** collects income taxes, and

    - monitors people's payments through **audits**

    - investigates and prosecutes in cases of tax evasion

- The income tax is **progressive**—people with higher incomes pay a greater percentage in taxes.

    - Opponents suggest a flat tax in which everyone pays an equal rate.

    - Others propose a sales tax to replace the income tax.

- Corporations also pay taxes on their income, but most tax money comes from individual income taxes.

Social insurance taxes: Social Security taxes are paid both by businesses and their employees.

- Money collected from this tax is used specifically to pay current monthly benefits to senior citizens.

- These taxes have grown significantly and now account for about one-third of the federal revenue.

- As the population ages, more people will be expecting payments from the government. Economists are concerned that the baby boom generation may drain the system.

Borrowing: The federal government has borrowed a huge amount of money over the years.

- It borrows from foreign investors, foreign governments, and the American people.

  - People can buy government bonds. The government gets the money but must pay it back to the bondholder with interest.

- The money the government owes is the **federal debt.**

  - About 10 percent of the federal budget is allocated to pay just the interest on the federal debt.

  - Future generations will have to pay for many policies enacted today.

- Lawmakers have considered proposing a **balanced budget amendment,** which would require Congress and the president to balance the budget each year.

  - Critics argue that it is too difficult to predict a balanced budget because of the uncertainties of the economy.

Taxes and Public Policy

Tax loopholes: Any tax break that allows a person to benefit from not paying a part of his or her taxes.

- Deductions for specific items are considered loopholes.

- Not everyone has the same access to loopholes.

Tax expenditures: The losses in federal revenues that result from tax breaks, deductions, and exemptions.

- They function as built-in subsidies—the government loses money by excusing a homeowner from paying taxes on a mortgage, but then the government does not have to pay for something like a homeowners' assistance program.

- Middle- and upper-income people benefit the most because they usually have more deductions and write-offs.

Tax reform: How much to tax is almost always a point of contention among Congress and the public.

- The most significant tax reform was President Reagan's **Tax Reform Act of 1986,** which cut taxes for everyone.

- eliminated many deductions and exemptions

- exempted many low-income families from paying

- Many cite these reforms as the cause of the enormous national debt.

- President Clinton raised tax rates on the wealthy.

- President George W. Bush enacted a series of tax cuts across all income levels, but that particularly benefitted the wealthy.

Federal Expenditures

The government must pay its own operational costs, which make up a significant percentage of its overall expenditures.

- **National security** was the biggest expenditure during the Cold War and Reagan era, but it had begun to decline before September 11, 2001.

- **Social services** are now the biggest expenditure: programs for people of low income and senior citizens make up one-third of the budget.

  - Social Security began with the **Social Security Act,** part of the New Deal.

  - **Medicare,** initiated in 1965, extends medical coverage to senior citizens.

  - Because people are living longer and the current generation of senior citizens is large, Social Security taxes have risen.

- **Uncontrollable expenditures** are a form of mandatory spending.

  - Pensions and payments toward the national debt are fixed and thus not subject to budgetary cuts or changes.

  - **Entitlements** are benefits the government must pay to people who are eligible according to federal rules, such as veterans' aid, Social Security, and welfare.

- **Incrementalism** is the basis on which the budget is adjusted every year.

  - A budget is calculated by assuming that the expenditures included in the budget of the previous year will rise for the next year.

  - One issue is how large the increment should be, and another concern is that this creates a system of an ever-increasing budget.

The Budgetary Process

The budget affects and involves agencies and departments in the federal, state, and even local governments.

- Each year the budget process begins with the "spring review" where the federal agencies review their programs and prepare their requests for the next fiscal year. Budget requests are submitted to the **Office of Management and Budget** (OMB). During the "fall review" the OMB reviews the requests and submits the final requests to the president.

- Interest groups and agencies often team up when making budgetary requests.

- Based on all of the agency requests, the president formally proposes a budget plan to Congress in February. Since 1922, the president has been required to prepare and submit a budget to Congress. In 1974, the **Congressional Budget and Impoundment Control Act** was passed by Congress to reform and regain some control over the budgetary process.

- The **House Ways and Means Committee** and the **Senate Finance Committee** write the tax codes that will determine how much revenue the government will have for the year.

- The House and Senate Budget Committees and the **Congressional Budget Office** review the proposal for its feasibility.

- Congress must agree on a **budget resolution,** the final amount of expenditures not to be exceeded for the year.

- The **Appropriations Committees** in both houses determine how federal funds within the total expenditure will be allotted among agencies and departments.

- Congress might make changes to existing laws to meet the budget resolution.

  - **Reconciliation:** Program authorizations are revised.

  - **Authorization bill:** The expenditures allowed for discretionary programs or the requirements for entitlement programs are changed.

- Congress must pass the final budget bill and the president must sign it for it to become law.

For Additional Review

Make a table of each step in the budgetary process. List the institutions involved in that step and their specific responsibilities. Make a note of any political motivations that influence each participant's role in making the budget.

Multiple-Choice Questions

1. Congress' authority to levy an income tax comes from which of the following?

    (A) Interstate Commerce Clause

    (B) Sixteenth Amendment

    (C) Budget Act (1974)

    (D) Bill of Rights

    (E) *Marbury* v. *Madison*

2. The institution responsible for compiling the president's budget proposal is the

    (A) Department of the Treasury

    (B) Congressional Budget Office

    (C) Senate Appropriations Committee

    (D) Office of Management and Budget

    (E) Council of Economic Advisors

3. The largest contribution to federal revenue comes from

    (A) taxes on businesses

    (B) interest on foreign debt

    (C) entry fees at national parks

    (D) individual income taxes

    (E) capital gains taxes

THE FEDERAL GOVERNMENT DOLLAR

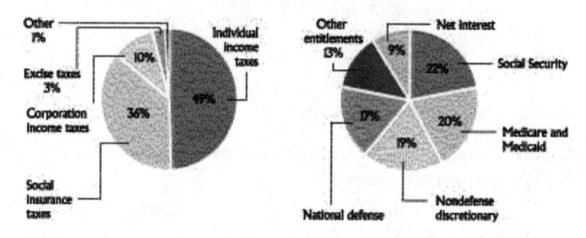

4. All of the following statements accurately describe the data in the above graphs EXCEPT

(A) Individuals pay five times more income taxes than corporations.

(B) The cost of social services for senior citizens outweighs the income from social insurance taxes.

(C) Nine percent of the budget is used to pay off interest on the national debt.

(D) National defense spending is only slightly less than the total spending for all other discretionary programs.

(E) The amount earned from corporate income taxes is enough to fund Medicare and Medicaid.

5. Which of the following statements is true about U.S. budget deficits?

(A) The first federal budget deficit did not occur until the 1990s.

(B) The Constitution requires a balanced federal budget.

(C) Large budget deficits make the U.S. government more financially dependent on foreign investors.

(D) Budget deficits have no practical effect on individual citizens.

(E) The Democratic and Republican parties have agreed that the deficit issue should not become an issue in presidential campaigns.

6. Two conditions associated with the dramatic government growth in the United States over the past half century are

   (A) growth in the national security state and growth in the social service state.

   (B) accelerated global warming and the rising cost of energy.

   (C) growth in the number of cabinet offices and growth in the number of unfunded mandates.

   (D) increased immigration and a growing birth rate.

   (E) increased use of presidential vetoes and new public works projects.

7. Which of the following initiates the budget process?

   (A) House Ways and Means Committee

   (B) President

   (C) Senate Finance Committee

   (D) Congressional Budget Office

   (E) Council of Economic Advisors

8. The biggest category of federal expenditures is spending for

   (A) foreign aid.

   (B) salaries and benefits for public employees.

   (C) interest on the national debt.

   (D) national defense.

   (E) aid to the elderly and the poor.

9. All of the following are examples of entitlement programs EXCEPT

   (A) Social Security.

   (B) Medicare.

   (C) defense contracts.

   (D) veteran's benefits.

   (E) agricultural subsidies.

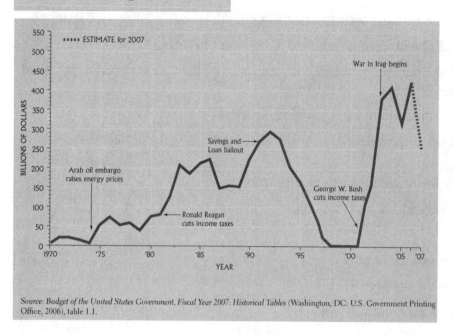

Fluctuating Deficits

····· ESTIMATE for 2007

War in Iraq begins

Arab oil embargo raises energy prices

Savings and Loan bailout

George W. Bush cuts income taxes

Ronald Reagan cuts income taxes

BILLIONS OF DOLLARS

YEAR

Source: Budget of the United States Government, Fiscal Year 2007: Historical Tables (Washington, DC: U.S. Government Printing Office, 2006), table 1.1.

10. Which of the following conclusions may be drawn from the graph above?

(A) The Clinton administration closed the budget deficit to reach a balanced budget in 1998.

(B) The federal deficit decreased dramatically during the Reagan administration.

(C) Between 1972 and 1992, the deficit grew by about five times the 1972 deficit.

(D) The federal deficit decreased significantly between 1975 and 1980.

(E) The administration of George W. Bush is primarily responsible for reversing the deficit and balancing the federal budget.

Free-Response Questions

1. The rise of the national security state and the rise of the social service state have long been associated with government growth and budget deficits in the United States.

    a. Briefly describe what is meant by growth in the national security state.

    b. Briefly describe what is meant by growth in the social service state.

    c. Identify one piece of legislation passed by Congress since 1970 that was designed to reform budget process and control the deficit spending by the government.

    d. For the legislation you identified in "c", briefly explain one goal it was designed to accomplish.

2. Budget deficits and increasing federal debt are perennial concerns for national policymakers.

    a. Define budget deficit.

    b. Define federal debt.

    c. Describe two negative consequences of a large federal debt.

ANSWERS AND EXPLANATIONS

Multiple-Choice Questions

- **1. (B) is correct.** The Sixteenth Amendment, ratified in 1913, explicitly gives Congress the authority to levy a tax on income.

- **2. (D) is correct.** The Office of Budget and Management was established to coordinate the budget proposals of all government agencies into the president's final proposal. It has a significant amount of budgetary power, but this is checked by Congress's approval of the president's nominee for its director.

- **3. (D) is correct.** The three major sources of federal revenue are individual income, corporate, and social security insurance taxes. Of these, the individual income tax provides the most revenue for the federal government. Nearly half of all federal revenues are generated by personal income taxes.

- **4. (E) is correct.** Corporate taxes generate only about 10 percent of federal revenues. Expenditures for Medicare and Medicaid, according to the second graph, are about 19 percent of all expenditures. Revenues are lower than expenditures. Corporate taxes are therefore too low to finance Medicare for senior citizens.

- **5. (C) is correct.** Large budget deficits make the U.S. government more financially dependent on foreign investors, governments as well as individuals. Foreign investors currently hold one-fifth of the U.S. national debt.

- **6. (A) is correct.** Two conditions associated with government growth in the U.S. are the rise in the national security state and the rise in the social service state. New military challenges and the cost of advanced technology are factors in the rising cost of the military state. Social service entitlements represent the largest expenditure in the federal budget.

- **7. (B) is correct.** Budgets are produced through a long and complex process that begins and ends with the president and has Congress squarely in the middle. The president submits a budget to Congress for consideration and decides whether to accept or reject the budget that ultimately emerges from Congress.

- **8. (E) is correct.** The biggest category of federal expenditures is spending for the elderly and the poor.

- **9. (C) is correct.** Entitlement programs are a form of mandatory spending because everyone entitled to the benefits of the program must be paid. Congress cannot control these expenditures unless it changes the eligibility requirements of the program, which it is unlikely to do unless such measures are absolutely necessary. Defense contracts clearly do not fit this definition.

- **10. (A) is correct.** The deficit was at its peak when President Clinton was elected in 1992. It decreased dramatically throughout the 1990s, however, and disappeared completely in 1998, when the United States experienced its first budget surplus in 30 years.

Free-Response Questions

This rubric provides examples of many, but not all of the possible correct responses to the free-response questions.

1.

a. Briefly describe what is meant by growth in the national security state.

- Growth in the national security state refers to the costs of supporting the military and national security establishment. The U.S. devoted a large share of its budget to military expenditures during WWII, the Cold War, and the immediate post-9/11 period.

b. Briefly describe what is meant by growth in the social service state.

- Growth in the social service state refers to dramatic increases in social welfare expenditures since the 1960s. Social welfare entitlement programs now make up the largest share of the federal budget.

c. Identify one piece of legislation passed by Congress since 1970 that was designed to reform budget process and control the deficit spending by the government.

- Congressional Budget and Impoundment Act (1974)

- Balanced Budget and Emergency Deficit Control Act (Gramm-Rudman-Hollings 1985)

d. For the legislation you identified in "c", briefly explain on goal it was designed to accomplish.

- The Congressional Budget and Impoundment Act was designed to make Congress less dependent on the president, by giving it some independent expertise on budget matters. It allows Congress to set and meet its own budget goals and bring spending in line with revenues.

- The Balanced Budget and Emergency Deficit Control Act was an attempt by Congress to gain control over growing budget deficits. It set maximum allowable deficits for each year. If Congress failed to meet the deficit goals, automatic across-the-board spending cuts were to be ordered by the president.

2.

a. Define budget deficit.

- A budget deficit occurs when expenditures exceed revenues.

b. Define federal debt.

- The federal debt is the cumulative amount of money borrowed by the federal government that is still outstanding.

c. Describe two negative consequences of a large federal debt.

- Government borrowing to service the debt may make it harder for individuals and businesses to get loans at favorable rates. The competition to borrow money increases interest rates, which makes it more difficult for businesses to invest in new equipment and buildings and create more jobs.

- Higher interest rates raise the costs to individuals of financing mortgages and credit card purchases.

- Large deficits make the American government for dependent on foreign investors, individuals and governments, to fund its debt. This is not a favorable position for a global superpower.

CHAPTER 15

The Federal Bureaucracy

The federal **bureaucracy** is composed of all of the agencies, departments, offices, and bureaus in the executive branch. These bodies are primarily responsible for implementing and enforcing laws.

The Bureaucrats

- Bureaucrats are hired in one of two ways:

1. Through the **civil service system**

- Entrance exam

- Promoted by **merit** rather than **patronage (Pendleton Civil Service Act)**

- Must be politically impartial and treated as such (**Hatch Act**)

  - The Civil Service Reform Act of 1978 created the **Office of Personnel Management (OPM),** which recruits and recommends individuals and oversees promotions and other employee issues.

2. **Presidential recruitment**

- Each new administration fills about 3,000 of the top posts.

- The president chooses people who will support the administration's policies.

- Cabinet department heads are presidential nominees who must be **approved by the Senate.**

  - The **Department of Defense** has the largest number of civil employees, followed by the **U.S. Postal Service.** Overall, federal civilian employment has not increased in decades, indicating that the federal bureaucracy is not actually growing.

- Bureaucrats are not easily removed from office.

How Bureaucracies Are Organized

1. Cabinet departments

- Fifteen cabinet departments oversee and administer various policy areas.

- Each is supervised by a secretary (with the exception of the Justice Department, headed by the Attorney General).

- Each has its own staff and budget.

2. Regulatory agencies

- Oversee a particular aspect of the economy

- Create regulations that protect people

- Can enforce regulations by judging disputes

- Usually headed by a commission (confirmed by Congress) rather than a secretary

- Closely involved with interest groups that want to influence regulations

3. Government corporations

- Perform services for a fee, like a private business

- The U.S. Postal Service is the largest; other examples include Amtrak and the Tennessee Valley Authority

4. Independent executive agencies

- All other executive bodies—most created for specific purposes, such as NASA

- Heads appointed by the president, so these usually have some partisan motivation

Bureaucracies as Implementers

- Enact and enforce rules and procedures for putting Congress's policy decisions into practice

- Work out details and guidelines, and assign responsibilities among bureaucrats

- Oversee day-to-day operation of the federal government

- **Policy implementation** is not always successful for various reasons.

  o Program design is flawed.

  o Congress was not clear enough about policy goals.

  o A department lacks staff or resources to carry out implementation.

  o An agency is so mired in its **standard operating procedures** that it fails to see what else needs to be done.

- Administrators use their discretion differently when the standard operating procedures do not sufficiently address a particular situation.

- There can be confusion when several departments are involved in the implementation of a particular policy.

- Reorganization of the bureaucracy for the sake of efficiency is unlikely, because this would disrupt well-established **iron triangles** of congressional committees, the agencies they oversee, and the affiliated interest groups.

Bureaucracies As Regulators

- Oversee policies once they are in place through regulation

1. Establish guidelines for a program or project

2. Enforce guidelines

   - through complaints registered by the public

   - through inspections

   - by issuing permits and licenses to people who meet the guidelines

3. **Bureaucratic institutions have the authority to change rules of a policy and apprehend violators**

   - All products and even many daily activities are shaped by regulation.

Bureaucracy and Democracy

- The governmental bureaucracy hires the most civilians but is not elected by the public.

- The governmental bureaucracy answers ultimately to the president, who:

    o Appoints agency heads who will support his policies

    o Issues **executive orders** to change or implement statutes

    o Manages budget of each agency (at least in his budget proposal)

    o Can reorganize an agency

- The governmental bureaucracy is partially controlled by Congress:

    o Congress ultimately determines each agency's budget

    o Can refuse to confirm a presidential appointment

    o Performs legislative oversight through hearings

    o Can change the legislation behind a program

Special procedures were created by Congress in 1996 in the Congressional Review Act, which allows Congress to express disapproval of the actions of agencies.

- The governmental bureaucracy is full of **iron triangles,** which may produce conflicting guidelines or regulations.

For Additional Review

Look through your textbook and make a list of federal agencies and departments. For each one, note the policy area that it handles and any other relevant information, such as which type of bureaucratic institution it is or how its administrators are selected.

Multiple-Choice Questions

1. All of the following are important official services performed by the federal bureaucracy EXCEPT

    (A) implementing laws passed by Congress.

    (B) implementing the president's policy initiatives.

    (C) solving disputes between the executive and legislative branches of government.

    (D) distributing information about public programs and services.

    (E) issuing rules and regulations.

2. The Pendleton Civil Service Act is significant because

    (A) it instituted an affirmative action policy for hiring and promoting federal bureaucrats.

    (B) it created the federal civil service and prescribed that the hiring of civil servants be based on merit.

    (C) it gave the president more control over federal agencies.

    (D) it reduced the number of federal civil servants working outside of Washington, D.C.

    (E) it established clear boundaries between state and federal bureaucracies.

3. Bureaucracies are often criticized as being undemocratic because

    (A) they are not directly accountable to the people.

    (B) they utilized a merit system for hiring.

    (C) citizens tend to have low opinions of them.

    (D) the courts have no influence over their actions.

    (E) they are overly influenced by campaign contributions.

4. Presidents attempt to exercise control over the bureaucracy through which of the following means?

  I. Appointing heads of federal agencies that are loyal to them.

  II. Issuing executive orders.

  III. Altering agencies' budgets.

  IV. Providing incentive pay to senior agency administrators.

  (A) I only

  (B) I and III only

  (C) III and IV only

  (D) I, II, and III only

  (E) All of the above.

5. Which of the following statements represent a prevalent myth about the federal bureaucracy?

  I. The bureaucracy is growing larger each year.

  II. Most federal bureaucrats work in Washington, D.C.

  III. Citizens are generally dissatisfied with the bureaucracy.

  IV. The bureaucracy makes government inefficient and cumbersome.

  (A) I only

  (B) IV only

  (C) I and II only

  (D) II, III and IV only

  (E) All of the above

6. An important tool Congress uses to influence the bureaucracy is

  (A) submitting *amicus curiae* briefs to the federal courts.

  (B) issuing executive orders.

  (C) hiring civil servants to head federal agencies.

  (D) frequently removing administrators from office.

  (E) requiring agency heads to routinely appear before congressional committees.

7. Iron triangles are made up of which of the following?

   (A) Congressional committees, independent executive agencies, and private corporations.

   (B) Bureaucratic agencies, congressional committees, and interest groups.

   (C) Regulatory commissions, the Office of Management and Budget, and interest groups.

   (D) The executive, the legislative, and the judicial branches of government.

   (E) The president's cabinet, interest groups, and private corporations.

8. All of the following are independent regulatory commissions EXCEPT

   (A) Federal Reserve Board

   (B) National Labor Relations Board

   (C) Security and Exchange Commission

   (D) Office of Management and Budget

   (E) Federal Trade Commission

9. The Hatch Act helps maintain a nonpartisan bureaucracy because it

   (A) creates a federal commission on which half the members are Democrats and half are Republican.

   (B) insures that federal employees are hired based on merit.

   (C) requires all federal employees to register to vote as independents.

   (D) requires all federal agencies to have staffs that are balanced along party lines.

   (E) prohibits government employees from active participation in partisan politics.

10. Implementation of public policy is most successful when

   (A) the goals of the policy and the authority of the implementers are clear.

   (B) there is a court order mandating compliance with the policy

   (C) the executive branch has pre-cleared the policy with the federal judiciary.

   (D) multiple agencies and bureaucrats are involved.

   (E) the policy originated in the executive branch as opposed to the legislative branch.

Free-Response Questions

1. Many political scientists believe that having a nonpartisan civil service increases the likelihood that government will operate in an effective and efficient manner.

    a. Define the merit principle and explain how it helps to insure that the civil service remains nonpartisan.

    b. Define the Hatch Act and explain how it helps to insure that the civil service remains nonpartisan.

    c. Although the federal bureaucracy is nonpartisan, the president is the person nominally in charge of it. Identify and describe two ways a president attempts to control the bureaucracy.

2. Policy implementation involves translating the goals and objectives of a policy into an operating, ongoing program. When policies are not successful, it often due to problems at the implementation stage of the policy process. Identify and explain three reasons that policy implementation might fail.

ANSWERS AND EXPLANATIONS

Multiple-Choice Questions

- **1. (C) is correct.** The bureaucracy does not referee or solve disputes between the executive and legislative branches of government. Bureaucracies are essentially implementers of policy.

- **2. (B) is correct.** The Pendleton Civil Service Act of 1883 created the federal civil service system. Hiring and promotions in this system are based on the merit system. With regards to hiring, applicants must take an exam, and those individuals in the highest scoring group are hired. Most federal bureaucratic positions are filled this way, though the president does appoint some people to high-level positions.

- **3. (A) is correct.** Although they make vital decisions and perform essential services for government and the people, bureaucrats are directly accountable to citizens the way the president and Congress are. This has led to the criticism that the bureaucracy is an undemocratic branch of government.

- **4. (D) is correct.** Presidents have no control over the compensation bureaucrats receive. There is a fairly rigid federal pay scale that is used to determine the level of pay and benefits to which federal employees are entitled.

- **5. (E) is correct.** All of these statements are false or misleading. The federal bureaucracy is not growing bigger and bigger each year. Only about 12 percent of federal bureaucrats work in Washington, D.C. California, with more than 245,000 federal employees leads the nation in the number of federal bureaucrats. Most citizens are generally satisfied with the service they receive from the bureaucracy.

- **6. (E) is correct.** Congress uses oversight committee hearings as a means to insure federal agencies are meeting the goals and objectives set in laws it passes, and to help keep federal agencies free of fraud, waste, and abuse.

- **7. (B) is correct.** An iron triangle is the mutually-dependent relationship between bureaucratic agencies, interest groups, and congressional committees. These relationships are often detrimental to the interests of taxpayers and ordinary citizens.

- **8. (D) is correct.** The Office of Management and Budget is part of the Executive Office of the President and is not an independent regulator commission.

- **9. (E) is correct.** The Hatch Act, originally passed in 1939 and amended most recently in 1993, prohibits civil service employees from actively participating in partisan politics while on duty. The act was intended to help insure a fair and impartial bureaucracy, and to protect bureaucrats from coercion on the part of superiors or political appointees.

- **10. (A) is correct.** If the goals of a policy are not clear to those who have to implement it, and if those who have to implement lack the authority to act definitively, then the policy in question is not likely to be well implemented or received.

Free-Response Questions

This rubric provides examples of many, but not all of the possible correct responses to the free-response questions.

1.

a. Define the merit principle and explain how it helps to insure that the civil service remains nonpartisan.

- The merit principle calls for the use of entrance exams and promotion ratings to hire and reward qualified civil servants. Under this principle individuals, are hired and promoted based on their qualifications, rather than patronage or partisan ties.

b. Define the Hatch Act and explain how it helps to insure that the civil service remains nonpartisan.

- The Hatch Act is a federal law that prohibits government employees from participating in partisan political activities while on duty. The law helps to protect civil service employees from pressures from political appointees and others to behave in a partisan manner in carry out their professional duties.

c. Ways a president attempts to control the bureaucracy.

- **Appoint the right people to head agencies**. Presidents control the appointments of federal agency heads and subheads. Appointing individuals who share their ideology and goals is one good way for presidents to influence what agencies do.

- **Issue executive orders.** Executive orders carry the force of law and can be used to get agencies to take or not take certain actions.

- **Alter and agencies budget**. The Office of Management and Budget (OMB) is instrumental in determining an agency's budget. Threats to cut or add to a budget usually get an agency's attention.

2. Identify and explain three reasons that policy implementation might fail.

- **Flawed program design.** It is difficulty to implement a policy that or program that is defective in its basic theoretical conception.

- **Lack of clarity.** Congress often states a broad policy goal in legislation and leaves the implementation of the policy to bureaucrats. Congress does this so that it can claim to be responsive to its constituents, while reserving the ability to blame others if specific policies fail to meet constituents' expectations. Similarly, bureaucrats sometimes receive unclear or even contradictory instructions from Congress. This makes knowing what to implement and how best to do it quite difficult.

- **Lack of resources.** If agencies have insufficient funds to carry out assign tasks, successful policy implementation will be difficult to achieve.

CHAPTER 16

The Federal Courts

In the American judicial system, courts apply the law to solve conflicts and disputes between two or more parties. The United States has a dual court system. Federal courts hear cases of federal law and cases involving two parties of different states. This amounts to only about two percent of all trials—most cases are heard in state and local courts. The sources of American law include the constitutions of the United States and the states, federal and state statutes and regulations, and case law (legal principles expressed in court decisions). Most of this law is based on the English system of common law which is judge-made law shaped by custom and applied to similar situations.

The Nature of the Judicial System

- **Criminal law:** Used when a person has violated a law.

- **Civil law:** Used to settle disputes between private parties

- Only about three percent of all cases actually go to trial; most are settled out of court.

- **Litigants:** The parties involved in a case

    - The **plaintiff** brings the charges (this name is listed first in the name of the case). In matters of criminal law, the government is the plaintiff.

    - The **defendant** is the party who has been charged (this name is listed second).

    - Plaintiffs must have **standing to sue,** or sufficient legal reason to bring charges.

    - Litigants in a **class action suit** sue on behalf of all citizens who are in the same situation.

- **Groups:** Interest groups become involved with court cases to influence decisions about the law.

    - May have their lawyers take up an appropriate litigant's case

    - Can submit *amicus curiae* briefs to influence a judge's decision

        - Explain the possible effects of the judge's decision

        - Bring new points of view to the case

- Provide additional information not presented in the case

- The federal government can also submit them

- **Attorneys:** Lawyers present a case in court.

  - Every citizen is guaranteed a lawyer in a criminal case.

  - **Public interest lawyers** and **legal aid groups** may represent poor people in some civil and criminal cases.

  - State and local governments hire public defenders to represent poor defendants in criminal cases.

  - Usually people with more money can hire lawyers with more time and resources, and therefore may have an advantage.

The Structure of the Federal Judicial System

- Courts of **original jurisdiction** are the first courts to hear a case, usually when it goes to **trial.**

  - The court assesses and decides a case based on the **facts of the case.**

  - Most cases do not continue after their first ruling.

- Courts of **appellate jurisdiction** hear cases that have been **appealed.**

  - The court interprets the case as it relates to the law; it does not review the facts.

  - The litigants do not appear before the court, and there is no jury.

- **District courts:** there are 94 federal district courts

  - Have original jurisdiction

  - Hold trials in which the litigants appear before the court

  - Federal district courts primarily handle the following types of cases:

    - Cases violating federal law or involving federal civil law

    - Civil suits in which the litigants are of different states

    - Bankruptcy proceedings and process of naturalization

  - The **U.S. attorney** in each district serves as the government's lawyer.

- The federal government is a plaintiff when prosecuting violators of federal laws.

- The government can be a plaintiff or defendant in a civil suit.

- **Courts of appeal:** Thirteen courts of appeal review cases appealed from the district courts.

    - Have appellate jurisdiction

        - Do not focus on the facts of the case

        - Evaluate the treatment of the case in the district court in terms of errors of procedure or the law

    - Usually three judges hear a case

    - Their ruling sets a **precedent** for the district courts within their geographic circuit

- **Supreme Court:** The ultimate authority on the law

    - Has original jurisdiction in cases between two states, the federal government and a state, or a state and a foreign country

    - Most cases fall under its appellate jurisdiction

        - It can choose which cases to hear

    - Consists of nine justices who rule on cases together

The Politics of Judicial Selection

- All federal judges and justices are appointed by the president.

- Nominations must be confirmed by the Senate.

    - Confirmation of district judges is determined by **senatorial courtesy,** in which Senators in the state where the district is located have a significant influence in appointing judges.

- Justices are carefully selected by the president when there is a vacancy on the Supreme Court.

    - Supreme Court cases set precedents for the law through the principle of *stare decisis.*

- Justices serve much longer than a president's term.

- The Court will be more closely aligned with the president's ideology.

The Courts as Policymakers

1. **Accepting cases:** The Supreme Court shapes policy by selecting which cases to hear.

   - Most likely to choose cases involving civil rights and civil liberties, a discrepancy in the lower courts' interpretation of the law, or disagreements between justices and the lower courts

2. **Making decisions:** The Court follows a regular process.

   - Justices read briefs pertaining to the case

   - Hear **oral arguments**

   - Meet to discuss cases and vote on decision

   - Write and announce opinions

   - Decisions are based heavily on **precedent;** lower courts must follow precedents set by higher courts.

   - Decisions often must clarify ambiguities in the law.

   - Justices usually rule *stare decisis:* "let the decision stand."

3. **Judicial implementation:** Decisions must be translated into policy.

   - This is accomplished by policymakers, the president, lower courts, lawyers, and administrators.

   - The public must become aware of its rights under the new decision.

   - Often implementers disagree with the decision and try to hinder implementation.

The Courts and the Policy Agenda

- Some justices have had a significant impact on the shaping of policy.

  - **John Marshall:** Initiated the practice of judicial review in the case of *Marbury* v. *Madison* and expanded the power of the Supreme Court significantly

200

- The **Warren court:** The Supreme Court became actively involved in expanding civil rights and civil liberties.

- The **Burger court:** Appointed by Nixon, Burger made the Court more conservative, though it still allowed abortion in *Roe* v. *Wade.*

- The **Rehnquist court:** The Court became even more conservative with Reagan's appointments and began to limit (though not reverse) previous rulings.

- Some critics think the Supreme Court is too powerful and favor **judicial restraint.**

- Others favor **judicial activism** to allow justices the freedom to forge new policies, especially concerning people largely underrepresented in the political process.

- Power of the courts is checked by the president's appointments and by Congress's ability to amend the Constitution despite—or in order to overrule—a Supreme Court decision.

For Additional Review

Select two Supreme Court cases that are of particular interest to you, or that had a major impact on politics or society. Read the opinion or opinions associated with the cases to better understand the reasoning on which the justices make important decisions.

Multiple-Choice Questions

1. Which of the following statement is true of the judicial system in the United States?

    (A) It is unitary court system.

    (B) Interest groups are forbidden from participating in criminal proceedings.

    (C) The system prescribes that criminal cases be decided by juries and civil cases be decided by judges.

    (D) Every defendant is entitled to a trial by a jury.

    (E) It is an adversarial system in which justice is supposed to emerge from the struggle between two contending points of view.

2. Which of the following is part of the federal court system?

   I. U.S. Supreme Court.

   II. State Supreme Courts.

   III. Court of Military Appeals.

   IV. U.S. Court of Appeals.

(A) I only

(B) IV only

(C) I and IV only

(D) I, II and IV only

(E) I, III and IV only

3. Federal district courts are the only federal courts in which

(A) the facts are presented by both parties in the case.

(B) *amicus curiae* briefs are registered with the court.

(C) the Solicitor General appears for oral argument.

(D) juries are impaneled to decide cases.

(E) three judge panels decide the outcome of cases.

4. Which of the following statements is true about Congress' influence over Supreme Court decision making?

(A) Congress can pass laws to prohibit judicial activism.

(B) The Senate can filibuster court decisions.

(C) Congress has significant control over the court's appellate jurisdiction.

(D) The Senate can decide which cases the Supreme Court will hear.

(E) District court judges are reviewed by Congress every ten years.

5. *Senatorial Courtesy* is

(A) the custom of the Supreme Court sharing its docket with the Senate Judiciary Committee before it is made public.

(B) a tradition whereby nominees for federal judgeships must meet the approval of senators of the president's party from the state in which the nominee will serve.

(C) the tradition of the full Senate approving all judicial nominees who win a majority vote in the Judiciary Committee.

(D) the practice of the Senate filling judicial vacancies with judges who share the same judicial philosophy as their most immediate predecessor.

(E) the tradition of the vice president hosting a formal reception to introduce Supreme Court nominees to members of the Senate.

6. All of the following influence the selection of federal judges and Supreme Court justices EXCEPT

(A) Campaign contributions.

(B) Partisanship.

(C) Ideology.

(D) Experience.

(E) Judicial philosophy.

7. Which of the following is true about the vast majority of cases decided by the Supreme Court?

(A) They are decided by unanimous decision.

(B) The decisions tend to significantly alter current policy.

(C) They tend to reverse the decision of the lower courts.

(D) They result in the payout of larger damage awards than decisions rendered by lower courts.

(E) They are decided based on how similar past cases have been decided.

8. One major weakness of federal courts as policymakers is

(A) judges are term-limited which affects their ability to implement their decisions.

(B) lower courts are not required to follow the decisions of superior courts.

(C) they must rely on other institutions to implement its decisions.

(D) they are shielded from the pressures of electoral politics.

(E) courts tend to lack legitimacy in the eyes of most citizens.

9. Interest groups play a role in the federal judicial process in all of the following ways EXCEPT by

(A) running advertisements endorsing a judicial nominee

(B) lobbying the Judiciary Committee about a judicial nominee

(C) filing *amicus curiae* briefs

(D) having their lawyers represent a plaintiff

(E) filing a class action suit

10. The power of courts to determine which acts of Congress, the executive branch, and state legislatures are constitutional is known as

(A) precedent.

(B) *stare decisis*.

(C) original jurisdiction.

(D) judicial implementation.

(E) judicial review.

Free-Response Questions

1. The framers of the Constitution desired a federal judiciary that was removed from the pressures and direct consequences of electoral politics.

    a. Identify and describe two provisions in the Constitution that were intended to shield the judiciary from electoral politics.

    b. The framers' intent notwithstanding, the federal judiciary is free of the influence of electoral politics. Identify and describe two ways electoral politics affect the federal judiciary.

2. The Constitution provides each of the three branches of government with the capacity to limit and trump the powers of the other two.

    a. Describe one way the president can check and balance the powers of the federal judiciary.

    b. Describe one way Congress can check and balance the powers of the federal judiciary.

    c. Describe one way the Supreme Court can check and balance the powers of the executive branch.

    d. Describe one way the Supreme Court can check and balance the powers of the Congress.

ANSWERS AND EXPLANATIONS

Multiple-Choice Questions

- **1. (E) is correct.** A bedrock principle underlying the American court system is justice will emerge from an adversarial system in which there is a struggle between two contending points of view.

- **2. (D) is correct.** All of the courts listed except state supreme courts are part of the federal judiciary. No state court is part of the federal court system.

- **3. (D) is correct.** There are no juries in the courts of appeal, the Supreme Court, and all other federal courts except the district courts.

- **4. (C) is correct.** In many instances federal courts' jurisdiction derives from Congress and not the Constitution. The Constitution provides Congress with the discretion to determine which category of cases appellate courts may hear.

- **5. (B) is correct.** Senatorial courtesy is a tradition whereby nominees for federal judgeships must meet the approval of senators of the president's party from the state in which the nominee will serve. This tradition began under George Washington, and since that time the Senate has tended not to confirm nominations for district court judges when senators of the president's party from the state in which the nominee will serve oppose them.

- **6. (B) is correct.** There is no evidence that campaign contributions to presidential races is a major factor in determining who president's nominate for federal judgeships.

- **7. (E) is correct.** Most Supreme Court rulings uphold the decision made by the lower court. This is the principle of *stare decisis,* meaning "let the decision stand."

- **8. (C) is correct.** Unlike with legislatures and the executive branch, the courts must always rely on other units of government to implement and enforce their rulings. This is widely viewed as a weakness for the courts as policymakers.

- **9. (A) is correct.** Interest groups do attempt to influence the appointment of federal judges, but not by running advertisements. The process of filling judgeships is far removed from the public—the only means of influence it has is by influencing the election of the president and members of the Senate, who, in turn, choose judges. Advertisements aimed at swaying public opinion therefore have little use in this case.

- **10. (D) is correct.** Judicial Review is the power of the courts to determine whether acts of Congress, the executive branch, and the states are constitutional. This power was established by the Supreme Court's decision in *Marbury* v. *Madison.*

This rubric provides examples of many, but not all of the possible correct responses to the free-response questions.

1.

a. Provisions in the Constitution that were intended to shield the judiciary from electoral politics

- **Federal judges are appointed not elected.** This feature allows judges to make reasoned decisions based on the rule of law without the fear of losing their jobs because some of their decisions may be unpopular with a group of constituents or the general public.

- **Lifetime appointment for federal judges**. Once confirmed by the Senate, federal judges have lifetime tenure on the bench, so long as they do not commit impeachable offenses. This lifetime tenure allows judges to make reasoned decisions based on the rule of law without the fear of losing their jobs because some of their decisions may be unpopular with other government officials or the general public.

- **Federal judges' salary cannot be reduced.** The Constitution expressly prohibits the reduction of judges' salaries during their time on the bench. This constitutional provision allows judges to make decisions without fear of reprisal from the executive and legislative branches.

b. Ways electoral politics affects the federal judiciary.

- **Federal judges are nominated by a president who is a political partisan.** Presidents seek to appoint judges to the bench who share their party affiliation, ideology, judicial philosophy, and their stances on specific issues. This makes federal judges products of a partisan political process.

- **The confirmation process.** The confirmation process for federal judges is sometimes highly partisan, with the Democrats and Republicans seemingly using the process as continuation of the last election or a precursor for the next.

- **Congress controls the appellate jurisdiction of federal courts.** Because of this authority, Congress has the capacity to prohibit the courts from hearing specific categories or classes of cases.

2.

a. Ways the president can check and balance the powers of the federal judiciary.

- **Appointment power.** The president nominates Supreme Court and other federal judges.

b. Ways Congress can check and balance the powers of the federal judiciary.

- **Confirmation process.** Supreme Court justice and all other federal judge nominees must be confirmed by the Senate.

- **Impeachment power.** Congress can impeach federal judges.

- **Jurisdiction authority over lower federal courts.** The Constitution created just one federal court, the U.S. Supreme Court. It gave Congress the authority to create any other subordinate courts that it saw fit to create. Thus in theory, the Congress could disband all federal courts except the Supreme Court. Congress also has the capacity to prohibit the courts from hearing specific categories or classes of cases.

- **Power of the purse.** Although the Constitution expressly prohibits the reduction of judges' salaries during their time on the bench, Congress determines if federal judges receive pay raises and how much any raise will be.

c. A way the Supreme Court can check and balance the powers of the executive branch.

- **Judicial Review.** Courts can declare acts of the president and federal agencies to be unconstitutional or unlawful.

d. A way the Supreme Court can check and balance the powers of the Congress.

- **Judicial Review.** Courts can declare laws passed by Congress to be unconstitutional.

CHAPTER 17

Economic Policymaking

The U.S. government and economy have always been closely entwined. The American economy is based on the principles of **capitalism** and **laissez-faire,** but in practice it is a **mixed economy** because the government plays a regulatory role. The regulatory role is evidenced by the activities of agencies like the **Securities and Exchange Commission (SEC),** which regulates stock fraud, and through the passage of laws such as the **minimum wage** law. The economic concerns of the government are changing due to the growth of **multinational corporations,** which have created a global economy.

It is very unlikely that you would be asked on an AP Free-Response Question to address one specific policy area. It is, however, important that you understand the public policymaking process in general and be able to draw appropriate examples from a variety of policy areas. Thus, there are two Free-Response Questions at the end of Chapter 20, which allow you to draw upon your knowledge of more than one policy-making process and topics covered in other parts of this book and your course.

Government and the Economy

Social problems arise as a result of economic downturns.

- **Unemployment** occurs when there are not enough jobs.

- Measured by the **unemployment rate**

- The Democratic coalition consists of groups concerned with unemployment (labor and the lower classes).

- Voters, especially Democrats, take the state of the economy into account when choosing candidates.

- Democrats generally sacrifice higher inflation to keep unemployment down.

- **Inflation** occurs when prices rise.

- Measured by the Consumer Price Index

- The Republican coalition includes businesspeople that are concerned about the cost of goods and services.

- Republicans generally try to prevent inflation, even at the risk of rising unemployment.

209

Instruments for Controlling the Economy

- Monetary policy: monitoring and controlling the amount of money in circulation; based on the economic theory known as monetarism, which states that controlling the money supply is the key to controlling the economy.

- If there is too much available cash or credit, inflation occurs.

- The Federal Reserve System was created to manage monetary policy. Its Board of Governors is appointed by the president and confirmed by the Senate but operates fairly independently. The Federal Open Market Committee is the most important body within the Federal Reserve; it decides how monetary policy is carried out. It regulates monetary policy by

  - 1. influencing the rate at which loans are given, which influences decisions about borrowing;

  - 2. controlling the amount of money banks have available, and, in turn, the rate at which people can borrow;

  - 3. adding to the money supply by selling bonds.

- **Fiscal policy:** Regulating revenues and expenditures through the federal budget; determined by Congress and the president

- **Keynesian economic theory** (liberal)

  - Encourages government's active participation in the economy

  - Government spending stimulates the economy by creating demand. Cutting taxes is another way the government can create demand. This is known as expansionary fiscal policy.

  - The government can decrease demand by cutting spending and increasing taxes, which is known as contractionary fiscal policy.

- **Supply-side economics** (conservative)

  - By decreasing government involvement in the economy, people will be forced to work harder and save more.

  - Cutting taxes increases the money supply.

Obstacles to Controlling the Economy

- It is difficult to predict the economy far enough in advance to make and implement policy.

- Events abroad can affect the economy. The U.S. economy is affected by actions taken by international organizations such as the **World Trade Organization (WTO),** which regulates such things as international trade. This has led some policymakers to support the idea of **protectionism** to protect the United States' economy from imports.

- The economy is grounded in the private sector, which is harder to regulate.

Arenas of Economic Policy

Business Policy

- A few **transnational corporations, often formed through mergers,** control most of the country's assets and play a large role in the world economy.

- **Antitrust laws** allow the Justice Department to bring suit against companies that have **monopolized** a certain product or service.

    o Breaks up the company

    o Opens the market to competition

- The government participates in the economy by assisting failing industries with subsidies and loans and by funding product research.

- Business lobbies are well established and influential.

Consumer Policy

- Consumer groups are fairly new.

- Have successfully lobbied for increased regulation over product safety and advertising.

- The **Federal Trade Commission** regulates trade and now advertising claims.

- The **Food and Drug Administration** monitors the health safety of food and approves new drugs for sale.

Labor and Government

- Prior to the twentieth century, the government traditionally favored business over labor.

- In the twentieth century, labor won some economic protection of the law.

- Unions have the power of **collective bargaining** with management.

- Unemployment compensation

- Minimum wage

- Safety standards

- The regular workweek

New Economy, New Policy Arenas

- The Internet is creating an economy based on information.

- The **"digital divide"** describes the inequality of access among socioeconomic groups.

For Additional Review

Unemployment and inflation are two social consequences of economic downturns. Brainstorm a list of some other social problems that may arise as a result of these two situations. What other consequences might result from a poor economy? Can you think of anything consumers can do to avoid or alleviate these problems?

Multiple-Choice Questions

1. Which of the following statements best describes the consumer price index (CPI)?
   (A) It is an index used to measure the trade deficit.
   (B) It is an index used to measure inflation.
   (C) It is an index used to measure budget deficits.
   (D) It is an index used to set prices for durable goods.
   (E) It is an index used to set interest rates that banks charge for credit.

2. Which of the following indicates that the United States has a mixed economy?

    (A) The Supreme Court regulates interstate commerce.

    (B) The federal government owns the means of production.

    (C) Congress plays no role in setting tariffs on imported goods.

    (D) The Justice Department can sue monopolistic companies.

    (E) Federal workers are not allowed to unionize.

3. The purpose of antitrust policy is to

    (A) ensure competition and prevent monopolies.

    (B) increase the amount of trust the public has in government.

    (C) to ensure a smooth relationship between the Federal Reserve Board and Congress.

    (D) increase tax revenue from private corporations.

    (E) reduce the likelihood of high unemployment.

4. One way the government attempts to overcome inflation is by

    (A) decreasing loan rates to make money more available to the public.

    (B) increasing the amount of credit available to the public.

    (C) decreasing the amount of money in banks, which raises loan rates and discourages people from borrowing.

    (D) limiting the number of bonds sold to the public.

    (E) increasing the amount of money in banks to help individuals and businesses acquire spending capital.

5. Which of the following statements accurately describe traditional Republican Party economic positions?

    I. Republicans place greater emphasis on full employment than Democrats.

    II. Republicans tend to worry about inflation more than Democrats.

    III. Republican economic positions tend to appeal to the working class and unions.

    IV. Republicans tend to favor higher income tax rates.

    (A) I only

    (B) II only

    (C) II and III only

    (D) I and IV only

    (E) I, II, and III only

213

6. Which of the following statements best describes the significance of the National Labor Relations Act?

(A) It prohibits labor unions within the federal bureaucracy.

(B) It guarantees workers the right to unionize and bargain collectively.

(C) It allows mediation to solve conflicts between public and private workers.

(D) It allows companies to disband labor unions after giving 30 days advanced notice.

(E) It prohibits labor unions from collecting union dues from federal workers.

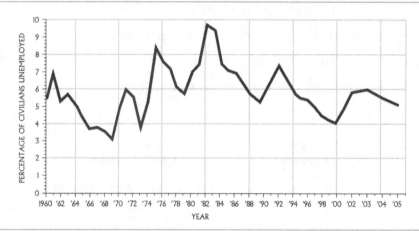

Figure 17.1   Unemployment: Joblessness in America, 1960–2005

Source: Economic Report of the President, 2006 (Washington, DC: U.S. Government Printing Office, 2006).

7. Which of the following statements accurately describes the data in the graph above?

(A) Unemployment decreased during the Clinton administration.

(B) Unemployment increased steadily through the 1970s.

(C) Unemployment rises only during a Republican presidency.

(D) Unemployment is higher in the United States than in other countries.

(E) Unemployment declined by about 50 percent during the 1980s.

8. All of the following are affected by actions of the Federal Reserve Board EXCEPT

(A) the federal budget deficit.

(B) the money supply.

(C) interest rates.

(D) the availability of jobs.

(E) inflation.

214

9. Which of the following segments of the population faces the most serious unemployment problems?

   (A) Middle-aged workers

   (B) Elderly workers

   (C) Women

   (D) Young adults

   (E) White collar workers

10. Labor unions usually oppose free trade policies because they

   (A) believe free trade policies lead to inflation.

   (B) believe free trade will force them to provide more benefits to their members.

   (C) believe free trade gives the government more control over union activities.

   (D) believe free trade will lead to growth in union membership at a rate too fast for unions to manage well.

   (E) believe free trade causes corporations to abandon workers in search of cheaper labor in foreign countries.

Free-Response Question (Refer to Chapter 20)

ANSWERS AND EXPLANATIONS

Multiple-Choice Questions

- **1. (B) is correct.** The consumer price index (CPI) is an index used by government and economists to measure inflation. It tracks the rise in prices of goods and commodities over time.

- **2. (D) is correct.** A mixed economic system is an economic system in which the government is deeply involved with, but does not command or control the economy. The Justice Department's ability to sue monopolistic companies is an indication of the government's ability to be involved in the economy.

- **3. (A) is correct.** Antitrust policy is designed to ensure competition in the marketplace and prevent monopolies. Antitrust policy is another example of the government's ability to be involved in the economy.

- **4. (C) is correct.** One way the government attempts to overcome inflation is by decreasing the amount of money in banks, which raises loan rates and discourages people from borrowing. The Federal Reserve Board controls how much money is issued from the Federal Reserve Bank to all other banks. When it limits those available funds, banks are forced to offer loans at higher rates. This discourages people from applying for loans, which are one cause of the over-circulation of money.

- **5. (B) is correct.** Republicans tend to worry about inflation more than Democrats. Republicans generally try to prevent inflation, even at the risk of rising unemployment.

- **6. (B) is correct.** The National Labor Relations Act, also know as the Wagner Act, is a 1935 law that guarantees workers the right to unionize and bargain collectively

- **7. (A) is correct.** Bill Clinton was president from 1993 to 2001. The unemployment rate dropped from 7.4 percent to 4 percent in his first seven years.

- **8. (A) is correct.** The Federal Reserve Board has either direct or indirect influence over money supply, interest rates, the availability of jobs, and inflation. It does not have control over the amount of money the government spends.

- **9. (D) is correct.** Of the groups listed, young people (16 to 24 years old) is the segment of the population that faces the most serious unemployment problems.

- **10. (E) is correct.** One of the primary reasons Labor unions usually oppose free trade policies is because they believe free trade causes corporations to abandon workers in search of cheaper labor in foreign countries.

CHAPTER 18

Social Welfare Policymaking

The United States has one of the largest income gaps in the world because **income distribution** is extremely unequal among different economic classes. The degree of government involvement in issues of **poverty** has resulted in a major political debate. The biggest factor in this debate is how people view the poor—as lazy people who are avoiding work, or as disadvantaged people with no opportunity to advance their economic situation. This policy area plays a key role during elections, because Americans feel strongly about it.

It is very unlikely that you would be asked on an AP Free-Response Question to address one specific policy area. It is, however, important that you understand the public policymaking process in general and to be able to draw appropriate examples from a variety of policy areas. Thus, there are two Free-Response Questions at the end of Chapter 20 that allow you to draw upon your knowledge of public policymaking and topics covered in other parts of this book and your course.

Income: Defining the Rich and the Poor

The rich have not only more **income** but also greater **wealth** in the form of stocks and other assets.

- A small number of Americans—1 percent of the total population—possess more than one-third of all wealth in the United States.

- The assets of that 1 percent are actually higher than the total worth of 90 percent of Americans.

The social welfare debate hinges on **how people view the poor.**

- Many view the poor as receiving too much government money

- Most government funds are given through **entitlement programs** to people who are not poor.

- Eligibility for **means-tested programs** depends on how narrowly poverty is defined.

- The poor are viewed as "deserving" if a family has lost its breadwinner or has a legitimate reason, such as a disability, for not being able to work.

- The poor are viewed as "undeserving" if they abuse the system or have created conditions of poverty themselves.

217

Poverty is defined by the government as family income that falls below the **poverty line.**

- Counts underestimate poverty, because millions of people hover around the line and continually fall just below or rise just above it.

- African Americans, Hispanic Americans, people living in inner cities, and unmarried women tend to be the groups most afflicted with poverty. The increase in the incidents of women and their children living in poverty is referred to as the **feminization of poverty.**

Income: Defining Government Involvement

Through **taxation**

- Types of taxes

  - **Progressive**: The wealthy are taxed at a higher rate.

  - **Proportional:** Everyone is taxed at the same rate.

  - **Regressive:** People of lower incomes are taxed at a higher rate.

  - **Earned Income Tax Credit:** Program, which provides very low-income workers with a cash credit, even if they paid no federal income tax.

  - State sales taxes are somewhat regressive, but the effect is counterbalanced by progressive federal income taxes.

Through **expenditures**

- **Transfer payments** are given by the government directly to citizens.

- Food stamps

- Student loans

- Social Security and Medicare benefits

- The elderly receive the most in transfer payments (Supplemental Security Income).

The Evolution of American Social Welfare Programs

- The **Great Depression** proved that poverty can be beyond anyone's control and encouraged the government to become more involved in welfare.

- Social Security began under the **New Deal (Social Security Act of 1935);** the poor become a part of the Democratic Party coalition.

- President Johnson initiated many **Great Society** programs to fight the **War on Poverty** during the civil rights era.

- President Reagan cut the growth of many of these programs in the 1980s.

- The system underwent a major overhaul during the Clinton administration (**Personal Responsibility and Work Opportunity Reconciliation Act of 1996**).

- Families receive small payments with a maximum of two years to find employment.

- People have a lifetime maximum of five years on welfare.

- States have more latitude and discretion in operating their own welfare programs.

- Welfare reform brought with it a name change for the cash payments to families from Aid to Families with Dependent Children (AFDC) to **Temporary Assistance for Needy Families (TANF).**

The Future of Social Welfare Policy

Social programs have become a major component of government. How they will continue to fare depends on future presidents, members of Congress, interest groups, and voters.

- **Social Security:** It is possible that the system will go bankrupt during the twenty-first century.

- More people will be of retirement age.

- The cost of living is rising, so monthly payments will increase.

- Either taxes will have to be raised or benefits will have to be cut.

- **Means-tested programs:** Their future is even more tenuous.

- Antipoverty programs have had mixed effects on lowering poverty rates; economic growth distributed across incomes has been more effective.

- Some argue that federal benefits encourage people to remain in poverty.

- Others contend that other problems such as recessions and a concentration of wealth have distorted the results.

Understanding Social Welfare Policy: Democracy and Social Welfare

Social welfare can be an emotionally charged issue.

- Influences voters' decisions

- Is a factor in choosing party identification

- The public participates in many active interest groups.

Social Security and Medicare for senior citizens receives much more political and public support than welfare for the poor.

- Interest groups for senior citizens (e.g., AARP) are much better organized and funded than groups for the poor.

- Senior citizens are more likely than the poor to vote.

- The size of the bureaucracy has grown to support such sweeping welfare programs.

For Additional Review

Do some research and then create a list of some of the key public and political institutions involved in making and implementing social welfare policy. Briefly describe the role of each one and then note any ideological motivations that might influence the actions or decisions of the institution.

Multiple-Choice Questions

1. The United States has one of the largest income gaps in the world because

   (A) it has one of the largest unemployment rates in the world.

   (B) the number of federal employees far outnumbers the number of private sector workers.

   (C) it is one of the few countries in the world without a federal minimum wage policy.

   (D) Americans tend to save a smaller proportion of their income than people in other countries.

   (E) income distribution is extremely unequal among different economic classes.

2. Which of the following is an accurate statement about social welfare policy?

    I.   The current system encourages beneficiaries to seek employment

    II. Programs usually have expanded under Republican presidents

    III. Most social welfare programs are noncontroversial.

    IV. The government gives more money to the nonpoor than to people below the poverty line.

    (A) I only.

    (B) II only.

    (C) I and IV only.

    (D) I, II, and IV only.

    (E) II, III, and IV only.

3. The feminization of poverty refers to

    (A) the increasing concentration of poverty among women.

    (B) a political advocacy campaign organized by the National Association of Women..

    (C) the disproportionate number of women in interest groups that represent the poor.

    (D) the tendency of the mass media to focus attention on poor women.

    (E) the alliance between women members of Congress and interest groups that represent poor women.

4. Which of the following groups has consistently had the highest rates of poverty?

    (A) Asian Americans.

    (B) African Americans.

    (C) Hispanic Americans.

    (D) Southern Whites..

    (E) Non-Hispanic White Americans.

WHO GETS WHAT? INCOME SHARES OF AMERICAN HOUSEHOLDS					
Income Quintile	1960	1970	1980	1990	2000
Lowest fifth	4.9	5.5	5.1	4.6	3.7
Second fifth	11.8	12.0	11.6	10.8	8.9
Third fifth	17.6	17.4	17.5	16.6	14.9
Fourth fifth	23.6	23.5	24.3	23.8	23.0
Highest fifth	42.0	41.6	41.6	44.3	49.6

SOURCE: U.S. Census Bureau.

5. Which of the following statements accurately describe the data in the chart above, "Who Gets What? Income Shares of American Households"?

   I.   The highest fifth was the only group to benefit from the economic boom of the 1990s.

   II.   Overall, all groups fared well in the 1970s and 1980s.

   III.   The third fifth has had the steadiest income of all of the groups.

   IV.   The lowest three fifths have fared the worst since the 1960s.

(A) II only

(B) I and II only

(C) I and III only

(D) I and IV only

(E) II, III, and IV only

6. The Social Security program is endangered primarily because

(A) the U.S. birth rate has increased dramatically over the past decade.

(B) the program has lost public support in recent years.

(C) the number of contributors to the program is growing at a much slower rate than the number of recipients.

(D) large federal budget deficits have reduced the amount of tax revenue collected in support of the program.

(E) the program has become more identified with racial minorities.

7. All of the following are examples of means-tested programs EXCEPT

(A) Temporary Assistance for Needy Families (TANF)

(B) Children's Health Insurance Program (CHIP)

(C) Food Stamps

(D) Medicaid

(E) Social Security

8. Which of the following is an accurate comparison of how citizens and governments in the United States and citizens and governments in European countries view social welfare?

(A) Americans are more willing to pay higher taxes to fund social welfare programs.

(B) Americans tend to support a broader range of social welfare programs.

(C) Americans tend to view social welfare needs as individual rather than governmental concerns.

(D) The American government spends a larger share of its Gross National Product (GDP) on social welfare programs.

(E) The American government provides more social benefits for the elderly.

9. The most expensive social welfare program in the United States is

(A) Social Security.

(B) Aid to Families with Dependent Children (AFDC).

(C) Food Stamps.

(D) Supplemental Security Income (SSI).

(E) Children's Health Insurance Program (CHIP).

10. Senior citizens fare better than the poor in social welfare budget battles for which of the following reasons?

(A) The Constitution requires a certain amount of spending for senior citizens, but not the poor.

(B) Most social services for senior citizens come from state governments.

(C) Lobbyists representing the poor are not allowed to make campaign contributions.

(D) Senior citizens are more organized and better represented politically than the poor.

(E) There are more senior citizens in the US than there are poor people.

ANSWERS AND EXPLANATIONS

Multiple-Choice Questions

- **1. (E) is correct.** The United States has one of the largest income gaps in the world because income distribution is extremely unequal among different economic classes. In fact, no industrialized country has wider extremes of income than the United States.

- **2. (C) is correct.** The government spends more money on the nonpoor than on people who live in poverty. Since the welfare reforms of 1996, welfare programs have included incentives, and sometimes requirements that beneficiaries seek employment as a condition of receiving aid.

- **3. (A) is correct.** The feminization of poverty refers to the increasing concentration of poverty among women, especially unmarried women and their children.

- **4. (B) is correct.** Although the poor are a varied group, poverty is more common among African Americans than the other groups listed here.

- **5. (D) is correct.** The income of all groups declined during the 1990s except for that of the highest fifth. Overall, the income of the lower three-fifths declined between the 1960s and 1999.

- **6. (C) is correct.** The Social Security dilemma is the number of Social Security contributors (the workers) is growing slowly, while the number of recipients (the retired) is growing rapidly.

- **7. (E) is correct.** A means-tested program is a program that is available only to individuals with a certain standard of living, usually below the poverty line. Social Security is an entitlement program. Entitlement programs benefit certain qualified individuals who are entitled by law, regardless of need.

- **8. (C) is correct.** Americans view social welfare with a greater degree of skepticism than do Europeans, who pay as much as 50 percent of their income in taxes to fund a wealth of social programs. Americans are generally more suspicious of big government and also tend to believe that poverty is more the fault of the individual than of society at large.

- **9. (A) is correct.** In part because it is an entitlement program, Social Security is the most expensive social program in the United States.

- **10. (D) is correct.** The elderly fare better than the poor in social welfare budget battles because they are more organized, more politically active and better represented than the poor. The elderly are also widely considered to be among the deserving poor.

CHAPTER 19

Policymaking for Health Care and the Environment

Both health care policy and environmental policy are becoming important issues on the public and political agendas. Many competing interests vie to influence these policies. The health care system is expensive, and not all people have access to it. Politicians and the public agree that the system needs major reforming, but no one has yet agreed on what those reforms should be. Environmental policies, while they help protect the environment, may hinder business. Furthermore, these two policy areas require a fair amount of technical expertise to be fully understood, so most Americans are unable to make informed policy choices and most decisions are left to policymakers, interest groups, and the industries.

It is very unlikely that you would be asked on an AP Free-Response Question to address one specific policy area. It is, however, important that you understand the public policymaking process in general and to be able to draw appropriate examples from a variety of policy areas. Thus, there are two Free-Response Questions at the end of Chapter 20 that allow you to draw upon your knowledge of public policymaking and topics covered in other parts of this book and your course.

Health Care Policy

The cost of health care in the United States is very high and is growing.

- Funding has focused on **technological advances,** that are extremely expensive.

- More facilities have been built than are being used, but their upkeep must be paid for.

- New drugs and procedures have been developed to treat more illnesses than ever before.

- The public is not pressed to be concerned about the cost of health care, since most of it is paid for by the **government, employers, and insurance companies.**

- **Malpractice lawsuits** are becoming more common, which raise doctors' insurance premiums and, in turn, raises the cost of their services.

Americans do not all have equal access to health care.

- Health care and insurance are mostly **privatized,** not **nationalized,** so they are not provided for everyone.

- Most people get **insurance** through their jobs.

- Unemployed people have to pay for health care themselves, and most cannot afford to pay.

- Companies feel they are bearing too much of the health care burden, but they do get significant tax breaks for contributing to their employees' insurance policies.

- Part-time employees are usually not eligible for benefits.

- Many small companies cannot afford to pay for their employees' health care.

- **Accessibility** is unequal among people of different races and incomes.

  - A greater percentage of minorities and lower-income families do not have insurance.

  - Members of minority groups and lower classes have poorer health because they often do not have regular family doctors.

- Health maintenance organizations (**HMOs**) have lowered the cost of health care but have not alleviated the problem of inaccessibility.

Debate continues over **who should pay for health care.**

- The **government** pays for about 50 percent of health care costs.

  - A nationalized system in which the government pays all health care costs has been proposed and rejected after lobbying by insurance and doctors' interest groups.

  - The government pays for Medicare and part of Medicaid, but the Medicare system is in danger of running out of money in the next decade.

- **Insurance companies** pay for about 30 percent of health care costs.

  - Have lobbied against **socialized medicine** because it would put them out of business

- Individuals pay about 20 percent.

Policymaking for Health Care

Policymaking for health care involves several political players and is a highly-charged issue.

- Senior citizens actively pursue federal funding for Medicare.

  - Lawmakers must fulfill the needs of their constituents, especially of those who vote.

226

- Interest groups representing the medical profession and insurance companies are well funded and very active in the political arena.

- Business groups try to persuade the government to take on more responsibility for health care so that businesses do not have to pay for it.

- Many groups, particularly the poor, are largely underrepresented in the health care policy debate.

- Policymakers in some cases choose which medical procedures to fund, because the money necessary to perform just a few very expensive procedures could be distributed more widely to provide basic services to more people.

Environmental Policy

Environmental policy and **economic policy** often conflict with each other.

- Industrial processes can harm the environment.

- A growing source of pollution comes from nonpoint sources, such as home fertilizers. Construction of ex-urb communities creates more runoff pollution and air pollution through increased use of highways for daily transportation.

- Environmental restrictions may inhibit economic growth and expansion.

- Environmental and business interest groups lobby strongly for conflicting policies.

  - Environmental groups call for preservation of wildlife and natural resources and for greater regulation of pollution.

  - Business groups demand fewer regulations and restrictions that inhibit industrial expansion.

- Private companies and federal agencies must file a report with the **Environmental Protection Agency,** citing the possible effects on the environment of every project they plan to undertake. The EPA was created in 1970 and is responsible for administering the government's environmental legislation. There are around 20 major pieces of federal environmental legislation. Among them are the **Water Pollution Control Act of 1972,** the **Endangered Species Act of 1973**, and the EPA's **Superfund,** which was created in 1980 to clean up toxic waste sites throughout the United States.

  - Interest groups have access to the reports, and even the threat of a lawsuit brought by one of them deters many companies from proposing projects that may be challenged by the environmental lobby.

Environmental and **energy policy** also may conflict but are dependent on each other.

- There is a growing demand for energy, but most energy is derived from sources with extraction and transportation methods that can harm the environment.

  - The government has tried to make industries more responsible for cleanups and environmental protection.

  - Energy providers argue that such restrictions are costly to the industry.

- The government funds research on **alternative energy** resources and sets standards for environmentally safe energy production and consumption.

- Policy debates continue over how to dispose of **nuclear waste.**

- Debate also continues over the possible consequences of **global warming** and what the government should do to prevent it.

- **"Environmental racism"** refers to the placing of factories and power plants in poor, minority neighborhoods, which meets with less organized opposition. Many of these neighborhoods now face "brownfield" problems, involving land occupied by empty factories that require very expensive cleanup before the land can be redeveloped.

For Additional Review

Make a table of the advantages and disadvantages of the current health care system. Then, in a third column, note reforms that have been attempted or suggested. Can you think of any other possibilities?

Multiple-Choice Questions

1. An interesting paradox about American health care is

   (A) the U.S. spends more money on healthcare than any other country, yet it is far from having the healthiest population.

   (B) Americans are healthier than people in most other countries even though the U.S. devotes relatively few resources to healthcare.

   (C) the cost of healthcare has been declining even though inflation in general is becoming more of a problem.

   (D) expenditures for healthcare for the elderly exceeds expenditures for healthcare for the young.

   (E) the rising costs of healthcare do not directly affect individuals because nearly all Americans have private insurance.

2. Most people in the U.S. get health insurance

   (A) from the federal government.

   (B) from state governments.

   (C) from private policies.

   (D) through their job.

   (E) through special cooperatives established by Congress.

3. Which of the following groups has the worst access to health care?

   (A) Federal employees.

   (B) Blue collar workers.

   (C) The elderly.

   (D) Children.

   (E) Racial and ethnic minorities.

4. All of the following are major pieces of federal environmental legislation EXCEPT

   (A) the Endangered Species Act.

   (B) the Environmental Protection Agency.

   (C) the Clean Air Act.

   (D) the Superfund.

   (E) the Water Pollution Control Act.

5. All of the following are accurate statements about the health care policy debate EXCEPT

   (A) Business interest groups represent employers who want the government to take greater responsibility for health care.

   (B) Groups like the American Medical Association lobby successfully for privatized health care because they are well funded and highly organized.

   (C) Senior citizens are the most active portion of the electorate in the health care debate because they stand to gain the most.

   (D) Many new interest groups have arisen to lobby for more health care assistance to people in poverty.

   (E) Disagreements between the government and private employers is pervasive.

6. Environmental concerns often become hotly contested political issues because

   (A) the number of environmental interest groups is shrinking.

   (B) the federal courts refuse to get involved in disputes involving the environment.

   (C) environmental concerns often conflict with other concerns like foreign trade and economic growth.

   (D) Congress has failed to enact any major environmental protection laws.

   (E) large corporations support any efforts by the government to clean up the environment.

7. Which federal program was designed to provide health care for poor Americans?

   (A) Medicare.

   (B) National Health Insurance.

   (C) Managed Care.

   (D) Endangered Species Act.

   (E) Medicaid.

8. One major reason that many groups' health needs go unmet is

   (A) there are too few well-organized groups that insist the government meets these needs.

   (B) there is confusion about what their health needs are.

   (C) the health care industry is overly centralized.

   (D) there are too few doctors in the United States.

   (E) the states have failed to reach agreements over what constitutes proper treatment.

9. Which of the following is the United States' most abundant fuel?

   (A) natural gas

   (B) coal

   (C) greenhouse gas

   (D) oil

   (E) nuclear energy

10. Environmental racism refers to

   (A) the practice of environmental interest groups refusing to let individuals join their causes on account of race.

   (B) the practice of establishing rigid racial quotas for hiring employees at the Environmental Protection Agency.

   (C) the locating of waste treatment facilities and power plants disproportionately in poor, minority neighborhoods.

   (D) the practice of the Environmental Protection Agency taking race into account when deciding where to locate its regional offices.

   (E) the tendency of minority neighborhoods to create more pollution than other neighborhoods do.

Free-Response Question (Refer to Chapter 20)

ANSWERS AND EXPLANATIONS

Multiple-Choice Questions

1. (A) is correct. There is a paradox about American health care: The U.S. spends more money on health care than any other country, yet it is far from having the healthiest population.

2. (D) is correct. Most Americans who have health insurance, get it through their job.

3. (E) is correct. There is uneven access to health care in the United States. Access to insurance and quality care is closely tied to race and income. Of the groups listed, racial and ethnic minorities have the worst access to health care.

4. (B) is correct. The Environmental Protection Agency (EPA) is not a piece of federal legislation. It is the federal agency charged with administering the government's environmental policies.

5. (D) is correct. Although there are many different interest groups who are extremely active in the health care debate, there has not been a significant rise in the number of such groups advocating for the poor,

6. (C) is correct. Environmental concerns often become heated political issues because the environmental concerns often conflict with other concerns like foreign trade and economic growth. For example, environmental restrictions may inhibit economic growth. As a consequence, business interest groups often oppose environmental groups on specific policy proposals.

7. (E) is correct. Medicaid is a public assistance program designed to provide health care for the poor. Medicaid is funded by both the national and state governments. It is often confused with Medicare, which is the part of the Social Security Program that provides hospitalization insurance for the elderly.

8. (A) is correct. One major reason that many groups' health needs go unmet is because there are relatively few advocacy groups pressuring the government to meet these needs. Single women, racial minorities, and the poor are worst off in this regard.

9. (B) is correct. Is the United States' most abundant fuel. About 90 percent of the country's energy resources are in coal deposits—enough to last hundreds of years.

10. (C) is correct. Environmental racism refers to the locating of waste treatment facilities and power plants disproportionately in poor, minority neighborhoods. Power plants tend to be located in poorer neighborhoods for two reasons: Land is cheaper there, and residents have less political clout with which to oppose new plants. Environmentalists have taken up the cause of environmental racism because pollution from the plants affects mostly people of low income who cannot afford medical care.

CHAPTER 20

Foreign and Defense Policymaking

Foreign policy has become crucial to governmental affairs in the past century, as the United States made the transition from isolationist country to world superpower. In this global era of high-speed connections, brief but deadly missile strikes, and free trade, it is apparent that this policy area will continue to hold an important place on every politician's agenda and in the public's mind as well.

It is very unlikely that you would be asked on an AP Free-Response Question to address one specific policy area. It is, however, important that you understand the public policymaking process in general and to be able to draw appropriate examples from a variety of policy areas. Thus, there are two Free-Response Questions at the end of this Chapter that draw upon your knowledge of public policymaking and topics covered in other parts of this book and your course.

American Foreign Policy: Instruments, Actors, and Policymakers

International organizations are becoming more necessary in today's global political and economic arenas.

- The **United Nations** is a global legislative body.

    - Nearly 200 countries are members, each with one vote in the General Assembly.

    - Mainly responsible for **peacekeeping,** but also international economic, education, and welfare programs.

    - The **Security Council** has the real power in the United Nations and therefore makes the most pressing decisions.

    - Five permanent members, each with veto power: the United States, China, Russia, France, and Great Britain.

    - Ten other seats are rotated each session.

Regional organizations combine blocs of countries in military and economic alliances.

- The **North Atlantic Treaty Organization (NATO)** is a military alliance formed by the United States and Western European countries during the Cold War.

- Since the end of the Cold War, some former Eastern bloc countries have been admitted.

- Members pledge to support each other in times of war.

- Helps prevent the threat of war

- The **European Union** is an economic alliance.

  - Most Western European countries share a common currency.

  - No trade barriers

  - No employment restrictions among countries

Multinational corporations contribute to about one-fifth of the global economy.

- Have significant influence over taxes and trade regulations

- Can be as powerful as governments

Non-governmental organizations (NGOs) unite people globally for common causes or goals.

- Churches, labor unions, environmental groups, human rights groups

American foreign policy is conducted mostly by the president and the executive branch, though Congress has some important responsibilities.

- The president serves as chief diplomat.

- Commander-in-chief of the armed forces

- Negotiates treaties and make executive agreements

- Appoints ambassadors

- Can act quickly and decisively

- The bureaucratic arm of foreign policy is the **State Department.**

- The **Secretary of State** is the president's top foreign policy advisor.

- American embassies fall under its jurisdiction.

- The **Department of Defense** works closely with the State Department in matters of national security.

- The **Joint Chiefs of Staff** represent each branch of the armed forces in an advisory committee to the President.

- The **Central Intelligence Agency** collects information in other countries to help the departments and the President make policy decisions.

- Sometimes plays a covert role in the governmental affairs of other nations.

- **Congress** helps to oversee foreign policy.

- The Senate ratifies treaties

- Authorizes declarations of war

- Appropriates funds for national security

American Foreign Policy: An Overview

- Foreign policy is made up of a nation's external policies and positions and the techniques for achieving those policies and positions. The goal of foreign policy is to achieve peace and prosperity in the international community. Foreign policy is typically a struggle to achieve a middle ground between political idealism and political realism.

- The United States practiced **isolationism** until World War I.

- During the ideological **Cold War,** the United States focused on the **containment** of **communism.**

- The Department of Defense grew in terms of size and responsibilities.

- The **military-industrial complex** came to play a major role in politics.

- The **arms race** between the United States and the Soviet Union caused an international arms buildup.

- The United States became involved in the **Vietnam War** to contain the spread of communism in Asia.

- The prolonged conflict resulted in massive troop commitments and heavy bombing of the North.

- Protests erupted at home, and Americans' faith in the government was shaken.

- The policy of **détente** brought greater cooperation among nations.

- Defense spending went up enormously under Reagan, higher than it had been through the previous decades of the Cold War.

- The Cold War came to an end with the fall of the Soviet bloc in the early 1990s, but international relations have yet to stabilize completely in a new system.

The Politics of Defense Policy

- Defense spending has decreased to one-sixth of the federal budget.

- There is some concern that defense spending detracts from social spending.

- Decreasing spending means fewer jobs for weapons builders.

- The standing army is large and costly.

- The extremely costly arms buildup has stopped, but new expenditures are focused on engagements in Afghanistan and Iraq, and on high-tech weapons systems.

- Treaties have reduced nuclear weapons reserves among several nations with nuclear arms.

The New Global Agenda

Attention has shifted away from long wars and formal military actions and alliances.

- **Economic sanctions** have become a powerful tool of foreign policy.

  - Embargoes, cutting off economic aid, and restricting imports are all forms of sanctions.

  - Are safer and cheaper than military alternatives

  - Are often initiated as a result of the efforts of human rights, environmental, and other political groups

- Stopping the proliferation of **nuclear weapons** is high on the international agenda.

- **Terrorism** has become a pressing international issue.

The international economy is now the highest priority on the international agenda.

- International trade has increased dramatically in the past few decades. International economic treaties have attempted to address the issue of international trade through such ideas as most favored nation status, where equitable trade and tariff policies are observed by nations.

- Capital can move more easily across borders with the internet and advanced communications systems.

- The use of tariffs has declined to allow free trade among nations.

- International protests against free trade have become common, because people fear the exploitation of less-developed countries by multinational corporations and because workers fear the loss of jobs.

- In the United States, imports exceed exports, so there is a **balance of trade deficit.**

- Labor is cheaper in other countries.

- This leads to unemployment, especially in blue-collar jobs.

- The North-South divide of wealthy nations and third world countries is becoming increasingly apparent.

- Less-developed countries are millions of dollars in debt to developed countries.

- Countries that receive aid usually have desirable natural resources.

- **Oil** and energy supplies are making economies more interdependent.

- The United States imports most of its oil from the Middle East. The policies of **OPEC (Organization of Petroleum Exporting Countries)** are therefore of real importance to the United States.

- The **environment** is a global concern that affects all nations, but economic progress usually dominates environmental priorities.

- There are also areas of regional conflict with which the United States must be concerned, such as Cuba, Haiti, and the Middle East.

For Additional Review

Make a time line of some of the most important foreign policy events of the twentieth century. Note important political actors and briefly describe the consequences of each event.

Multiple-Choice Questions

1. Which of the following is the United Nations' most powerful policymaking entities?

   (A) Joint Chiefs of Staff

   (B) North Atlantic Treaty Organization (NATO)

   (C) European Union (EU)

   (D) Security Council

   (E) Organization of American States (OAS)

2. American foreign policy is conducted mostly by the

   (A) Senate Foreign Relations Committee.

   (B) President and the Executive Branch.

   (C) National Security Agency.

   (D) Joint Chiefs of Staff.

   (E) House Foreign Affairs Committee.

3. All of the following contribute directly to the development of U.S. foreign policy EXCEPT

   (A) the United Nations' General Assembly.

   (B) the Joint Chiefs of Staff.

   (C) the Central Intelligence Agency.

   (D) the State Department.

   (E) the Department of Defense.

4. Congress exercises influence over foreign policy in which of the following ways?

   I. Declaring war

   II. Confirming ambassadors

   III. Appropriating money

   IV. Ratifying treaties

   (A) I only.

   (B) III only.

   (C) I, II, and III only.

   (D) I, III, and IV only.

   (E) All of the above.

5. Which of the following is an accurate statement about the role regional organizations have played in U.S. defense and foreign policy?

   (A) Regional organizations have contributed large sums of money to U.S. defense budgets.

   (B) In times of war, regional organizations have gained complete control over U.S. armed forces.

   (C) Regional organizations have largely been ignored by U.S. presidents.

   (D) The U.S. ended its involvement in most regional organizations after the Cold War ended.

   (E) Regional organizations have been used to promote economic as well as national security interests.

6. All of the following can be used to characterize U.S. foreign policy at various times during past century EXCEPT

   (A) isolationism.

   (B) unilateral disarmament.

   (C) détente.

   (D) containment.

   (E) arms race.

7. Which of the following is a true statement about the U.S. and foreign aid?

   (A) The Constitution limits the amount of money that can be spent on such aid.

   (B) The U.S. can only provide nonmilitary aid.

   (C) The U.S. is the world's largest donor of foreign aid.

   (D) The president can provide such aid without congressional approval.

   (E) The U.S. provides no foreign aid European countries.

8. Which of the following is the most important national security issue the United States has faced since the end of the Cold War?

   (A) The spread of terrorism.

   (B) A dramatic increase in nuclear proliferation.

   (C) An increasing isolationist Sate Department.

   (D) The inability to secure cooperation and commitments from allies.

   (E) The strengthening of the Warsaw Alliance's military forces.

9. Which of the following bureaucratic institutions has primary responsibility for coordinating U.S. foreign and military policies?

   (A) Department of Defense

   (B) Federal Bureau of Investigation

   (C) Central Intelligence Agency

   (D) National Security Council

   (E) State Department

10. Which of the following statements best describes today's international economy?

    (A) It is dominated by trade between the United States and the European Union.

    (B) It is remarkably similar to the international economy prior to World War II.

    (C) It is controlled and dominated by regional nongovernmental organizations.

    (D) Mutually assured destruction is its underlying operating principle.

    (E) It is characterized by greater interdependency than ever before.

Free-Response Questions

1. Foreign policy involves choices about relations with the rest of the world. The instruments or tools presidents use to conduct foreign policy are different from the instruments or tools they use to conduct domestic policy.

   a. Identify three types of instruments or tools mostly commonly used by presidents to conduct foreign policy.

   b. For two of the instruments or tools you identified in "a", describe how they are used to help accomplish foreign policy objectives.

   c. Identify two executive branch bureaucratic institutions involved in U.S. foreign policy and describe the role they play in the foreign policy process.

2. Congress shares with the president constitutional authority over foreign and defense policy.

   a. Identify and describe two constitutionally-derived powers Congress has in foreign policymaking.

   b. Identify and describe two constitutionally-derived powers the president has in foreign policymaking.

   c. Identify and describe a limitation on Congress in foreign policymaking.

ANSWERS AND EXPLANATIONS

Multiple-Choice Questions

- **1. (D) is correct.** The Security Council is the seat of real power in the UN. Five of its 15 members (the United States, Great Britain, China, France, and Russia) are permanent members of the council; the other 10 are chosen on a rotating basis. The five permanent member states on the Security Council and have veto power over all Security Council decisions.

- **2. (B) is correct.** The president is the chief initiator of foreign policy in the U.S. Presidents are aided in foreign policy decision making by several executive branch agencies including the State Department, the Department of Defense, the National Security Council, and the Central Intelligence Agency.

- **3. (A) is correct.** The UN General Assembly plays no direct role in formulating American foreign policy.

- **4. (E) is correct.** Although the president is the chief initiator of foreign policy in the U.S., Congress exercises influence over foreign policy through its powers to declare war, appropriate funds, ratify treaties, and confirm ambassadors to foreign nations. Congress has full authority over all military expenditures, including foreign aid and the budgets of the State Department, the Department of Defense, and the CIA.

- **5. (E) is correct.** Regional organizations have proliferated since the end of World War II. The United States has used them to help to promote its economic and national security interests.

- **6. (B) is correct.** Although the U.S. has entered into several arms control agreements over the years, it has never had a foreign policy predicated on unilateral disarmament.

- **7. (C) is correct.** The U.S. is the world's largest donor of foreign aid. However, the U.S. ranks lower than almost all other industrialized nations in the percentage of its gross domestic product it spends on economic development aid for need nations.

- **8. (A) is correct.** The spread of terrorism is the most troublesome national security issue the U.S. faced in the post Cold War era. Terrorism takes on many forms, including the bombing of buildings and the assignation of political leaders. It is difficulty and costly to defend against terrorism, especially in an open society like the United States.

- **9. (D) is correct.** Created in 1947, the National Security Council (NSC) is charged with the responsibility of coordinating American foreign and military policies. The NSC is composed of the president, vice president, the secretary of defense, and the secretary of state. The president's national security advisor manages the NSC staff.

- **10. (E) is correct.** Interdependency is the word that best describes today's international economy. The health of the American economy depends increasingly on the prosperity of its trading partners and on the smooth flow of trade and finance across borders.

Free-Response Questions

This rubric provides examples of many, but not all of the possible correct responses to the free-response questions.

1.

a. Types of instruments or tools mostly commonly used by presidents to conduct foreign policy.

- **military**

- **diplomacy**

- **economic**

b. Describe how the instruments above are used to help accomplish foreign policy objectives.

- **Military**. War and the threat of war are among the oldest instruments of foreign policy. Among other things, the United States has used its armed forces to help topple enemy governments, protect friendly governments, insure the delivery of humanitarian aid, protect American business interests and prevent ethnic cleansing.

- **Diplomacy**. Diplomacy is the least obvious instrument of foreign policy. It takes place when national leaders meet in summit talks or when less prominent negotiators meet to work out treaties covering all kinds of national contracts, like economic relations, arms control agreements, and cease fires in armed conflicts.

- **Economic**. Economic instruments can be as potent as war. For example, the control of oil can be a major source of power. Trade regulations, embargos, tariffs, and monetary policies can all be economic instruments of foreign policy.

c. Identify executive branch bureaucratic institutions involved in U.S. foreign policy and describe the role they play in the foreign policy process.

- **State Department**. The State Department is the main foreign policy agency of the U.S. government. It is the home of the diplomatic corps, and its head, the secretary of state, is the president's chief diplomatic advisor.

- **Department of the Defense**. The Department of Defense is a key foreign policy actor. It is the administrative home to the U.S. military, the army, air force, and navy. U.S. strategic and tactical military planning takes place at the Department of the Defense.

- **National Security Council (NSC)**. The NSC is the committee that links the president's key foreign and military policy advisors. Its formal members are the president, vice president, secretary of defense, and secretary of state. The NSC coordinates U.S. national security policy for the president.

- **Central Intelligence Agency (CIA).** The CIA is responsible for collecting and analyzing military, economic, and political data and information from foreign countries. This information can be used for both military and diplomatic planning. Information gathered by the CIA can also be used to prevent attacks on U.S. interests.

2.

a. Identify and describe constitutionally derived powers Congress has in foreign policymaking.

- **Power to declare war**.

- **Power of the Purse.** A president's national security agenda requires a willingness on the part of Congress to appropriate the necessary funds to support it.

- **Treaty Ratification**. Treaties that presidents negotiate with foreign countries must be approve by a two-thirds vote in the Senate.

- **Approval of key personnel**. The secretaries of state and defense, the director of the CIA, and ambassadors to foreign nations must be confirmed by the Senate.

b. Identify and describe constitutionally derived powers the president has in foreign policymaking.

- **Commander in Chief.** Because the framers wanted civilian control of the military, they made the president commander in chief of the armed forces. As commander in chief, the president controls where and how the military is deployed. The president also commands the vast arsenal of weapons of mass destruction.

- **Appointment power.** The president selects the persons who serve in key foreign policy decision making positions like the secretaries of state and defense, the national security advisor, and the director of the CIA.

- **Diplomatic powers.** The president alone extends diplomatic recognition to foreign governments. The president can also terminate relations with other countries. The president is also responsible for choosing U.S. ambassadors to foreign countries.

- **Power to make treaties with other nations**. The president has the sole power to negotiate treaties with other countries, although the Constitution requires the Senate to approve them by a two-third vote.

c. Identify and describe limitations on Congress in foreign policymaking.

- Congress is a relative large and decentralized institution, which makes it difficult for it to speak with one unified voice.

243

- There is a common perception that the Constitution vests foreign policy decision making solely in the president. This often makes it difficult for the Congress to effectively assert itself in matters of foreign policy.

- Congress has to rely on the president for important intelligence information about other countries. This can sometimes result in Congress receiving misleading or wrong information, like what happened in the period leading up to the 2003 Iraqi war.

CHAPTER 21

The New Face of State and Local Government

State and local governments (**sub national governments**) are the governments with which citizens most often come into contact. They employ thousands of people to perform all kinds of regular daily tasks, many of which are often taken for granted. In the past few decades, the responsibilities of both state and local governments have grown. The governments themselves have become increasingly diverse and more active in social policy than ever before.

The AP exam does not cover state and local government *per se*, but sub national governments are obviously very important in the federal system. Because of the way the AP exam is structured, there are no Free Response Questions at the end of this chapter. You should refer back to Chapter 3, "Federalism," where material covered in this chapter could enrich your responses to those questions.

State Constitutions

Each state is governed by a constitution that lays out the structure of the government and the laws of the state.

- Most state constitutions authorize a **governor** and a **bicameral legislature.**

- Most provide for the separation of powers and include a **bill of rights.**

- The U.S. Constitution requires each state to have a republican form of government, and has supremacy over all state constitutions.

State Elections

Citizens usually have the opportunity to vote for many political officials, including state judges.

- Some states allow residents to vote on laws (referred to as referenda, or ballot initiatives) directly during elections.

- Gubernatorial elections, like presidential elections, are becoming more candidate-centered.

- Political parties are declining in influence in state elections.

- Voters are less likely to vote by **party identification.**

- Gubernatorial campaigns are fairly independent and rely heavily on television advertising.

- This leads to **ticket splitting** and **divided government** at the state level.

- Voters also elect their state's lieutenant governor, attorney general, treasurer, and often many department secretaries.

- In *Baker* v. *Carr,* the Supreme Court decreed that state House (and later Senate) districts must be based on population counts.

- Shifted political focus away from rural agendas

- Suburban areas win new political representation.

- State representatives tend to be less known because their campaigns are smaller and receive less media attention.

- Incumbents usually have a great advantage over challengers.

- Some states have attempted to set term limits for state legislators and executive officers.

- More women and minorities are being elected to state-level positions.

The Job of Governor

Each state's governor has different powers and responsibilities, and some governors have more power than others.

- **Governors and most statewide elected officials (excluding the judiciary) are limited in the number of terms they can serve consecutively.**

- Some governors exercise a great deal of power through the **line-item veto**.

- Can veto specific parts of an appropriations bill, which gives the governor the last word in legislation

- Governors also have significant **budgetary** power.

- State legislatures do not have the time and the staff to devote much effort to amending the governor's budget proposal.

- The **line-item veto** allows governors to fine-tune budgetary legislation.

State Legislatures

State legislatures are becoming increasingly important to the political activity of each state.

- They have undergone a great deal of reform to make them more professional and more representative of their constituents.

- Many states have enacted term limits for legislators.

- **Legislative sessions** have been lengthened to allow legislatures to be more critical and more active in policymaking.

- A raise in salaries allows legislators to devote more attention to policymaking rather than relying on another job.

- Legislatures now have **larger administrative staffs.**

- Many people criticize the reforms for engineering too much politicking and failing to achieve greater representation.

- State legislatures have many of the **same responsibilities as Congress.**

- Pass laws in the same process

- Appropriate money

- In many states, the legislature confirms the governor's appointments

- State legislators are more closely in contact with their **constituents** than federal politicians are.

State Court Systems

State court systems developed with little organization but have recently been reformed to mirror the federal court system.

- **Trial courts** oversee civil and criminal cases.

- **Intermediate courts of appeal** hear routine appeals.

- The **state supreme court** handles appeals that may have a greater impact on state law or involve state constitutional issues.

- In some states, voters elect judges; in others, judges are appointed.

- Many states use the **merit plan.** According to this plan, judges are appointed from a list of recommendations, serve a trial term, and then are put on a ballot for voters to decide if they should stay in office.

Direct Democracy

Some states, particularly in the West and Midwest, offer voters the ability to participate in politics directly.

- **Initiatives** allow citizens to propose a piece of legislation, petition to have it placed on the ballot, and then vote on whether to make it law.

- Elected politicians are bypassed in the legislative process.

- Not all initiatives are well planned, and some do not succeed.

- Many initiatives are backed by interest groups.

- A **referendum** is a proposal passed by the state legislature that is then placed on the ballot to be approved by voters rather than by the governor.

- Voters can use a **recall** to call for a special election to remove a politician from office.

- This is difficult and costly and therefore occurs infrequently.

Local Governments

Local governments are completely subservient to the state government. However, because they work closely with constituents, they still have significant political clout.

- **County**—mostly administrative

- Keep birth, death, marriage, and property records

- Responsible for law enforcement, roads, education, elections, collecting taxes

- Provide local welfare services, particularly in urban counties

- Usually have only limited legislative powers to make laws

- **Township**—also administrative

- Most have limited responsibilities assisting county governments.

- Some function like city governments, but they have no lawmaking powers.

- **Municipality**—the most common type of government, which does have legislative capabilities

- Responsible for all public works, education, and public services

- **Mayor-council government:** Both a mayor and city council are elected.

- **Council-manager government:** The city council is elected and chooses a manager to implement policies.

- **Commission government:** Members of the commission are elected by voters. Each has an area of jurisdiction over which he or she has both legislative and executive authority.

- **School district:** A special type of government that deals specifically with public education

- Residents elect a board of education, pay taxes to support their schools, and make decisions about their schools.

- There are many pressing issues about social and economic inequalities among school districts.

- **Special district**: Any other special government set up to handle a specific issue, such as waste disposal or public libraries

State and Local Finance Policy

- States get most of their revenues from sales and income taxes.

- State expenditures go mostly to statewide social programs and public services or to local governments.

- Local governments get most of their funds from the state, local income, property, and sales taxes, and certain service fees for residents.

For Additional Review

Draw a diagram of the major federal, state, and local governmental institutions. Draw arrows to show where authority is directed and briefly describe the responsibilities of each institution you have included.

Multiple-Choice Questions

1. Which of the following is a true statement about state constitutions?

   (A) They tend to provide more details about specific policies than the U.S. Constitution.

   (B) They must be recertified by popular vote every ten years.

   (C) They must be recertified by state legislatures every ten years.

   (D) Most states have no method for amending their constitution.

   (E) There are no checks and balances in state constitutions.

2. Which of the following is a procedure for direct democracy?

   I. a recall

   II. an initiative

   III. a line-item veto

   IV. a referendum

   (A) IV only.

   (B) I and II only.

   (C) I, II, and IV only.

   (D) II, III, and IV only.

   (E) All of the above.

3. Compared to members of Congress, state legislators generally

   (A) represent more constituents.

   (B) have smaller districts.

   (C) receive more media coverage.

   (D) are more likely to be nonpartisan.

   (E) spend more money on their campaigns.

4. In 42 states, the governor has line-item veto powers that allow her or him to

   (A) veto state supreme court decisions.

   (B) veto referenda.

   (C) veto laws previously signed into law.

   (D) veto unfunded federal mandates.

   (E) veto specific parts of a bill.

5. Legislative professionalism refers to

(A) a set of reforms designed to enhance the capacity of state legislatures to perform their policymaking role more effectively and more efficiently.

(B) the growing tendency of legislative elections being won by upper income white-collar professionals.

(C) the trend of state legislatures imposing dress codes on legislators and legislative staff.

(D) the recent trend of state legislatures assuming primary governing responsibility in policy areas like education, crime, and social welfare.

(E) a set of rules of professional conduct that have been adopted by all fifty state legislatures.

6. Which can you infer from the data in the two graphs below?

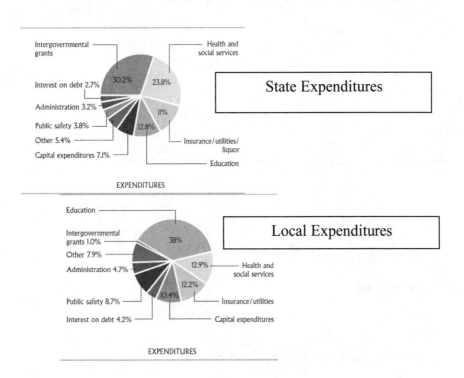

(A) The cost of health and social services is divided almost equally between state and local government.

(B) Thirty-four percent of local government's revenue is from state grants.

(C) Local government's debt is larger than state government's.

(D) A school that wants money to buy computers should ask the local government for funds.

(E) State government has fewer administrators than local government does.

7. Which of the following is an important change among state elected officials over the past forty years?

I. More women have been elected to state legislatures.

II. The number of women elected governor has increased.

III. More racial minorities have been elected to state legislatures.

IV. More women have selected for leadership positions in legislatures.

(A) I only.

(B) I and III only.

(C) II and III only.

(D) I, II, and III only.

(E) All of the above.

8. Which of the following is the largest source of revenue for state governments?

(A) state lotteries

(B) public utilities

(C) taxes

(D) federal grants

(E) transfers from local governments

9. Dillon's Rule is the idea that

(A) state governments should maintain balanced budgets in order to govern most efficiently.

(B) counties and municipalities should be empowered to determine local tax rates.

(C) laws passed by the legislature can be invalidated by a majority vote of the council of governments.

(D) the use of the patronage system in state governments is beneficial for public morale.

(E) local governments have only those powers that are explicitly given to them by the states.

10. All of the following are true statements about special districts EXCEPT

(A) They are the fastest growing form of local governance in the U.S.

(B) They usually exist to provide only a single service.

(C) They tend to be highly flexible units of government.

(D) They are highly accountable to the general public.

(E) They help local governments carry out their responsibilities more efficiently.

Free-Response Question (Refer to Chapter 3)

ANSWERS AND EXPLANATIONS

Multiple-Choice Questions

- **1. (A) is correct.** Each state is governed by a separate and unique constitution. The key difference between the federal and state constitutions is that the state documents often provide far more details about specific policies.

- **2. (C) is correct.** Direct democracy is government controlled directly by citizens. In some states, procedures such as the initiative, recall elections, and referenda give voters a direct impact on policymaking by means of the voting booth.

- **3. (B) is correct.** State legislators usually represent smaller districts than members of Congress.

- **4. (E) is correct.** The line-item veto allows a governor to veto only certain parts of a bill while allowing the rest of it to pass into law. Fort-two governors have this power.

- **5. (A) is correct.** Legislative professionalism refers to a set of reforms designed to enhance the capacity of state legislatures to perform their policymaking role more effectively and more efficiently. The three most significant reforms have been the lengthening of legislative sessions, increasing legislators' salary, and increasing the size of the legislative staff.

- **6. (D) is correct.** Remember that circle (or pie) graphs compare parts of a whole (100 percent); the figures do *not* describe dollar amounts. Since the state "pie" is so much bigger than a local "pie," 3 percent of state expenses can be much more than six percent of local expenses. Education is by far the biggest priority of local governments, and they would be in charge of the needs of individual schools.

- **7. (E) is correct.** One of the most noticeable and significant changes among state elected officials over the past forty years has been the growth in the number of women and racial minorities in positions of power. During this period, more women have been elected governor and more women and minorities have been elected to state legislatures. More women also assumed leadership positions within state legislatures.

- **8. (C) is correct.** State government revenues are derived from a variety of sources, but the largest share comes from taxes. Taxes make up almost 43 percent of state revenue.

- **9. (E) is correct.** Dillon's Rule, named after an Iowa judge who expressed the idea in a court decision, is the principle that local governments have only those powers that are explicitly given them by the states. This means local governments are totally subservient to the state government.

- **10. (D) is correct.** Special districts are the fast growing form of local governance. Generally they provide only a single service like flood control, fire protection, or public transportation. Special districts tend to be highly flexible units of government because their boundary lines can be drawn across county and municipal borders. They help local governments carry out their responsibilities more efficiently. One criticism of special districts is that they are not accountable to the voters. There is little direct public participation in their decision making.

Part III

Sample Tests with Answers and Explanations

On the following pages are two sample exams. They mirror the actual AP exam in format and question types. Set aside a time to take these exams, timing yourself as you will be timed when you take the real test, to prepare yourself for your actual test-taking experience.

United States Government & Politics Section I

Time: 45 minutes
60 Questions

Directions: Each of the questions or incomplete statements below is followed by five suggested answers or completions. Select the one that is best in each case and then fill in the corresponding oval on the answer sheet.

1. Political action committees were created by campaign reform laws to

   (A) involve the public more directly in presidential campaigns.

   (B) regulate how groups such as business and labor contribute to campaigns.

   (C) finance challengers' campaigns to eliminate the advantages of incumbency.

   (D) pay for candidates' air time because it has become the most expensive feature in a campaign.

   (E) limit the influence of political parties over election outcomes.

2. All of the following are examples of entitlement programs EXCEPT

   (A) Social Security.

   (B) Medicare.

   (C) defense contracts.

   (D) veteran's benefits.

   (E) agricultural subsidies.

Political Action Committees—Number of Committee Type: 1980 to 2001 (As of December 31)									
Committee type	1980	1985	1990	1995	1997	1998	1999	2000	2001
Total	2,551	3,992	4,172	4,016	3,844	3,798	3,835	3,706	3,907
Corporate	1,206	1,710	1,795	1,674	1,597	1,567	1,548	1,523	1,545
Labor	297	388	346	334	332	321	318	316	317
Trades/membership/health	576	695	774	815	825	821	844	812	860
Nonconnected	374	1,003	1,062	1,020	931	935	972	902	1,026
Cooperative	42	54	59	44	42	39	38	39	41
Corporation without stock	56	142	136	129	117	115	115	114	118

Source: U.S. Federal Election Commission, press release of January 2002.

3. Which of the following generalizations is supported by the information in the chart above?

   (A) Nonconnected PACs grew in number more sharply between 1980 and 2001 than any other kind of PAC.

   (B) The most dramatic change in the number of PACs occurred between 1985 and 1990.

   (C) There are only a few cooperative PACs because these are the most difficult type to meet the approval of the Federal Election Commission.

   (D) Business PACs spend the most money on congressional elections.

   (E) All types of PACs have increased in number dramatically since 1980.

4. Federal district courts are the only federal courts in which

   (A) the facts are presented by both parties in the case.

   (B) *amicus curiae* briefs are registered with the court.

   (C) the Solicitor General appears for oral argument.

   (D) juries are impaneled to decide cases.

   (E) three judge panels decide the outcome of cases.

5. The government began to pursue civil rights in the 1950s when

   (A) Congress passed the Voting Rights Act.

   (B) civil rights activists marched on Washington to demand government action.

   (C) the Supreme Court declared public school segregation unconstitutional.

   (D) states agreed to discontinue their use of poll taxes as a means of preventing people from voting.

   (E) the president issued an executive order to desegregate all public transportation.

6. Which of the following statements about the president as commander in chief is true?

   (A) The president has the authority to declare war for up to 60 days without consulting Congress.

   (B) The president can decide if and when to use weapons of mass destruction in times of war.

   (C) Presidents with no prior military experience are not allowed to make major military decisions alone.

   (D) The president is required by law to consult with the Joint Chiefs of Staff before deploying the military.

   (E) The president is a nonvoting member of the Senate Armed Services Committee.

7. Interest groups play a role in the federal judicial process in all of the following ways EXCEPT by

   (A) giving campaign contributions to judicial nominees.

   (B) lobbying the Judiciary Committee about a judicial nominee.

   (C) filing *amicus curiae* briefs.

   (D) having their lawyers represent a plaintiff.

   (E) filing a class action suit.

8. Presidents exercise their influence over the ideology of federal courts by

   (A) trying to appoint only judges who agree with their ideology and political views.

   (B) ordering Congress to impeach judges who are too liberal or too conservative.

   (C) demoting judges to lower courts.

   (D) allowing them to hear only those cases on which judges are likely to agree with the president's point of view.

   (E) meeting with members of the Senate Judiciary Committee when they are performing oversight.

9. The electoral votes of most states are allocated by which of the following methods?

(A) Each party's candidate receives electoral votes based on his or her percentage of the state's popular vote.

(B) Each elector chooses the candidate whom he or she feels is best suited to represent the needs of the state.

(C) The winner of the popular election in the state receives 75 percent of the state's electoral votes and the loser receives 25 percent.

(D) All of the state's electors cast their votes for whichever candidate won the state's popular vote.

(E) The loser in the popular election receives one electoral vote and the winner receives the rest of the state's electoral votes.

10. Which of the following groups is most likely to vote in elections?

(A) People under the age of 21

(B) Senior citizens

(C) People without a college degree

(D) People with no party affiliation

(E) Men with low-income jobs

11. The Supreme Court asserted which of the following principles in *Marbury* v. *Madison?*

(A) The Fourteenth Amendment guarantees all individual freedoms under state laws.

(B) Freedom of religion is guaranteed, but some religious practices may violate the establishment clause.

(C) Under the Tenth Amendment, the federal government can regulate commerce among states.

(D) The exclusionary rule must be upheld in all state court trials.

(E) The Supreme Court has the power to declare laws passed by Congress unconstitutional.

12. In the process of political socialization, individuals

(A) form their political beliefs.

(B) participate in a direct democracy.

(C) attend functions organized by political parties.

(D) evaluate and select their representatives.

(E) engage in political protest against a law.

13. The failure of the Articles of Confederation and necessity for a new Constitution were made evident by the

(A) success of the American Revolution.

(B) legislature's inability to select a president.

(C) need for a bicameral legislature.

(D) government's inability to subdue Shays' Rebellion.

(E) excess of centralized power in the national government.

14. Voter turnout in the United States is low in part because

(A) minority groups still struggle for the right to vote in southern states.

(B) registering to vote has become more difficult.

(C) voters see little difference between the platforms of the two parties' candidates.

(D) many low-income people are not able to pass the literacy test required to vote.

(E) candidates do little to try to attract voters.

15. Which of the following statements is true about U.S. budget deficits?

(A) The first federal budget deficit did not occur until the 1990s.

(B) The Constitution requires a balanced federal budget.

(C) Large budget deficits make the U.S. government more financially dependent on foreign investors.

(D) Budget deficits have no practical effect on individual citizens.

(E) The Democratic and Republican parties have agreed that the deficit issue should not become an issue in presidential campaigns.

16. Congress performs legislative oversight over executive departments by

(A) hiring and firing department heads.

(B) determining departments' budgets.

(C) vetoing department proposals.

(D) issuing impoundment bills.

(E) coordinating department activities with the president.

17. Members of Congress most often vote according to

    (A) their own policy preferences.

    (B) the needs of their constituents.

    (C) their relationship with the president.

    (D) their party affiliation.

    (E) the ideology of their geographic region.

18. Which of the following is NOT specifically prohibited by the Constitution?

    (A) Gender bias in the workplace

    (B) Self-incrimination

    (C) Slavery

    (D) National religion

    (E) Cruel and unusual punishment

19. Regulatory agencies are most likely to turn to the industries they oversee when they

    (A) have leaders who need campaign contributions.

    (B) want to deregulate.

    (C) have an unambiguous policy to implement.

    (D) are making budget proposals to Congress.

    (E) are trying to win general public approval.

20. The largest federal expenditure is

    (A) national defense.

    (B) public education.

    (C) Social Security.

    (D) grants to the states.

    (E) political campaigns.

OUTLAYS BY MAJOR SPENDING CATEGORY, 1970–2002 *(in billions of dollars)*				
Year	Discretionary Spending	Entitlements and Other Mandatory Spending	Net Interest	Total Outlays
1970	120.3	72.5	14.4	195.6
1975	158.0	169.4	23.2	332.3
1980	276.3	291.2	52.5	590.9
1985	415.8	448.2	129.5	946.4
1990	500.6	626.9	184.3	1,253.2
1995	544.9	818.5	232.1	1,515.8
2000	614.8	1,029.8	223.0	1,788.8

SOURCE: Congressional Budget Office.

21. Which of the following are true of the data in the table above?

I. Entitlements and mandatory spending are the fastest-growing federal expenditures.

II. Since 1975 it would require congressional action not to spend a majority of federal outlays.

III. The federal government spends about one-third of its revenues on entitlements and mandatory spending.

IV. Payments made toward interest on the national debt typically double every five years.

(A) III only

(B) I and II only

(C) II and III only

(D) III and IV only

(E) I and IV only

22. The two main responsibilities of congressional committees are

    (A) making and implementing policies.

    (B) setting the dates for federal elections and confirming the appointment of federal judges.

    (C) writing guidelines for federal programs and educating the public.

    (D) reviewing proposed legislation and performing legislative oversight.

    (E) suggesting candidates for cabinet positions and writing tax codes.

23. All of the following are recent trends in presidential nominations and campaigns EXCEPT

    (A) declining party identification among voters.

    (B) increasing costs of campaigning.

    (C) decreasing importance of national conventions.

    (D) increasing reliance on PACs to sustain campaigns.

    (E) infrequency of presidential primaries among states.

24. Single-issue groups, as opposed to other types of groups, represent people in the electorate who

    (A) have little political access and influence.

    (B) donate money to political campaigns.

    (C) pressure candidates to be less ambiguous about their ideology.

    (D) feel strongly about a certain cause.

    (E) advocate campaign finance reform.

25. Which of the following presidential appointments requires Senate confirmation?

    (A) The National Security Council.

    (B) The Chief of Staff.

    (C) The White House Counsel.

    (D) The Council of Economic Advisors.

    (E) The Secretary of State.

26. According to the Constitution, the vice president

    (A) chairs all cabinet meetings

    (B) is ineligible to run for president after two terms as vice president

    (C) is the president of the Senate

    (D) must be of the same party as the president

    (E) is an ex-officio member of the Council of Economic Advisors

27. The Social Security program is endangered primarily because

    (A) the U.S. birth rate has increased dramatically over the past decade.

    (B) the program has lost public support in recent years..

    (C) the number of contributors to the program is growing at a much slower rate than the number of recipients.

    (D) large federal budget deficits have reduced the amount of tax revenue collected in support of the program..

    (E) the program has become more identified with racial minorities.

28. The Supreme Court has upheld which of the following in its interpretation of the freedom of speech?

    (A) All forms of speech, including obscenity, are protected under the First Amendment.

    (B) The government cannot under any circumstances censor information.

    (C) Protests against the government are not protected under the First Amendment.

    (D) Forms of symbolic speech are protected under the First Amendment.

    (E) The freedom of speech is guaranteed by federal law, but it does not have to be upheld by the states.

29. The rise of the primary election system has led to

    (A) the increasing role of political parties in presidential elections.

    (B) the public's more direct involvement in the election of the president.

    (C) a decline in media coverage of presidential campaigns.

    (D) a shift in power from national to state party organizations.

    (E) fewer candidates seeking each party's nomination.

30. Congress exercises influence over foreign policy in which of the following ways?

    I. Declaring war

    II. Confirming ambassadors

    III. Appropriating money

    IV. Ratifying treaties

    (A) I only.

    (B) III only.

    (C) I, II, and III only.

    (D) I, III, and IV only.

    (E) All of the above.

31. Unlike members of the House of Representatives, senators can influence policy debates by

    (A) relying on partisan support.

    (B) calling for a vote.

    (C) using a filibuster.

    (D) forming a presidential coalition.

    (E) running televised ads.

32. Bureaucracies are often criticized as being undemocratic because

    (A) they are not directly accountable to the people.

    (B) they utilized a merit system for hiring.

    (C) citizens tend to have low opinions of them.

    (D) the courts have no influence over their actions.

    (E) they are overly influenced by campaign contributions.

33. All of the following influence the selection of federal judges and Supreme Court justices EXCEPT

    (A) Campaign contributions.

    (B) Partisanship.

    (C) Ideology.

    (D) Experience.

    (E) Judicial philosophy.

34. A president can be removed from office in which of the following ways?

(A) The Supreme Court rules that he is incompetent or has violated the law.

(B) In a recall, citizens can vote to remove the president from office.

(C) The House votes to impeach him, and the Senate tries and convicts him.

(D) The Senate votes to impeach him, and the Supreme Court tries the president.

(E) Both houses of Congress vote to remove the president by a simple majority.

Average Yearly Presidential Approval

Source: George C. Edwards, III, *Presidential Approval* (Baltimore, MD: Johns Hopkins University Press, 1990); updated by the authors.

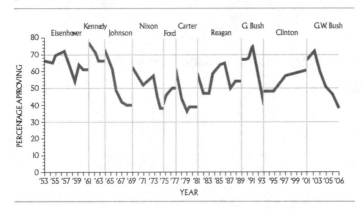

35. All of the following statements accurately describe the data in the graph EXCEPT

(A) Most presidents experience a drop in public approval ratings over their terms.

(B) Presidents G. Bush, Johnson, and G.W. Bush lost the most public approval during their presidencies.

(C) Ronald Reagan was our most popular president ever.

(D) On average, most presidents have approval ratings of more than 50 percent.

(E) Democratic presidents usually have higher public approval ratings than Republicans.

36. Proponents of the pluralist theory argue that for the most part, power is evenly distributed among interest groups because

(A) the public participates equally in different types of interest groups.

(B) all interest groups receive the same amount of federal funds.

(C) each policy area is assigned a limited number of related interest groups.

(D) interest groups each get the same attention from politicians.

(E) competition prevents any one group from becoming more influential.

37. The government institution responsible for the drawing of congressional district lines is the

    (A) state's governor.

    (B) Senate Committee on Governmental Affairs.

    (C) state's legislature, or its delegated body (Ohio has an apportionment board).

    (D) House Rules Committee.

    (E) Department of the Interior.

38. All of the following are true of two-party systems, EXCEPT

    (A) they encourage moderation in policymaking and discourage change.

    (B) they offers voters no choice among ideologies.

    (C) they usually include a liberal and a conservative party.

    (D) they rely on popular elections to change the party in power.

    (E) they allow parties to choose their own leaders in the legislature.

39. The media has the most influence over which of the following aspects of the presidential selection process?

    (A) The way electoral votes are distributed

    (B) The outcome of the popular election

    (C) Who decides to run for office

    (D) The outcome of primary elections

    (E) The party's national convention

40. The Framers' distrust of the public when writing the Constitution is best illustrated by the

    (A) Electoral College.

    (B) Bill of Rights.

    (C) process of electing members of the House of Representatives.

    (D) creation of a bicameral legislature.

    (E) ability to amend the Constitution.

41. Congress increased the power of the federal government to enforce regulations in employment by passing the

    (A) Fourteenth Amendment.

    (B) Civil Rights Act.

    (C) Fifteenth Amendment.

    (D) Equal Rights Amendment.

    (E) Voting Rights Act.

42. The Hatch Act helps maintain a nonpartisan bureaucracy because it

    (A) creates a federal commission on which half the members are Democrats and half are Republican.

    (B) insures that federal employees are hired based on merit.

    (C) requires all federal employees to register to vote as independents.

    (D) requires all federal agencies to have staffs that are balanced along party lines.

    (E) prohibits government employees in their official capacities from active participation in partisan politics.

43. In *Miranda* v. *Arizona*, the Supreme Court ruled that persons accused of a crime

    (A) cannot be denied bail.

    (B) have the right to a fair trial.

    (C) have rights during police questioning.

    (D) have equal protection under the law.

    (E) cannot be searched illegally.

44. The principle that the Constitution gives states all powers neither granted to the federal government nor denied the states refers to

    (A) states' rights.

    (B) reserved powers.

    (C) federal supremacy.

    (D) concurrent powers.

    (E) federalism.

45. Critical elections tend to occur under which of the following circumstances?

(A) When a third-party candidate wins some electoral votes

(B) After a presidential scandal has been exposed in the media

(C) When the United States engages in a military operation

(D) After a serious domestic crisis alters the political agenda

(E) When one of the parties suffers a major defeat in a congressional election

46. Which of the following statements is true about Congress' influence over Supreme Court decision making?

(A) Congress can pass laws to prohibit judicial activism.

(B) The Senate can filibuster court decisions.

(C) Congress has significant control over the court's appellate jurisdiction.

(D) The Senate can decide which cases the Supreme Court will hear.

(E) District court judges are reviewed by Congress every ten years.

47. Which of the following statements are true of political parties?

I. The United States has a multiparty system.

II. The electorate is becoming increasingly independent of political parties.

III. The use of television advertising allows candidates more independence from their political parties.

IV. Political party organizations are exercising greater control over the choice of candidates.

(A) II only

(B) III only

(C) II and III only

(D) I, III, and IV only

(E) II, III, and IV only

48. Each of the following helps explain the incumbency advantage of members of Congress EXCEPT

(A) the franking privilege

(B) the pattern of campaign contributions

(C) casework

(D) the low standing of Congress in public opinion

(E) name recognition

49. Implementation of public policy is most successful when

   (A) the goals of the policy and the authority of the implementers are clear.

   (B) there is a court order mandating compliance with the policy

   (C) the executive branch has pre-cleared the policy with the federal judiciary.

   (D) multiple agencies and bureaucrats are involved.

   (E) the policy originated in the executive branch as opposed to the legislative branch.

50. Interest groups differ from political parties in which of the following ways?

   (A) Interest groups link the public to the political process.

   (B) Interest groups pursue general policy goals in the political arena.

   (C) Interest groups try to shape specific policy goals.

   (D) Interest groups are not allowed to play any part in political campaigns.

   (E) Interest groups unite politicians with the same political ideology.

51. Which of the following is true of relationships between the president and Congress?

   (A) Presidents usually have little success in forming presidential coalitions in Congress.

   (B) Presidents work most with minority party leaders to win minority support.

   (C) Policy gridlock results when the president's party is not the majority in Congress.

   (D) Members of Congress almost always vote in favor of presidential initiatives.

   (E) Presidents usually have closer relationships with members of the House than they do with senators.

52. The elderly fare better than the poor in social welfare budget battles for which of the following reasons?

   (A) The Constitution requires a certain amount of spending for the elderly, but not the poor.

   (B) Most social services for the elderly come from state governments.

   (C) Lobbyists representing the poor are not allowed to make campaign contributions.

   (D) The elderly are more organized and better represented politically than the poor.

   (E) There are more elderly people in the US than there are poor people.

53. Which of the following statements accurately describes iron triangles?

(A) Iron triangles are composed of members of the military-industrial complex, Congress, and the Defense Department.

(B) Iron triangles are formed in specific policy areas to advance policies among groups that benefit each other mutually.

(C) Iron triangles are formed to generate support for presidential proposals in Congress.

(D) Iron triangles help coordinate policy among the executive, legislative, and judicial branches.

(E) Iron triangles help perform policy implementation among the local, state, and federal levels of government.

54. Which of the following statements represent a prevalent myth about the federal bureaucracy?

   I. The bureaucracy is growing bigger and bigger each year.

  II. Most federal bureaucrats work in Washington, D.C.

 III. Citizens are generally dissatisfied with the bureaucracy.

 IV. The bureaucracy makes government inefficient and cumbersome.

(A) I only

(B) IV only

(C) I and II only

(D) II, III and IV only

(E) All of the above

55. The Establishment Clause, as interpreted by the Supreme Court, prevents

(A) states from passing laws that conflict with federal laws.

(B) the government from violating the rights of individuals.

(C) Congress from exercising any powers beyond those necessary to execute the law.

(D) gender discrimination in the workplace.

(E) the incorporation of religion into policy.

56. *Regents of the University of California* v. *Bakke* is a Supreme Court case that addressed

    (A) affirmative action.

    (B) prayer in school.

    (C) the rights of the accused.

    (D) the right of privacy.

    (E) desegregation through busing.

57. One of a president's most powerful tools for gaining support of his proposals is

    (A) his financial resources.

    (B) executive privilege.

    (C) "going public" to sway public opinion.

    (D) senatorial courtesy.

    (E) his cabinet.

58. Which of the following statements accurately describe traditional Republican Party economic positions?

    I. Republicans place greater emphasis on full employment than Democrats.

    II. Republicans tend to worry about inflation more than Democrats..

    III. Republican economic positions tend to appeal to the working class and unions.

    IV. Republicans tend to favor higher income tax rates.

    (A) I only

    (B) II only

    (C) II and III only

    (D) I and IV only

    (E) I, II, and III only

59. Members of Congress are more likely to vote according to their personal ideology when

    (A) the issue is not well known by their constituents.

    (B) they are up for reelection.

    (C) the piece of legislation was introduced by the president.

    (D) they are on the committee responsible for the piece of legislation.

    (E) interest groups have been actively involved with the piece of legislation.

60. In the era of globalization, which of the following presidential powers is becoming important?

   (A) Vetoing legislation

   (B) Negotiating economic agreements

   (C) Declaring war

   (D) Authorizing the use of weapons of mass destruction

   (E) Appointment of Supreme Court Justices

END OF SECTION I.

IF YOU FINISH BEFORE TIME IS CALLED, YOU MAY CHECK YOUR WORK ON THIS SECTION.

DO NOT GO ON TO SECTION II UNTIL YOU ARE TOLD TO DO SO.

United States Government & Politics
Section II

Time: 100 minutes

Directions: You have 100 minutes to answer all four of the following questions. It is suggested that you take a few minutes to plan and outline each answer. *Spend approximately one-fourth of your time (25 minutes) on each question.* Illustrate your essay with substantive examples where appropriate. Make certain to number each of your answers as the question is numbered below.

1. In the American democracy, political parties use two different systems for selecting delegates to the national party conventions that nominate presidential candidates.

   a. Explain how caucuses select delegates to the national convention.

   b. Explain how primaries select delegates to the national convention.

   c. Discuss one consequence of "frontloading" the delegate selection process.

2. The mass media has a major effect on politics in the United States. It has both positive and negative consequences for the political process.

   a. Identify and describe 2 positives effects that the media has on the political process.

   b. Identify and describe 2 negative effects that the media has on the political process.

Would you say the government is pretty much run by a few big interests looking out for themselves or that it is run for the benefit of all the people?

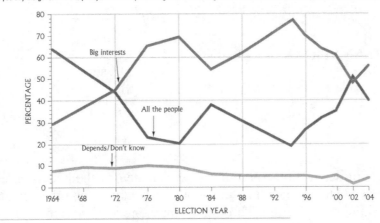

Source: Authors' analysis of 1964–2004 American National Election Study data.

3. The above graph shows the results of a survey in which respondents answered whether they perceive the government as being run for the benefit of a few big business interests rather than for the benefit of the public. Using this information and your knowledge of U.S. politics:

   a. Briefly describe a trend in public opinion depicted in this graph.

   b. Identify two factors that may have produced the trend you describe.

   c. Explain how each of these factors you identify has had an impact of the trend you describe.

4. The Tenth Amendment reserves for the states all powers neither denied nor designated to the federal government in the Constitution. For decades, this afforded states a good deal of freedom in writing their state laws. However, the ratification of the Fourteenth Amendment allowed the Supreme Court to exercise its authority over the states in an attempt to advance the civil liberties of all Americans.

   a. What provision of the Fourteenth Amendment has been used by the Supreme Court to exercise its authority over the states for the purpose of advancing civil liberties?

   b. Identify two areas in which civil liberties protections have been extended to the states, and discuss the specific case which accomplished this task in each area.

ANSWERS AND EXPLANATIONS

Practice Test 1

Section I

- **1. (B) is correct.** Political action committees were created by the Federal Election Campaign Act of 1974 to regulate how much business, labor, and other groups could contribute to a candidate's election. Through them, the federal government can better regulate campaign financing, because all PACs must register with the Federal Election Commission and report all of their spending activities to the government and the public.

- **2. (C) is correct.** Entitlement programs are a form of mandatory spending because everyone entitled to the benefits of the program must be paid. Congress cannot control these expenditures unless it changes the eligibility requirements of the program, which it is unlikely to do unless such measures are absolutely necessary. Defense contracts clearly do not fit this definition.

- **3. (A) is correct.** According to the data in the chart, the number of nonconnected PACs nearly tripled between 1980 and 1985 alone, increasing from 374 to 1,003. Although this number did not change much in the next few decades and even declined a bit, in 2001 nonconnected PACs were the third most predominant type, totaling 1,026.

- **4. (D) is correct.** There are no juries in the courts of appeal, the Supreme Court, and all other federal courts except the district courts.

- **5. (C) is correct.** The Supreme Court's 1954 landmark decision in *Brown* v. *Board of Education* was a dramatic reinterpretation of what the Constitution required. This began "the Second Reconstruction," in which the Court, Congress, and the executive took steps to advance civil rights.

- **6. (B) is correct.** As commander in chief of military forces, the president decides if and when American armed forces use weapons of mass destruction in times of war.

- **7. (A) is correct.** Interest groups do attempt to influence the appointment of federal judges, but not by running advertisements. The process of filling judgeships is far removed from the public—the only means of influence it has is by influencing the election of the president and members of the Senate, who, in turn, choose judges. Advertisements aimed at swaying public opinion therefore have little use in this case.

- **8. (A) is correct.** Presidents work hard to seek and appoint judges who agree with their own political ideology. Not only would the judges be more likely to favor the president's agenda, but also (because they have no term limit) they would continue to influence policy long after the president's term has ended. The appointment of Supreme Court

276

justices is a golden opportunity for presidents, but it is also one that is highly scrutinized by Congress.

- **9. (D) is correct.** Most states award their electoral votes in a "winner-take-all" system. Whichever candidate wins the popular vote in the state receives all of that state's electoral votes. One criticism of the electoral system is that this gives larger states an unfair advantage because they have more electors than smaller states.

- **10. (B) is correct.** Senior citizens have a high voter turnout rate. They tend to be the most active and informed group in the electorate, especially because Social Security and health care have become major political issues. People with college degrees or any party affiliation also vote in higher percentages, but young people and people of low income do not.

- **11. (E) is correct.** In the 1803 case of *Marbury* v. *Madison,* the Supreme Court under Chief Justice John Marshall first asserted its power of judicial review. Judicial review allows the Supreme Court, whose responsibility is to interpret the Constitution, to declare laws passed by Congress unconstitutional. This power helped solidify the system of checks and balances among the three branches of government.

- **12. (A) is correct.** Political socialization is the process through which citizens learn about government and form their political beliefs. Family, school, the media, and religion play major parts in influencing how people see the government and with which party they identify themselves.

- **13. (D) is correct.** Shays' Rebellion occurred when a group of Massachusetts farmers raided several courthouses in protest of the government's foreclosure of their farms. Under the Articles of Confederation, the national government was not able to raise a militia to stop the group, and so the rebellion was an embarrassing failure for the new government. It served as the final proof that the government established by the Articles lacked centralized power and legitimacy.

- **14. (C) is correct.** People who have not voted often cite the generally indistinguishable ideologies of the candidates of the two parties as one major reason for their inaction. This perception may be partly the result of the media's focus on the campaign game rather than on the two candidates' platforms, but it is also due to the fact that, because there are only two major parties in the United States, each one must remain near the center of the political spectrum to win elections.

- **15. C) is correct.** Large budget deficits make the U.S. government more financially dependent on foreign investors, other governments, and individuals. Foreign investors currently hold one-fifth of the U.S. national debt. **C) is correct.** Large budget deficits make the U.S. government more financially dependent on foreign investors, governments, and individuals. Foreign investors currently hold one-fifth of the U.S. national debt.

- **16. (B) is correct.** One of the ways Congress oversees the activities of the departments in the executive branch is by determining their budgets. Each department submits its budget proposal to the president, who in turn coordinates them and submits his proposal to Congress. Congress makes the final decision about how much each department can spend on its programs and activities.

- **17. (D) is correct.** Members of Congress do sometimes vote according to their own ideology. However, they most often vote according to their party affiliation. In doing so, they may presume that the constituents who elected them as a Democrat or Republican probably agree with that party's political ideology. By voting along the party line, they may also be voting according to their constituency's preferences.

- **18. (A) is correct.** Gender discrimination is not specifically addressed in the Constitution or its amendments. However, it is prohibited by law as a form of civil rights discrimination.

- **19. (D) is correct.** Regulatory agencies and industries are most likely to work together when Congress is appropriating funds during the budgetary process. Industries therefore increase their lobbying pressure during the budgetary process to convince the relevant committees of their need for the money they have requested.

- **20. (C) is correct.** In the past few decades, Social Security has become the largest federal expenditure. It alone accounts for nearly a quarter of all expenditures.

- **21. (B) is correct.** Statement I is correct: by 2000 expenditures for entitlements and other forms of mandatory spending grew to 14 times the amount in 1970. According to the table, these are now the biggest federal expenditures by far; no other expenditures grew nearly that much. Statement II is also correct. It would require congressional action not to spend either "Entitlements and Other Mandatory Spending" and "Net Interest." This spending is sometimes called "uncontrollable" because it will occur unless action is taken.

- **22. (D) is correct.** Congressional committees play an important role in the legislative process. They review and assess bills for their feasibility and consequences, and they either revise or kill them. If they pass a bill on to the floor, they make a recommendation for it, and many other congresspeople are likely to vote according to the recommendation. The other major function of a committee is to perform oversight of all the federal departments and agencies under its jurisdiction. Committees do this by setting agencies' budgets and by assessing their performance and activities in committee hearings.

- **23. (E) is correct.** The use of presidential primaries has been increasing, not decreasing. Almost every state now holds a primary election. These have, in turn, led to a much longer campaign season and have added significantly to the cost of campaigning. They make the nomination of presidential candidates a process that involves voters directly, at least in some states.

- **24. (D) is correct.** Single-issue groups attract people who feel very strongly about one particular issue. These issues, such as abortion or gun control, often incite emotional responses. Single-issue groups pressure senators and representatives to vote according to that one issue, and members themselves often vote for political officials based solely on their stand on the issue.

- **25. E) is correct.** Because they are a member of the president's cabinet, nominees for Secretary of State, must be confirmed by the Senate. The National Security Council, the Chief of Staff, the White House Counsel, and the Council of Economic Advisors are considered to be part of the president's personal staff of advisors and are not required to be approved by the Senate.

- **26. (C) is correct.** The Constitution assigns vice presidents the relatively minor tasks of presiding over the Senate and voting in case of a tie among the senators. the process of removing a president from office is as follows: 1) the House votes to impeach the president; 2) the Senate carries out the impeachment trial; and 3) the Senate must have a two-thirds majority vote to convict and remove the president. Statements I, III, and IV describe these steps.

- **27. (C) is correct.** The Social Security dilemma is the number of Social Security contributors (the workers) is growing slowly, while the number of recipients (the retired) is growing rapidly.

- **28. (D) is correct.** In the 1989 case of *Texas* v. *Johnson,* the Supreme Court determined that flag burning, a form of symbolic speech, is protected under the First Amendment. Symbolic speech is that which communicates nonverbally; participating in parades or protests is another form of symbolic speech.

- **29. (B) is correct.** Primary elections give voters the opportunity to participate more directly in the presidential election process. In their state's primary election, people can nominate either a candidate or delegates pledged to that candidate. This process circumvents the traditional role of political parties in the nomination process, especially when a blanket primary is used.

- **30. (E) is correct.** Although the president is the chief initiator of foreign policy in the U.S., Congress exercises influence over foreign policy through its powers to declare war, appropriate funds, ratify treaties, and confirm ambassadors to foreign nations. Congress has full authority over all military expenditures, including foreign aid and the budgets of the State Department, the Department of Defense, and the CIA.

- **31. (C) is correct.** Only senators have the ability to use a filibuster to hold up debate on a bill. The Senate imposes no restrictions on the length of time for debate over a piece of legislation, so senators are free to talk as long as it takes for their colleagues to lose interest and choose not to vote on the bill. Southern senators made effective use of the filibuster during debates over civil rights legislation.

- **32. (A) is correct.** Although they make vital decisions and perform essential services for government and the people, bureaucrats are not directly accountable to citizens the way the president and Congress are. This has led to the criticism that the bureaucracy is an undemocratic branch of government.

- **33. (B) is correct.** There is no evidence that campaign contributions to presidential races is a major factor in determining who president's nominate for federal judgeships.

- **34. (C) is correct.** The Constitution sets forth the process of removing a president from office. First, the House votes to impeach the president. Then the Senate tries the president, with the chief justice of the Supreme Court presiding. The Senate must reach a two-thirds vote to remove the president from office. Only two presidents have been impeached, but neither was removed from office through this process.

- **35. (E) is correct.** John Kennedy and George Bush achieved the highest approval ratings in the graph. Bush was a Republican, so it is not true that Democratic presidents have the highest ratings. Eisenhower, another Republican, also maintained fairly high approval ratings. In fact, overall, Democrats have achieved the lowest approval ratings.

- **36. (E) is correct.** Pluralists believe that interest groups have about the same amount of power because they must compete with each other for influence. If, for example, one group increases its efforts to reach politicians, other groups will quickly follow suit to catch up and will, therefore, balance the system again.

- **37. (C) is correct.** State legislatures have the task of drawing congressional district lines for their state. Every 10 years, the population count of the national census determines how many House seats each state receives. If seats must be reapportioned or redistricted, the state legislature, or a body it designates, redraws district lines.

- **38. (A) is correct.** With only two parties offering policy alternatives, there is little opportunity or incentive for political change. Each party, to draw in a majority of the electorate, stays toward the middle of the road and maintains the status quo. If it were to move too far left or right, or to take a risk in introducing a radically new policy, it would probably lose the support of some voters.

- **39. (D) is correct.** One of the major criticisms held against the primary system is that it allows the media too much influence over election results, particularly in the early primaries. Media attention skews the results by branding winners and losers so early in the campaign process that losers have little chance to score victories in later primaries.

- **40. (A) is correct.** The authors of the Constitution were a group of elite intellectuals who distrusted leaving government too much in the hands of the uneducated masses. Therefore, they arranged for the president to be chosen by the Electoral College, a group of chosen electors, rather than by the public at large. Although today citizens cast individual votes for president, the Electoral College still casts the final vote. In fact, Al Gore won the popular vote in the 2000 election but lost the presidency because of the distribution of electoral votes.

- **41. (B) is correct.** By passing the Civil Rights Act of 1964, Congress outlawed discrimination in the workplace. Consequently, the Justice Department was granted authority to enforce equality in employment and to pursue violators of the Civil Rights Act.

- **42. (E) is correct.** The Hatch Act, originally passed in 1939 and amended most recently in 1993, prohibits civil service employees from actively participating in partisan politics while on duty. The act was intended to help insure a fair and impartial bureaucracy, and to protect bureaucrats from coercion on the part of superiors or political appointees.

- **43. (C) is correct.** The Supreme Court enhanced the rights of the accused in its decision in *Miranda* v. *Arizona*. This decision required that all people arrested for a crime be informed of their rights before questioning.

- **44. (B) is correct.** The Tenth Amendment articulates the reserved powers of the states. All powers not denied by the Constitution or specifically designated to the federal government are held by the states. Many states have used this principle of reserved powers to their advantage, particularly in the case of civil rights. Many Supreme Court cases of the twentieth century focused on limiting the power of states to make laws that conflict with federal law.

- **45. (D) is correct.** Most critical elections follow a serious domestic problem that significantly alters the political landscape. The Great Depression is one such crisis that generated a critical election. Republicans lost power to a new coalition of Democrats that included workers, minority groups, and southerners.

- **46. C) is correct.** In many instances federal courts' jurisdiction derives from Congress and not the Constitution. The Constitution provides Congress with the discretion to determine which category of cases appellate courts may hear.

- **47. (C) is correct.** Political parties are losing power because both candidates and voters have come to rely less on them. Because candidates can address voters directly through television, the public does not have to fall back on party identification to choose candidates. At the same time, candidates who use television do not need their party to help attract voters as much as in the past.

- **48. (D) is correct.** More than 90 percent of all congressional incumbents seeking reelection win. This occurs in spite of the fact that people hold a low opinion of Congress as an institution.

- **49. (A) is correct.** If the goals of a policy are not clear to those who have to implement it, and if those who have to implement lack the authority to act definitively, then the policy in question is not likely to be well implemented or received.

- **50. (C) is correct.** Interest groups concentrate most of their efforts on shaping policy during the political process. They maintain frequent contact with lawmakers while Congress is in session. Political parties, on the other hand, try to shape the policy agenda by having their candidates elected to office. They therefore apply their efforts mostly to campaigns.

- **51. (C) is correct.** The relationship between the president and Congress tends to be strained when the president's party is not the majority party in Congress. The two often have conflicting policy goals and work together less often than do a president and

Congress of the same political party. Policy gridlock has occurred more frequently in recent years because this kind of divided government has been more common.

- **52. (D) is correct.** The elderly fare better than the poor in social welfare budget battles because they are more organized, more politically active and better represented than the poor. The elderly are also widely considered to be among the deserving poor.

- **53. (B) is correct.** Iron triangles are unofficial political entities composed of interest groups, agencies, and legislative committees that are all concerned with the same policy area. Each group helps the others to help itself in the policy arena. For example, interest groups lobby committee members for larger agency budgets so that the interest groups will benefit from the agency's money.

- **54. (E) is correct.** All of these statements are false or misleading. The federal bureaucracy is not growing bigger and bigger each year. Only about 12 percent of federal bureaucrats work in Washington, D.C. California, with more than 245,000 federal employees leads the nation in the number of federal bureaucrats. Most citizens are generally satisfied with the service they receive from the bureaucracy.

- **55. (E) is correct.** The Establishment Clause, located in the First Amendment of the Constitution, establishes the separation of church and state in all levels of government. Religious qualifications cannot be imposed on public officials, and the government cannot regulate, restrict, or endorse religious worship.

- **56. (A) is correct.** Both cases dealt with the constitutionality of affirmative action. In *Bakke,* the Supreme Court upheld the principle of affirmative action but banned the use of quotas to establish racial diversity.

- **57. (C) is correct.** A president relies heavily on the power of public opinion, because, with the backing of the public, members of Congress have little recourse but to support him as well. This power has grown in recent decades as presidents have been able to communicate directly with the public through television.

- **58. (B) is correct.** Republicans tend to worry about inflation more than Democrats. Republicans generally try to prevent inflation, even at the risk of rising unemployment.

- **59. (A) is correct.** Because their constituents usually are familiar with only the most publicized issues, members of Congress have many opportunities to vote according to their own ideology on smaller, less publicized issues. In theory, because they were elected by people who share their ideology, representatives and senators would still be voting according to the wishes of their constituents.

- **60. (B) is correct.** In the recent era of globalization, foreign policy is shifting toward economic concerns. The president, as chief diplomat, has both increasing power and responsibility as the nation's negotiator of treaties and executive agreements. Many of today's agreements focus on expanding free trade among nations around the world.

This rubric provides examples of many, but not all of the possible correct responses to the free-response questions.

1.

a. Explain how caucuses select delegates to the national convention.

In some states, delegates are chosen for the national conventions by caucuses. Caucuses are when members of political parties meet (i.e. caucus) in town hall like meetings to discuss and debate about their party's nominees for the presidency. Individuals attending the caucus vote for their preferred candidate. Candidates are awarded delegates to the state and national party conventions based on the number of votes they receive.

b. Explain how primaries select delegates to the national convention.

In some states, delegates are elected for the national party conventions in a primary vote. In states that have primaries, voters go to the poll to vote for a particular candidate. When people vote for the presidential candidate they prefer, they are most often voting for a delegate to the state or national convention who, at the convention, is obligated to vote for the candidate they represent.

c. Discuss one consequence of "frontloading" the delegate selection process.

Frontloading is when several states hold their primary or caucus early in the primary election cycle. With frontloading, one candidate often is able to gain an insurmountable lead in the delegate count long before primaries and caucuses are held in other states. Frontloading has led to a race to the front of the line, with many states moving their primary or caucus to earlier dates.

2.

a. Identify and describe positive effects that the media has on the political process.

   • Citizens have access to important information about candidates for public office, elected officials, and public policy.

   • Through investigative reporting the media performs a watchdog role for the political process. In this role the media uncovers governmental fraud, waste, and abuse and helps voters hold public officials accountable for their actions.

b. Identify and describe negative effects that the media has on the political process.

   • The media tend to provide superficial coverage of complex public policy issues.

   • Because mass media outlets tend to be owned by profit seeking corporations, the choice of what news they cover might be influenced by how well it will sell rather than how important it is to the public.

- The media (especially television) are biased towards stories that generate good pictures.

- In political campaigns the media tends to focus more on the horse race than the issues positions of the candidates.

3.

a. Briefly describe a trend in public opinion depicted in this graph.

- The graph indicates, people have increasingly felt that government is no longer of and by the people, but that it serves the interests of big business and influential interest groups. In 1964, just 25 percent of people polled expressed their suspicions about the government, but by 2000, that number had reached nearly 60 percent.

- Since 1970, at least half of all Americans have shared this distrust of the government.

b. Identify two factors that may have produced the trend you describe.

- Increase in the number or the visibility of business related lobbyists or interest groups.

- Increase in the number or the influence of business related political action committees (PAC)s.

- Increased media attention to the role big businesses play in the political process.

c. Explain how each of these factors you identify has had an impact of the trend you describe.

- **Increase in the number or the visibility of business related lobbyists or interest groups**. Business interest groups are the most common type of interest groups and they also tend to be the group with the most money. According to elite theorists, it is the wealthiest groups that have the most influence over public policy. Americans tend to view lobbyists with great distrust. Interest groups have become more visible to the public because they use media advertisements to endorse their causes or to refute the claims of opposing interests. So, Americans are well aware of their increasing presence in government. This is a possible explanation for the increase in the number of people who believe that government is run mostly for the benefit of a few big business interests.

- **Increase in the number or the influence of business related political action committees (PAC)s.** During the time period represented on the graph, there was a sharp rise in the number of political action committees (PACs). PACs were created by campaign finance reforms in the early 1970s as a means of making campaign financing more open. PACs represent a variety of interests, including big business, and they channel money from these interests to presidential and congressional campaigns. It is widely believed that PACs have disproportionate influence over politicians and policymakers because of their campaign contributions.

- **Increased media attention to the role and influence of big businesses in the political process.** As the number of PACs and lobbyists has grown, the mass media has paid more attention to the potential influence that business interests have on politics and government. This increased attention by the media, including uncovering unlawful and or unethical behavior on the part of government officials and businesses, has increased public distrust of the business government relationship.

4.

a. What provision of the Fourteenth Amendment has been used by the Supreme Court to advance civil liberties?

- The due process clause of the Fourteenth Amendment was used to make the provisions of the federal Bill of Rights applicable to state governments.

b. Identify two areas in which civil liberties protections have been extended to the states, and discuss the specific case that accomplished this task in each area.

- **Freedom of speech** (*Gitlow v. New York*)

- **Freedom of press** (*Near v. Minnesota*)

- **Right of Privacy** (*Griswold v. Connecticut*)

- **Right to Counsel in felony cases** (*Gideon v. Wainwright*)

United States Government & Politics Section I

Time: 45 minutes
60 Questions

Directions: Each of the questions or incomplete statements below is followed by five suggested answers or completions. Select the one that is best in each case and then fill in the corresponding oval on the answer sheet.

1. In which of the following elections are voters allowed to choose candidates from either party for different offices?

   (A) open primary

   (B) initiative

   (C) closed primary

   (D) blanket primary

   (E) recall election

2. All of the following play a role in an impeachment of the president, EXCEPT

   (A) Court of Appeals

   (B) Judiciary Committee

   (C) U.S. House of Representatives

   (D) Chief Justice of the United States

   (E) U.S. Senate

3. Popular elections are held for all of the following governmental offices EXCEPT

   (A) senator

   (B) president

   (C) federal judge

   (D) member of the House of Representatives

   (E) governor

4. In general, Democrats are more likely than the Republicans to advocate for which of the following?

(A) lower capital gains tax rates

(B) reduced spending for social services

(C) prayer in public schools

(D) increased military spending

(E) restrictions on handgun ownership

THE INCUMBENCY FACTOR IN CONGRESSIONAL ELECTIONS

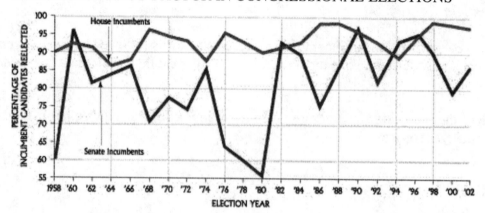

5. Which of the following conclusions may be drawn about incumbents based on the data in the graph above?

(A) In the past 40 years, at least half of incumbents consistently have won reelection.

(B) Senate incumbents are reelected at a greater rate than House incumbents.

(C) The most congressional incumbents were reelected in 1960.

(D) Almost no senatorial incumbents won reelection in 1980.

(E) House incumbents tend to win elections more often than senatorial incumbents because their elections are less publicized.

6. The Elastic Clause grants Congress the authority to

(A) amend the president's budget proposal as it sees fit.

(B) make any laws that enable it to carry out its assigned responsibilities.

(C) raise taxes.

(D) create any number of legislative committees and subcommittees.

(E) reapportion seats based on the nation's changing population.

7. The most common way that ordinary citizens participate in politics is by

    (A) participating in political protests.

    (B) writing letters to the editor of a local newspaper.

    (C) voting in elections.

    (D) contacting their elected representatives.

    (E) joining an interest group.

8. The Constitution authorizes Supreme Court justices to be appointed for life for which of the following reasons?

    (A) To shield judges from political influence and pressure

    (B) To reward judges for their distinguished careers

    (C) To create a strong relationship between the Court and Congress

    (D) To allow politicians to use the patronage system

    (E) To limit the power of presidents to appoint judges too frequently

9. One common criticism of the media's participation in politics is

    (A) its bias in favor of outsiders and third parties.

    (B) its focus on the Supreme Court to the exclusion of the other branches.

    (C) its live and uncensored coverage of committee hearings.

    (D) its tendency to focus more on personalities than issues.

    (E) its failure to shape the public agenda through its news coverage.

10. Which of the following groups is the least likely to participate in politics?

    (A) 65-75 year olds

    (B) high school graduates

    (C) women

    (D) Protestants

    (E) 18 to 25 year olds

11. Which of the following statements about the budgetary process is true?

(A) The president submits a budget proposal to Congress, which ultimately decides how to allocate money.

(B) The president assigns a spending minimum and maximum to each agency in the executive branch.

(C) Interest groups have little influence over this aspect of policymaking.

(D) The Office of Management and Budget handles the entire budgetary process.

(E) Committees submit their internal budget requests to the Congressional Budget Office.

12. According to the Supreme Court's decision in *Lemon* v. *Kurtzman* (1971) which of the following is true about public aid to church-related schools ?

(A) Any use of public funds for church-related schools violates the separation of church and state doctrine.

(B) Only local governments may allocate public money to church-related schools.

(C) Public aid to church-related schools must be matched by an equal amount of privately raised funds.

(D) Public aid to church-related schools must have a primary effect that neither advances nor inhibits religion.

(E) Religious schools are not allowed to receive any public funds.

13. Which of the following powers are granted to Congress by the Constitution?

   I. Appropriate money

   II. Confirm justices

   III. Send troops into war

   IV. Enforce laws

   V. Regulate commerce

(A) I and IV only

(B) II and III only

(C) III and V only

(D) I, II, and V only

(E) III, IV, and V only

14. Which of the following authorized the Justice Department to send federal officials to oversee state elections?

    (A) Fifteenth Amendment

    (B) Voting Rights Act

    (C) Motor Voter Act

    (D) Thirteenth Amendment

    (E) Civil Rights Act

15. In which of the following cases is a congressional candidate most likely to be elected?

    (A) If he or she has a good television presence

    (B) When a state has just gained seats due to reapportionment

    (C) If he or she is new to politics

    (D) After a critical election for the presidency

    (E) If he or she is an incumbent

16. Which of the following is true of iron triangles?

    (A) An iron triangle is composed of the president, the speaker of the House, and the chief justice.

    (B) Iron triangles inhibit the policy process by interfering with the debate over a piece of legislation.

    (C) Iron triangles help unify the three branches of government in pursuit of a single, clear policy agenda.

    (D) Iron triangles help advance legislation and implementation in a particular policy area.

    (E) Iron triangles rarely form in government at the federal level because they lack sufficient resources for sustainability.

17. An environmental lobby would be LEAST likely to exert its influence by meeting with a

    (A) federal judge hearing a case on the constitutionality of an environmental regulation.

    (B) member of the House committee that authorizes money for the building of power plants.

    (C) staff member of the Environmental Protection Agency.

    (D) newspaper in the town where environmental laws are being violated.

    (E) staff member of the White House who is known to be sympathetic to environmental concerns.

18. Who a voter chooses to vote for is influenced most by

   (A) campaign finance laws.

   (B) political advertisements.

   (C) party identification.

   (D) the media.

   (E) radio talk shows.

19. Many Supreme Court cases of the 1960s involved issues of

   (A) gender discrimination.

   (B) economic regulation.

   (C) constitutional powers of the president.

   (D) rights of the accused.

   (E) campaign finance reform.

20. If the Supreme Court rules that a newly-passed law is unconstitutional, Congress can

   (A) ask the president to appoint new justices.

   (B) try to amend the Constitution to override the Supreme Court's interpretation.

   (C) appeal the Court's decision to the Senate Judiciary Committee.

   (D) issue a referendum to allow the public to vote on the Supreme Court's decision.

   (E) vote to override the Supreme Court's decision.

21. Which of the following are types of elections held in the U.S.?

   I.   run-off election

   II. national primary

   III. general election

   IV. initiative petition

   V.   referendum

   (A) III only

   (B) II and III only

   (C) I, II and III only

   (D) I, III, IV, and V only

   (E) All of the above

22. If the House and Senate pass two different versions of a bill,

    (A) the Senate version has seniority and is sent to the president.

    (B) the Supreme Court chooses the better version.

    (C) the two versions are sent to a conference committee to work out a compromise bill.

    (D) the president has the authority to choose which version he will sign into law.

    (E) each house must amend its bill and take another vote.

23. One tool that allows the president to sidestep congressional approval of his diplomatic duties is the

    (A) power to negotiate treaties.

    (B) authority to enter into executive agreements.

    (C) ability to send troops into war.

    (D) freedom to appoint ambassadors.

    (E) privilege of receiving foreign diplomats.

24. Which of the following is an accurate statement about the caseload of the Supreme Court?

    (A) Only a small portion of cases seeking review are heard by the Supreme Court.

    (B) The Senate Judiciary Committee selects which cases will be placed on the docket.

    (C) Most cases that reach the Supreme Court are appealed from state courts.

    (D) The solicitor general is responsible for assigning cases to the Supreme Court.

    (E) The Supreme Court attempts to hear every case appealed to it.

25. The Supreme Court has extended federal supremacy over state laws through its interpretation of the

    (A) Tenth Amendment.

    (B) Eminent Domain Clause.

    (C) First Amendment.

    (D) Fourteenth Amendment.

    (E) Establishment Clause.

26. Which of the following is an incumbent's greatest advantage during an election?

(A) automatic endorsement from the president

(B) a clean political record

(C) name recognition

(D) more campaign resources and funding

(E) a large number of undecided voters in the constituency

27. Television has had which of the following effects on political parties?

(A) It has helped lower the cost of campaigning, thereby saving the parties money.

(B) It has forced candidates to rely more heavily on their parties.

(C) It has caused a decrease in party identification among the electorate.

(D) It has led to the declining importance of national conventions.

(E) It has caused party realignment because parties can appeal to new groups in the electorate.

Questions 28 and 29 refer to the table below.

Congressional Campaign Finances—Receipts and Disbursements: 1995 to 2000

[Covers all campaign finance activity during 2-year calendar period indicated for primary, general, run-off, and special elections, for 1999-2000 relates to 2,083 House of Representatives candidates and 333 Senate candidates. Data have been adjusted to eliminate transfers between all committees within a campaign. For further information on legal limits of contributions, see Federal Election campaign act of 1971, as amended]

Item	House of Representatives						Senate					
	Amount (mil. dol.)			Percent distribution			Amount (mil. dol.)			Percent distribution		
	1995-96	1997-98	1999-00	1995-96	1997-98	1999-00	1995-96	1997-98	1999-00	1995-96	1997-98	1999-00
Total receipts [1]	505.4	493.7	610.4	100	100	100	285.1	287.5	437.0	100	100	100
Individual contributions	272.9	253.2	315.6	55	52	52	166.9	166.5	252.1	59	58	58
Other committees	155.0	158.5	193.4	31	32	32	45.6	48.1	52.0	16	17	12
Candidate loans	42.0	46.8	61.9	8	10	10	40.3	52.2	89.0	14	18	20
Candidate contributions	7.0	5.3	6.3	1	1	1	16.4	1.3	18.7	6	(Z)	4
Democrats	233.1	233.4	286.7	46	47	47	126.5	134.1	230.4	44	47	53
Republicans	266.9	255.8	317.7	53	52	52	157.7	153.0	203.8	55	53	47
Others	5.4	4.5	6.0	1	1	1	0.9	0.4	2.8	(Z)	(Z)	1
Incumbents	279.6	293.8	361.8	55	60	59	81.8	135.5	130.6	29	47	30
Challengers	119.1	92.8	127.4	24	19	21	79.2	113.9	99.6	28	40	23
Open seats [2]	101.1	102.7	121.1	14	21	20	124.1	37.7	206.7	44	13	47
Total disbursements	477.6	452.5	572.3	95	100	100	287.4	287.9	434.7	100	100	100
Democrats	221.1	211.1	266.8	44	47	47	127.4	134.6	226.3	44	47	52
Republicans	251.4	237.2	299.7	50	52	52	159.1	152.9	205.7	55	53	47
Others	5.3	4.2	5.7	1	1	1	0.9	0.4	2.7	(Z)	(Z)	1
Incumbents	258.1	257.2	327.0	51	57	57	85.4	137.3	130.2	30	48	30
Challengers	119.6	94.7	125.6	24	21	22	78.9	112.5	99.3	27	39	23
Open seats [2]	100.2	100.6	119.7	20	22	21	123.1	38.1	205.1	43	13	47

Z Less than $50,000 or 0.5 percent. [1] Includes other types of receipts, not shown separately. [2] Elections in which an incumbent did not seek reelection.

Source: U.S. Federal Election Commission, FEC Reports on Financial Activity, Final Report, U.S. Senate and House Campaigns, biennial.

28. The data in the table above supports which of the following statements?

    (A) Spending on congressional campaigns has stabilized.

    (B) There was a particularly high number of open Senate seats in the 2000 election.

    (C) Democrats consistently outspend Republicans in congressional elections.

    (D) Challengers for House seats are at a greater financial advantage than are challengers in senatorial campaigns.

    (E) PACs made the largest contributions to congressional campaigns.

29. What happens if no presidential candidate receives an Electoral College majority?

    (A) The election is decided by the U.S. House of Representatives.

    (B) The winner is decided by a conference of the state governors.

    (C) A run-off election is held to determine the winner.

    (D) The U.S. Supreme Court determines the winner.

    (E) The winner is decided by a vote of super delegates.

30. Which of the following is a trend in American elections?

    (A) Fewer candidates are seeking elective office.

    (B) Campaigns are becoming less expensive to run.

    (C) Political pundits are becoming more influential.

    (D) Fewer citizens are making financial contributions to candidates.

    (E) More states are allowing early voting.

31. Article II of the Constitution grants the president power to do all of the following EXCEPT

    (A) authorize troop movements during war

    (B) appropriate funds for agencies

    (C) veto proposed legislation

    (D) appeal to Congress and make legislative requests in a state of the union address

    (E) establish or discontinue relations with foreign governments

32. The Civil Rights Act articulated which of the following?

(A) The requirement that all public schools desegregate

(B) A prohibition on states instituting poll taxes or literacy tests when administering elections

(C) The illegality of discrimination in employment and public accommodations

(D) The creation of the Justice Department to investigate civil rights violations

(E) The right of all Americans, regardless of race or gender, to vote in federal elections

33. Which of the following statements accurately describes the procedure of debate in the House?

(A) The Rules Committee determines the order in which bills will be heard and the length of debate for each one.

(B) Representatives who are introducing a bill are allowed the privilege of unlimited debate.

(C) The speaker and the Sergeant at Arms together determine the schedule of debate

(D) The minority party is allowed an automatic 10 minutes of debate time to refute legislation introduced by the majority party.

(E) Only members of the party whose representative introduced the bill are allowed time on the floor to discuss it.

34. Which of the following statements characterize the relationship between congressional committees and federal agencies?

I. Committees appropriate funds for each agency to spend during the year.

II. Agencies regulate committees by holding hearings to assess their performance.

III. Committees perform oversight of the agencies that fall under their jurisdiction.

IV. Both committees and agencies can be influenced by the lobbying efforts of interest groups.

(A) II only

(B) III only

(C) I and III only

(D) II and IV only

(E) I, III, and IV only

35. In *Texas* v. *Johnson,* the Supreme Court determined that

   (A) the drawing of unreasonable school district lines cannot be used as a means of integrating schools.

   (B) symbolic speech is protected under the First Amendment.

   (C) affirmative action quotas are unconstitutional.

   (D) the death penalty is not a form of cruel and unusual punishment.

   (E) obscenity is not protected by the First Amendment.

36. Which of the following is usually a result of a critical election?

   (A) party dealignment

   (B) divided government

   (C) policy implementation

   (D) party realignment

   (E) policy gridlock

37. A weakness of the Articles of Confederation was that a government was established that was unable to

   (A) remain a democracy.

   (B) be recognized by foreign governments.

   (C) represent the views of the various states.

   (D) centralize its powers.

   (E) make decisions through a legislative process.

38. The Federal Reserve Board oversees which of the following policy areas?

   (A) social welfare policy

   (B) foreign policy

   (C) monetary policy

   (D) health care policy

   (E) domestic policy

39. Which of the following is a major difference between the Democratic and Republican parties?

(A) The Democratic Party campaigns fairly, but the Republican Party does not.

(B) A wider variety of groups in the electorate vote for Republican candidates.

(C) The Republican Party is much older than the Democratic Party.

(D) The Republican Party endorses raising taxes, whereas the Democratic Party favors cutting taxes.

(E) The Democratic Party has a more liberal ideology, whereas the Republican Party has a more conservative ideology.

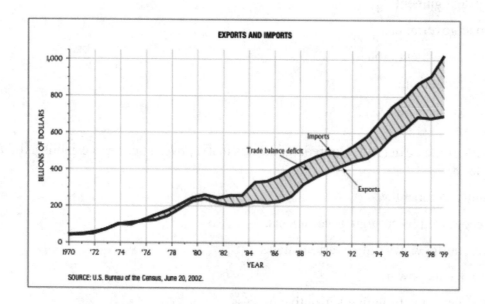

EXPORTS AND IMPORTS

SOURCE: U.S. Bureau of the Census, June 20, 2002.

40. The shaded area of the graph indicates that

(A) there is a growing balance-of-trade deficit.

(B) the national debt is growing.

(C) free trade agreements are damaging the U.S. economy.

(D) lowering tariffs has resulted in decreased exports.

(E) interdependency is becoming common in a new global economy.

41. A unitary system of government is one in which

    (A) an executive, legislative, and judicial branch share equal powers.

    (B) political officials are elected by the public in a popular election.

    (C) legislative committees and federal agencies work together to make and implement policy.

    (D) more than one level of government oversees a body of people.

    (E) all power resides in a central government.

42. The rise of the Social Security system has had which of the following effects on the federal budget?

    (A) It has led to cutbacks in defense spending and the building of new weapons.

    (B) It has become the largest federal expenditure.

    (C) It has increased Americans' trust in a government that provides for all Americans.

    (D) It has caused income tax rates to double since its initiation.

    (E) It has discouraged senior citizens from participating in politics.

43. One way federal agencies regulate an industry is by

    (A) hiring corporate leaders in the industry.

    (B) issuing bonds to the industry.

    (C) fixing stock prices in the industry.

    (D) limiting its ability to trade internationally.

    (E) sending inspectors to investigate an industry's regular activity.

44. Members of Congress are most likely to endorse a president's proposal when

    (A) one party holds the majority in Congress by only a slim margin.

    (B) the congressional session is nearing its end.

    (C) the president has a high public approval rating.

    (D) the issue at hand is not well publicized.

    (E) it involves amending the federal tax codes.

45. Which of the following is a basic weakness inherent in the presidency?

(A) Except in military affairs, presidents must rely on the support of other people to influence policy decisions.

(B) Because they are limited to only two terms, presidents rarely have enough time to achieve any of their policy goals.

(C) Media attention focuses heavily on the president, which leads the public to hold him accountable and, in turn, deprives him of power.

(D) The president is commander-in-chief, yet he cannot act in military situations without congressional approval.

(E) Because the Electoral College officially elects the president, presidents usually lack legitimacy among the electorate.

46. Despite their influence over the political agenda, interest groups may be seen as democratic institutions in that they

(A) help voters decide how to cast their ballots in an election.

(B) fund campaigns through political action committees.

(C) run advertisements to generate public support for a presidential proposal.

(D) promote equal representation of citizens' political beliefs.

(E) represent the concerns of groups in the electorate in the political arena.

47. The power of the president has expanded for which of the following reasons?

  I. Increasing importance of foreign relations

 II. The shift toward candidate-centered politics as a result of television

III. The use of primaries in presidential elections

IV. The easing of tensions among social groups as a result of the civil rights movement

(A) II only

(B) IV only

(C) I and II only

(D) III and IV only

(E) I, II, and III only

48. Which of the following is true of federal systems of government?

   (A) The central government completely regulates the activities of state governments.

   (B) Citizens vote for central government officials only.

   (C) The central government shares power with the states.

   (D) Most democracies are federal systems.

   (E) Federal systems tend to have just two major political parties.

49. The House of Representatives differs from the Senate in all of the following ways EXCEPT

   (A) House seats are distributed according to each state's population, whereas each state has the same number of senators

   (B) House debates are scheduled, whereas the Senate allows unlimited debate

   (C) representatives tend to act more independently, whereas senators usually vote according to party lines

   (D) power is distributed more hierarchically in the House than it is in the Senate

   (E) senators have the ability to filibuster, but representatives do not

50. An American citizen's approval of the president depends most heavily on

   (A) the president's ability to stand up to Congress.

   (B) whether the president is of the same party with which the citizen identifies himself or herself.

   (C) whether the president has balanced his attention to foreign and domestic policy.

   (D) how accessible the president is to members of the public.

   (E) the media's bias in favor of or against the president.

51. One way the executive branch may attempt to influence the outcome of a Supreme Court case is by

   (A) filing an *amicus curiae* brief.

   (B) selecting which justices will hear the case.

   (C) having the solicitor general preside over the justices.

   (D) requesting the chief justice to meet with the president.

   (E) issuing an opinion on the case.

52. The president may exercise authority over the federal bureaucracy in all of the following ways EXCEPT by

   (A) advising cabinet members and agency heads on department activities

   (B) proposing budgets for each department to Congress

   (C) appointing department secretaries who share his political goals

   (D) creating or dismantling agencies and departments

   (E) holding hearings on the departments' activities and performance

53. In some states, citizens can participate directly in lawmaking by

   (A) appointing legislators to committees.

   (B) presenting a budget proposal in the state legislature.

   (C) approving legislation through referenda.

   (D) writing letters to the governor.

   (E) setting the requirements for who can run for office.

54. Which of the following is a true statement about the Voting Rights Act of 1965?

   (A) It resulted in increased discrimination against women voters.

   (B) It allowed literacy tests to be administered as a prerequisite for voting.

   (C) It gave the states more control over federal elections.

   (D) It was the first voting rights law to pass Congress with no opposition.

   (E) It resulted in dramatic increases in the number of African American voters.

55. In a state that has six electoral votes, the Republican candidate wins the popular vote by 54 to 46 percent. The electoral votes would most likely be allocated in which of the following ways?

   (A) The Republican and Democrat would each get three electoral votes.

   (B) The Republican would get five electoral votes, and the 1 electoral vote reserved for a third-party candidate would go unused.

   (C) The Republican would get four electoral votes, and the Democrat would get two.

   (D) The Republican would get six electoral votes.

   (E) The Republican would get five electoral votes, and the Democrat would get one.

56. Senators are often more willing to allow a filibuster than they are to vote for cloture because

(A) voting for cloture looks bad on the senator's congressional record.

(B) they want to ensure that their colleagues will not vote for cloture when they choose to filibuster.

(C) voting for cloture does little to stop a filibuster.

(D) they fear losing public approval by refusing to hear the full debate.

(E) filibusters often generate well-developed, successful policies.

57. The president exercises influence over policymaking most by

(A) vetoing legislation passed by Congress.

(B) setting the congressional agenda.

(C) introducing legislation for debate.

(D) participating in committee hearings.

(E) appointing party leaders in both houses of Congress.

58. Which of the following sets of states has the most Electoral College votes?

(A) California, New York, and Texas

(B) Iowa, New Hampshire, and South Carolina

(C) Florida, New Jersey, and Ohio

(D) Maine, Massachusetts, and Vermont

(E) North Carolina, Oregon, and Pennsylvania

59. If one sees candidates from more than one political party on a ballot, one may be voting in a(n)

I.   open primary
II.   closed primary
III. blanket primary
IV.   general election

(A) I only

(B) I and III only

(C) I, III, and IV only

(D) III and IV only

(E) IV only

60. Which of the following is the presiding officer of the U.S. Senate?

    (A) Speaker

    (B) Majority Leader

    (C) Majority Whip

    (D) Chief Clerk

    (E) Vice President

END OF SECTION I.

IF YOU FINISH BEFORE TIME IS CALLED, YOU MAY CHECK YOUR WORK ON THIS SECTION.

DO NOT GO ON TO SECTION II UNTIL YOU ARE TOLD TO DO SO.

United States Government & Politics
Section II

Time: 100 minutes

Directions: You have 100 minutes to answer all four of the following questions. It is suggested that you take a few minutes to plan and outline each answer. *Spend approximately one-fourth of your time (25 minutes) on each question.* Illustrate your essay with substantive examples where appropriate. Make certain to number each of your answers as the question is numbered below.

1. The writers of the Constitution favored the ideals of democracy, yet they feared putting too much power in the hands of the people.

   a. Identify TWO changes from the original Constitution that increased the democratic nature of government.

   b. Explain how each of the two factors identified in part A has resulted in a more democratic nation.

2. Incumbent members of Congress have a tremendous advantage over challengers in elections.

   a. Identify 3 possible sources of incumbency advantage.

   b. Describe how each of the items you identified in "a" works to incumbents' advantage.

   c. The many advantages notwithstanding, incumbents do sometimes lose elections. Identify and explain 2 reasons why incumbents tend to lose elections.

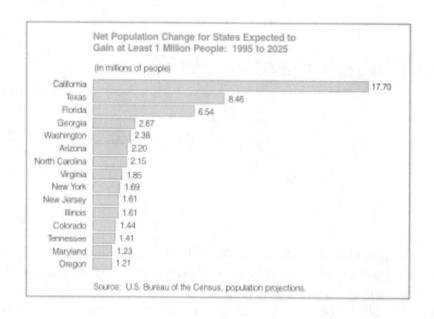

Net Population Change for States Expected to Gain at Least 1 Million People: 1995 to 2025

(In millions of people)

California	17.70
Texas	8.46
Florida	6.54
Georgia	2.67
Washington	2.38
Arizona	2.20
North Carolina	2.15
Virginia	1.85
New York	1.69
New Jersey	1.61
Illinois	1.61
Colorado	1.44
Tennessee	1.41
Maryland	1.23
Oregon	1.21

Source: U.S. Bureau of the Census, population projections.

3. The above graph shows population projections for the first quarter of the twenty-first century. All of the states listed are expected to gain at least a million people in the next few decades.

   Using the data above and your knowledge of U.S. government and politics, identify and explain THREE ways that these shifting populations will have an impact on government and politics.

4. During the budgetary process, Congress weighs revenues and expenditures to determine how to allocate money within the federal government. Social spending has become a major component of the federal budget in recent decades, but in some cases Congress is not able to adjust spending for it.

   a. Identify TWO items in the budget that cannot usually be amended during the budgetary process.

   b. For each one, explain why spending is not cut.

END OF EXAMINATION

ANSWERS AND EXPLANATIONS

Practice Test 2

Section I

- **1. (D) is correct.** In a blanket primary, candidates of all parties are listed on the ballot. A voter may choose a candidate from one party for one office and a candidate from another party for a different office. This is called ticket splitting. Two consequences of ticket splitting are a decline in the power of political parties and an increase in divided government.

- **2. (A) is correct.** The Court of Appeals plays no role in the impeachment process.

- **3. (C) is correct.** Federal judges are not elected by the public—they are appointed by the president and confirmed by the Senate. This process is intended to insulate them from the political pressures of campaigning so that, in office, they are free to make unbiased decisions without having to return favors or worry about reelection.

- **4. (E) is correct.** Democrats more than Republicans tend to favor polices like background checks and mandatory safety classes that make it more difficult for individuals to own handguns.

- **5. (A) is correct.** In 1960, senatorial incumbency was at 60 percent and House incumbency at 90 percent. In 2000, the numbers were still high, at close to 80 percent and 100 percent, respectively. Even when incumbency dropped to its lowest point—senatorial incumbency in 1980—incumbents were still elected at a rate of about 55 percent. This graph clearly shows how advantageous incumbency can be in congressional elections.

- **6. (B) is correct.** Located in Article I of the Constitution, the Elastic Cause enumerates the implied powers of Congress. It gives the legislature full authority to make any laws "necessary and proper" to carry out those responsibilities assigned to it by the Constitution.

- **7. (C) is correct.** Voting is the most common way people express their political views. By participating in an election, voters choose those candidates whom they feel agree with their political beliefs, and these candidates therefore act on their behalf in government.

- **8. (A) is correct.** Supreme Court justices are granted life terms on the condition that they remain in good conduct. This allows them to make judicial decisions objectively without the pressures of political influence. They do not have to appeal to the public or represent any one interest if they are guaranteed their position of authority.

- **9. (D) is correct.** The media tends to focus more heavily on candidates' personality than their policy platforms for the sake of achieving higher viewer ratings. However, this may distort the public's perception both of candidates and the party they represent.

- **10. (E) is correct.** Young people (18 to 25 year olds) are the least likely group in the electorate to vote. This is partially because young people have not yet formed their political beliefs or determined their needs from government. As people age and bear more responsibilities, they tend to participate more actively in politics.

- **11. (A) is correct.** In the budgetary process, federal agencies and departments in the executive branch submit their budget proposals to the president and the OMB, which amend and combine them into a single proposal. Then the president sends this proposal to Congress, which, through its committees, ultimately decides how much money each department or agency gets to spend in the coming year.

- **12. (D) is correct.** In *Lemon* v. *Kurtzman* the Supreme Court ruled that aid to church-related schools must (1) have a secular purpose (2) must have a primary effect that neither advances nor inhibits religion and (3) not foster excessive government entanglement with religion.

- **13. (D) is correct.** Some of Congress's enumerated powers are to appropriate money, confirm the appointment of justices, and regulate commerce. Congress also has the power to declare war, but it cannot send troops into war. It can make laws, but it cannot enforce them. These two responsibilities instead belong to the president, who is both commander-in-chief and head of the executive branch.

- **14. (B) is correct.** The Voting Rights Act was passed to enable the government to enforce African Americans' right to vote as guaranteed by the Fifteenth Amendment. Southern states had employed a variety of means, including intimidation, to prevent African Americans from voting. As a result of its new power to enforce the law, the Justice Department sent in federal officials to oversee elections in southern states.

- **15. (E) is correct.** Incumbents have enormous advantages in congressional elections. They have better exposure, a political record with the constituency, and more campaign money with which to eliminate any chance of their challengers' success. As a result of these advantages, usually more than 50 percent of congressional incumbents are reelected.

- **16. (D) is correct.** Iron triangles, or sub governments, often work like well-oiled machines to produce and implement policies in a specific policy area. Interest groups may suggest policies or lobby Congress to pass legislation, and then federal agencies and interest groups work together to implement the policy.

- **17. (A) is correct.** Lobbyists have the least influence over judges, because they have no leverage with which to influence judges who hold their offices for life. However, interest groups can file *amicus curiae* briefs to try to influence a judge's decision.

- **18. (C) is correct.** Political science research has consistently found party identification to be the strongest predictor of vote choice.

- **19. (D) is correct.** Many important and controversial Supreme Court cases in the 1960s addressed the rights of the accused. *Miranda* v. *Arizona* is one well-known case in which the Fifth Amendment right of protection from self-incrimination was enforced by the Court. Other cases also extended the right of counsel to the poor and confirmed the exclusionary rule, preventing the use of evidence gained through unreasonable search and seizure from being used in trials.

- **20. (B) is correct.** The Supreme Court is the interpreter of the Constitution, but Congress is the keeper of it. If the Supreme Court finds a law unconstitutional, Congress has the authority to amend the Constitution to suit the law. Then the Supreme Court would have no choice but to interpret the law in light of the amendment to the Constitution.

- **21. (D) is correct.** General and run-off elections are elections use to select governing officials. Initiative petitions and referenda are elections in which voters play a role in deciding whether a specific policy proposal becomes law. There is no national primary election in the United States.

- **22. (C) is correct.** A bill may be amended or altered during debate in either the House or the Senate. It is often the case that the two houses pass different versions of the same bill. When this happens, the bill is sent to a conference committee composed of members of both houses. The committee works to develop a compromise between the bill's two versions. If the compromise is accepted by a majority of each house, the final piece of legislation is sent to the president for his signature.

- **23. (B) is correct.** The president has the power to negotiate executive agreements as well as treaties. Treaties are more formal and tend to address major issues; these require the approval of Congress. Executive agreements, however, deal with smaller matters, so it is often easier for the president to handle them independently.

- **24. (A) is correct.** Thousands of cases are appealed to the Supreme Court each year, but only a few are actually placed on the docket. The justices meet regularly to review appeals and, as a group, choose to hear only those cases they feel are most deserving of appeal or may have the greatest impact on the interpretation of the law. Answer C is true, but it does not answer the question.

- **25. (D) is correct.** The Tenth Amendment reserves many unwritten powers for the states, so states have made their own laws, which (especially in the case of civil liberties) have at times conflicted with federal law. The passing of the Fourteenth Amendment, however, offered the Supreme Court the opportunity to assert federal supremacy over such state laws. This amendment grants all people the right to due process of the law. The Court has cited the Fourteenth Amendment in numerous civil liberties and civil rights cases.

- **26. (D) is correct.** Although incumbents do often benefit from a record of good service to their constituency or a clean political record, their *greatest* advantage in an election is name recognition. Incumbents receive a great deal of press coverage from local media outlets. As a consequence, their names are more easily recognized by voters. This leads to a tremendous advantage because on election day most voters can do little more than recall a candidate's name.

- **27. (C) is correct.** Television allows viewers to see and judge political candidates without the structure of a political party. Candidates too can address the public directly without having to channel their campaigns through the party machine. As a result, both candidates and the electorate have become more independent from political parties. While most people still vote according to their party identification, they are more frequently considering themselves political independents.

- **28. (B) is correct.** Receipts and disbursements for open seats in the Senate in the 2000 election were unusually high. Candidates received and spent twice as much as they had in 1996—and nearly six times as much as they had in 1998. This is a good indication that there were many competitive races for open seats in 2000.

- **29. (A) is correct.** If no candidate receives an electoral college majority, then the election moves to the House of Representatives, which must choose from among the top three electoral vote winners. Each state delegation has one vote, which means small and large states have equal voice in the process.

- **30. (E) is correct.** More and more states are allowing early voting, which is voting that takes place before the announced election day. Registered voters are allowed to either vote by mail or show up a specially designated polling places to cast their vote.

- **31. (B) is correct.** Presidents do have a significant amount of influence over the federal budget, because they compile the budget proposal for all of the departments in the executive branch. However, Congress plays an equal, if not greater, role authorizing and appropriating funds.

- **32. (C) is correct.** The Civil Rights Act officially prohibited discrimination in any public facilities and in employment. It also authorized the Justice Department to enforce the act by investigating and suing any company that violated civil rights as outlined by the law.

- **33. (A) is correct.** The Rules Committee is very influential on legislation, because it determines the length of debate for each piece of legislation. It also has the authority to declare whether or not a bill may be amended during debate. The less flexibility it affords a piece of legislation, the greater the likelihood that the bill will not be passed easily.

- **34. (E) is correct.** Committees oversee agencies, both by holding hearings and by setting their budgets. These are two ways the legislative branch checks the power of the executive branch. However, both committees and agencies are lobbied regularly by interest groups that hope to influence either policymaking or policy implementation.

- **35. (B) is correct.** *Texas* v. *Johnson* brought the issue of flag burning to the Supreme Court. The Court ruled that flag burning is protected under the First Amendment as a form of speech. The case therefore set a precedent that symbolic speech is considered "free speech" in the eyes of the law.

- **36. (D) is correct.** Party realignment often accompanies a critical election. Such elections are noteworthy because they initiate a new party era. Such major changes often are a result of new party affiliations among the electorate.

- **37. (D) is correct.** The Articles did prevent the new United States from raising militias and paying its war debts. However, these were consequences of the fact that the government simply was too weak—it did not have enough centralized power to give it legitimacy and, ultimately, to allow it to function.

- **38. (C) is correct.** The Federal Reserve Board oversees monetary policy. It is an executive institution that regulates the economy by controlling the flow of currency. For example, it has the authority to determine how much money banks have at their disposal and how much credit is available to the public.

- **39. (E) is correct.** One basic difference that defines the two parties against each other is their contrasting ideologies. Democrats tend to favor liberal policies such as social spending, whereas Republicans usually endorse more conservative policies, such as those that limit the role of the federal government.

- **40. (A) is correct.** A balance of trade occurs when a country's imports equal its exports. The shaded area of the graph shows that U.S. imports are exceeding exports. This is known as a balance-of-trade deficit. It is partially the result of lower tariffs and increasing free trade among nations around the world.

- **41. (E) is correct.** In a unitary system all power resides in a central government. State and local governments have duties and powers that are delegated to them by the central government. Most governments in the world are unitary governments.

- **42. (B) is correct.** Social Security has replaced national defense as the government's biggest expenditure. To pay for Social Security, social insurance taxes have risen somewhat comparably.

- **43. (E) is correct.** Regulatory agencies set industry standards to ensure both the quality of products and the safety of industrial workers. To oversee industries, agencies often send inspectors to determine whether specific companies are complying with industry standards. For example, the Food and Drug Administration send inspectors to test the quality of meat at meatpacking plants.

- **44. (C) is correct.** Public approval can be a powerful tool for the president. If public opinion is high, Congress is more likely to endorse his proposals. To go against a president who is well liked by voters might hurt a representative or senator's own chances for reelection.

- **45. (A) is correct.** Presidents are not legislators. They may propose policies indirectly or try to influence the policy process. This means that they must rely heavily on the support of other people to help them pursue their political agenda.

- **46. (E) is correct.** Interest groups play a role in democratizing government by serving as linkage institutions between politicians and the public. Interest groups represent the needs of different groups of people to lawmakers, so these groups help the constituency to be heard. Although not all groups may be heard equally, they at least have the opportunity to try to affect policymaking for the benefit of some citizens.

- **47. (C) is correct.** The new global economy and frequent military crises have increased the president's power and prominence as chief diplomat. The president has also become more powerful because he may act more independently than ever before. Television allows presidential candidates to reach the public directly without having to rely on political parties, and it also provides presidents with a means to address the public directly and to gain its support.

- **48. (C) is correct.** Federalism imposes a tiered structure on government. More than one level shares authority over the people. In the United States, people are subject to the laws of both state and federal governments, and they also may elect their leaders in both the state and federal governments.

- **49. (C) is correct.** Senators actually act more independently of their party. This is partially due to the fact that they have longer terms than representatives do. Party affiliations and party leadership are also much stronger in the House, so representatives tend to vote along party lines.

- **50. (B) is correct.** Party identification plays a large role in the public's perception of the president. An American citizen is more likely to approve of a president who is of the same party. By virtue of being of the same party, it is assumed that the president is advancing political views with which the citizen agrees.

- **51. (A) is correct.** Once justices have been appointed to the bench, there is little that the government can do to directly influence their decisions. It may, however, through the solicitor general, submit briefs stating the official position of the federal government on the issue at hand. State governments, interest groups, and members of the public are also allowed to file *amicus curiae* briefs to endorse their views.

- **52. (E) is correct.** Congress, not the president, is responsible for conducting oversight of federal agencies. The president and agencies together make up the executive branch, and in this case, it is the legislative branch that maintains the system of checks and balances.

- **53. (C) is correct.** Some states allow citizens to participate directly in policymaking at the state level. A bill is listed on the ballot, and voters can either choose to approve or kill it. If they approve it by a simple majority, the bill bypasses the state legislature and becomes law—or in some states, it goes directly to the governor for his or her signature or veto.

- **54. (E) is correct.** The Voting Rights Act of 1965, a law designed to help end formal and informal barriers to African American suffrage, resulted in dramatic gains in African American voter registration, voting, and engagement in politics more generally.

- **55. (D) is correct.** Generally, the winner of a state's popular election receives all of that state's electoral votes. This makes the more populous states powerful, because they have more electoral votes to wield. In this case, the Republican would receive all six of the electoral votes.

- **56. (B) is correct.** Senators like to reserve the power of filibustering, so they are unlikely to do anything to encourage their colleagues from trying to prevent them from using it. If a senator were to move for cloture, the next time he or she attempted to filibuster, the same might be done to him or her.

- **57. (A) is correct.** The veto is one of the president's strongest legislative tools. Most of the time, it allows him the final say on every piece of legislation. The veto also encourages legislators to shape policy in such a way that the president will not choose to reject it, so it gives the president some say in policy formation.

- **58. (A) is correct.** According to the Constitution, each state has as many electoral votes as it has U.S. senators and representatives. Since the number of representatives each state has is based on the size of its population, more populous states have more electoral college votes. California, New York, and Texas are the top three most populous states in the U.S.

- **59. (D) is correct.** Blanket primaries list candidates from all parties, and voters are free to participate in the nomination of candidates from different parties. The general election generally features the nominees of the different parties. Open and closed primaries have candidates from only one party on the ballot. The difference is that only people registered with the party can vote in closed primaries, while in open primaries, voters may "cross over" and vote in a party primary different from their registration.

- **60. (E) is correct.** The Constitution makes the vice president of the United States the president of the Senate. This is the vice president's only constitutionally defined job.

Free-Response Questions

This rubric provides examples of many, but not all of the possible correct responses to the free-response questions.

1.

a. Identify changes from the original Constitution that increased the democratic nature of government.

- **Seventeenth Amendment.**

- **Nineteenth Amendment.**

- **Twenty-third Amendment.**

b. Explain how each of the two factors identified in part A has resulted in a more democratic nation.

- **Seventeenth Amendment.** Under the original Constitution, U.S. senators were selected by state legislators. The Seventeenth Amendment, ratified in 1913, provides for the direct election of senators by the people.

- **Nineteenth Amendment.** Women were disenfranchised in the original Constitution. The Nineteenth Amendment, ratified in 1920, gave women the right to vote.

- **Twenty-third Amendment.** The Twenty-third Amendment, ratified in 1961, provided the District of Columbia with electoral college votes in presidential elections. This gave the citizens of the District of Columbia a voice and influence in presidential politics.

2.

a. Identify possible sources of incumbency advantage

- **Advertising**

- **Credit Claiming**

- **Position taking**

- **Weak opponents**

- **Campaign spending**

b. Describe how each of the items you identified in "a" works to incumbents' advantage.

- **Advertising.** Incumbents gain visibility and name recognition from communicating with their constituents. Members of Congress have franking privileges which allow them to use congressional funds to send newsletters, memos, and emails to voters and potential voters in their district. The name recognition that is gained from this, gives incumbents an advantage on election day.

- **Credit Claiming.** Members of Congress engage in credit claiming, which involve enhancing their standing with constituents through service to individuals or the district. Casework and so-called pork barrel projects are two common ways representatives service their constituency.

- **Position taking.** Members of Congress often take policy stances that enhance their public image and might affect the outcome of an election. Because of the office they hold, they generally receive media coverage for such actions.

- **Weak opponents.** Another advantage for incumbents is they are likely to face weak opponents.

- **Campaign spending.** Incumbents tend to have a tremendous advantage in campaign fundraising. In House races, typical incumbents usually outspend challengers by a ratio of 15 to 1. Among other things, money buys name recognition.

c. Identify and explain 2 reasons why incumbents lose elections, notwithstanding the advantages they have.

- **Corruption/Scandal**. An incumbent tarnished by scandal or corruption is almost instantly vulnerable.

- **Redistricting.** Incumbent House members may be redistricted out of their district as a result of the reapportionment and redistricting processes that take place after each census.

3. Identify and explain ways that shifting populations will have an impact on government and politics.

- The graph clearly indicates that Florida, Texas, and especially California are expected to see the largest increase in population in the next 20 to 25 years. These states will therefore experience a significant increase in political clout, as well. With more seats in the House, they will have more influence over national policy and may bring new issues that are pertinent to them to the federal agenda.

- A state's number of electors is equal to the total of its representatives and senators, so if these states gain seats, they will also gain electoral votes. As a result, presidential candidates will focus their campaign efforts on these states.

- The increasing power as a result of migration to these three states in particular may have other political consequences, because all three of these states have sizable populations of Hispanic Americans. This minority group, which is itself growing, may therefore win a greater voice in government. More Hispanic Americans may be elected to public office to represent largely Hispanic constituencies. They may also bring new social and economic issues particular to Hispanic Americans to the political agenda.

4.

a. Identify items in the budget that cannot usually be amended during the budgetary process.

- **Social Security**

- Medicare

b. For each of the items in "a", explain why spending is difficult to cut.

- **Social Security** issues benefits to senior citizens who have paid into the system during their careers because they no longer work to earn an income. The government must pay benefits to those entitled. Not only are Social Security recipients more likely to vote than other citizens, there are also a number of well organized interest groups who oppose reductions in spending for Social Security. This makes it difficult for members of Congress to go on record supporting cuts in this program.

- **Medicare**. Medicare is an entitlement program that helps pay for medical care for the elderly. The number of recipients has grown steadily. Congress, again, finds it difficult, if not impossible to amend Medicare funding during the budgetary process. Senior citizens are very protective of their claim to health care benefits, which places members of Congress under significant pressure to not cut Medicare services.